Internet BASICS

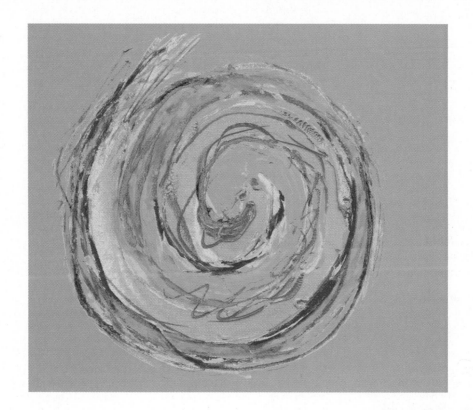

Karl Barksdale
Technology Consultant, Provo, Utah
Michael Rutter
Christa McCauliffe Fellow,
Brigham Young University
Ryan Teeter
Utah Valley State College

COURSE
TECHNOLOGY
™
THOMSON LEARNING

Australia • Canada • Mexico • Singapore • Spain • United Kingdom • United States

COURSE TECHNOLOGY

THOMSON LEARNING ™

Internet BASICS

by Karl Barksdale, Michael Rutter, Ryan Teeter

Publisher:
Kristen Duerr

Sr. Product Manager:
Dave Lafferty

Development Editor:
Anne Chimenti,
Custom Editorial Productions

Marketing Manager:
Kim Wood

Editorial Assistant:
Jodi Dreissig

Print Buyer:
Denise Sandler

Production:
Christine Spillett

Design:
Abby Scholz

Compositor:
GEX Publishing Services

Printer:
Banta

TABLE OF CONTENTS

WELCOME TO THE INTERNET: THE

UNIT 1   ## TOOLS OF THE TRADE

UNIT 2   ## E-COMMUNICATION: E-MAIL, ETC.

The end of lesson exercises focus on review and reinforcement of the skills you have learned in that lesson. They provide a comprehensive review of the ways you can apply your Net skills. The end of lesson features include the following:

- Lesson summary.

- Net Terms review of the new terms presented in the lesson.

- Review questions to assess your comprehension of what you have studied.

- Projects for applying the concepts and tools you have learned in the lesson.

- Teamwork projects that you can participate in with other members of your class.

- Critical thinking activities that require you to analyze and express your own ideas on a variety of Internet related topics.

The Unit Reviews are designed to evaluate your overall comprehension of the lessons. Each Unit Review includes the following:

- Review questions that cover topics from each lesson in the unit.

- Cross-curricular projects that discuss a broad range of subjects such as music, science, social studies, language arts, and technology. On-the-job projects that provide real-world business tasks.

These activities reinforce basic skills and ask you to complete realistic projects using the Internet as your source of information.

Glossary

A glossary is provided at the end of the text to provide you with definitions of those tricky Internet terms we all need to learn.

PREFACE

The Internet has put the information of the world at your fingertips. With a few mouse clicks or voice commands, you can access the knowledge of the planet Earth.

The Net is the door to what some have called the *information superhighway*. The world's information is online and connected by a group of computers networked together. This information is accessible to anyone with a computer and a connection to the Web. With an Internet connection, you can view a museum, dissect a virtual frog, discover the weather in Moose Jaw, Saskatchewan, visit a library, or peruse the home page of your favorite store catalog in a matter of seconds!

But, you ask, how does this all apply to me? How will the Internet affect what I do at school and at work? What practical use is all this information, and how can I find what I need? How can the Internet help me study or do research? How is the Internet used in business and how might it affect the way I do my job?

This book can answer your questions. Each lesson will teach you a new set of skills that you can begin using immediately. Each lesson presents basic Internet concepts and language. Then, it builds upon this new understanding with hands-on activities that will help you become an effective Internet user!

Once you develop your knowledge and skills, you will understand how the Internet is dramatically affecting the way companies do business, students learn, and people interact. You will feel confident using the Internet for research. You will locate online reference materials and insights relating to specific academic areas as varied as the humanities, science, and mathematics.

The Internet is more than a vast playground and storehouse of information; it's the future, and you should be a part of it. Mastering the Net isn't hard, but there are tools that will speed up the task. You will learn how to use these tools so you'll be in control.

Organization and Features of the Text

*I*nternet BASICS is organized into units and lessons that range from general concepts to specific facts. You will learn a concept and apply it through hands-on activities. This book will take you through each step in a logical easy-to-follow manner. Each lesson includes the following:

■ Lesson objectives that specify learning goals.

■ Estimated time of completion.

■ Net Terms that introduce new terms used in the lesson.

■ Step-by-Step exercises that will teach the basic skills you need to know.

■ Screen illustrations that provide visual reinforcement of what you are learning.

■ Sidebars with Net Tips, Net Concepts, and other information related to the lesson topics.

■ Special features such as Internet Milestone and Net Etiquette that provide information about Internet history, Net ethics, and basic online communication skills.

■ SCANS correlations.

How to Use this Book

Summary—At the end of each lesson, you will find a summary to prepare you to complete the end-of-lesson activities.

Vocabulary Review—Review vocabulary terms presented in the lesson.

Review Questions—Review material at the end of each lesson and each unit enables you to prepare for assessment of the content presented.

Critical Thinking Activity—Each activity gives you an opportunity to apply creative analysis to solve problems.

Cross-Curricular Activities—End-of-unit activities apply Internet concepts to topics across the curriculum.

Simulation—End-of-unit hands-on jobs provide opportunity for a comprehensive review.

Summary

Lesson ⊗ Sample Lesson

VOCABULARY REVIEW

LESSON X REVIEW QUESTIONS

LESSON X PROJECT

CRITICAL THINKING

COMMAND SUMMARY

REVIEW QUESTIONS

CROSS-CURRICULAR ACTIVITIES

SIMULATION

3

How to Use this Book

What makes a good text about the Internet? Sound instruction and hands-on skill-building and reinforcement. That is what you will find in *Internet BASICS*. Not only will you find a colorful and inviting layout, but also many features to enhance learning.

Objectives— Objectives are listed at the beginning of each lesson, along with a suggested time for completion of the lesson. This allows you to look ahead to what you will be learning and to pace your work.

Net Terms List— A list of new vocabulary terms to watch for as you progress through the lesson.

SCANS (Secretary's Commission on Achieving Necessary Skills)—The U.S. Department of Labor has identified the school-to-careers competencies. The eight workplace competencies and foundation skills are identified in exercises where they apply.

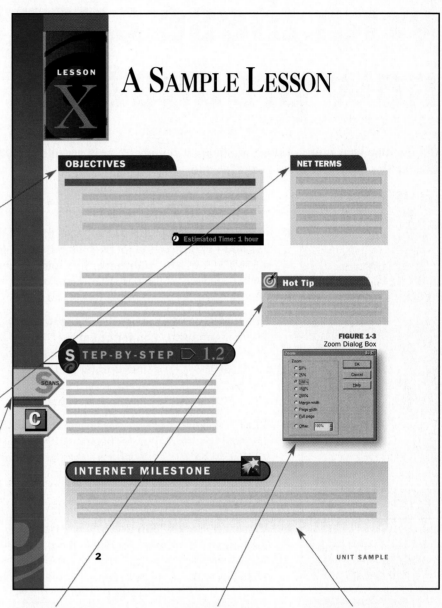

LESSON X

A SAMPLE LESSON

OBJECTIVES

Estimated Time: 1 hour

NET TERMS

Hot Tip

STEP-BY-STEP 1.2

SCANS

C

FIGURE 1-3
Zoom Dialog Box

INTERNET MILESTONE

2

UNIT SAMPLE

Marginal Boxes— These boxes provide additional information about the topic of the lesson.

Screen Shots— Numerous screen shots help clarify the text.

Special Feature Boxes— These boxes provide interesting additional information about the Internet.

Get Back to the Basics...
With these exciting new products!

Our exciting new series of short, application suite books will provide everything needed to learn this software. Other books include:

UNIT 3   FINDING A NEEDLE IN THE GLOBAL HAYSTACK

UNIT 4   EXPLORING THE NET FOR FACT AND FICTION

SPRECHEN SIE INTERNET: HOW THE INTERNET SPEAKS AND SPARKLES

UNIT 5

WELCOME TO THE INTERNET: THE TOOLS OF THE TRADE

UNIT 1

QUICK BROWSER AND OPERATING SYSTEM KNOW-HOW

OBJECTIVES

Upon completion of this lesson, you should be able to:

- Open your Web browser.
- Manipulate your browser's buttons, menus, toolbars, and scroll bars.
- Change the size and shape of your browser's window.
- Save, move, and delete files and folders.
- Organize your computer using file-management tips and tricks.
- Copy and paste Web information.

⏱ Estimated Time: 2.5 hours

NET TERMS

Active server pages

Client

Dialog box

Directory

Drives

File

File Transfer Protocol (FTP)

Folder

Graphical User Interface (GUI)

Hypertext links

Icons

Network

Newbies

Operating system (OS)

Peer-to-peer networks

Server

Server-client network

Speech recognition

Welcome to the Internet

T he Internet can be a complicated place for beginners. In fact, newly initiated users of the Net are called *newbies*. Net rookies make a lot of mistakes as they first explore the Web. In this section, we will show you how to avoid the rookie mistakes.

Net Tip

The Internet is often called the Web or the Net. Connecting to the Net is called going online. Exploring the Net is sometimes called surfing.

Communicating with the Internet

Your primary Internet tool will be your Web browser. Your browser is your looking glass to the Net.

Two Web browsers dominate: Microsoft's Internet Explorer and Netscape's Navigator. These tools have changed the way we use our personal computers. We will help you become very comfortable with your browser. This lesson introduces you to this user-friendly Web tool.

Today's browsers are based on a *GUI* interface. GUI, pronounced "gooey," stands for *graphical user interface*, a system that allows users to control their computer by clicking on pictures called *icons* or underlined words called *hypertext links*, as shown in Figure 1-1. And, it doesn't matter if you're on a Windows, Macintosh, or Linux computer system. Browsers work in a similar way on nearly every computer.

Net Tip

Web surfing has gone vocal! You can talk your way around the Web or do word searches using *speech recognition* software. With your speech software installed, simply speak the *hypertext links*, say the numbers that appear next to hyperlinked graphics, or speak search words into a search tool, as shown in Figure 1-1. Speaking the links is the same as clicking with your mouse.

FIGURE 1-1

You can surf the Web by clicking or speaking

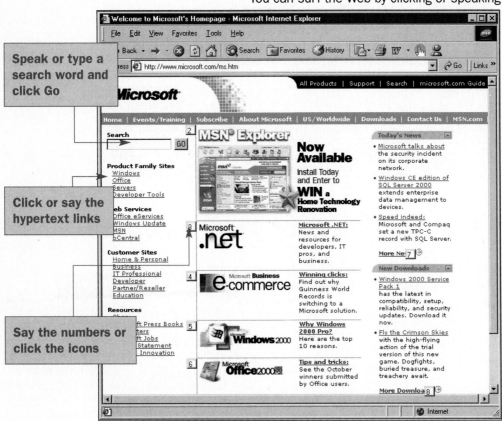

1. Windows users, open your browser by selecting its icon  on your desktop. Click the icon on your taskbar or choose the **Start** button, then **Programs**, followed by **Internet Explorer** or **Netscape Navigator** (see Figure 1-2A). In the Macintosh operating system (OS), select the browser icon on the dock (Figure 1-2B). You can also select **Go** and then **Applications** and choose **Internet Explorer** or **Netscape Navigator**.

2. Leave your browser open for the next Step-by-Step.

Net Tip

A toolbar is a set of icons that provide one-click access to frequently used menu items. Figures 1-3A and 1-3B illustrate menus and toolbars for both the Windows and Macintosh operating systems.

FIGURE 1-2A
Windows taskbar

Browser icon

FIGURE 1-2B
Macintosh dock

Browser icon

Review the Key Parts of Your Browser

As your browser opens, take a look at its various parts. Browsers share some common elements, including pull-down menus and toolbars, as shown in Figures 1-3A and 1-3B.

Net Tip

Menu options that are followed by an ellipsis (three dots ...) will open a dialog box when selected. A *dialog box* is a window that requires you to enter information before the software can execute a command. For example, the Open dialog box asks you to choose a file before you can go on.

FIGURE 1-3A

Pull-down menu bar and toolbar in Internet Explorer for Windows

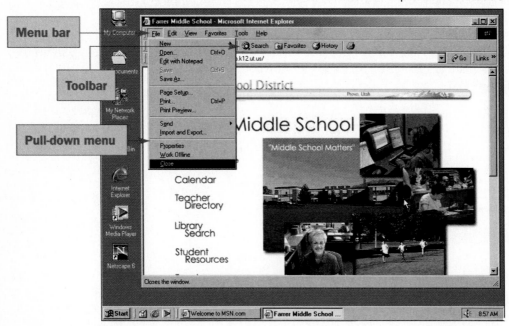

FIGURE 1-3B

Pull-down menus and toolbars in a Macintosh browser

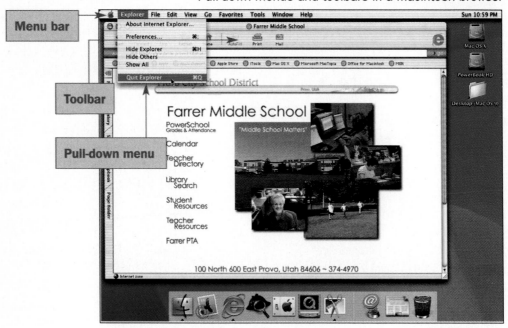

Pull-down menus and toolbar icons are the easiest way to execute browser commands. You can choose an option on a pull-down menu by clicking on it or speaking a command. Once you click with your mouse or speak a menu command, the menu opens, giving you a choice of commands.

Most browsers share at least three common pull-down menus: File, Edit, and Help.

Net Tip

There are subtle differences between the way the Windows, Macintosh, and Linux GUI *operating systems* (*OS*) work. If you can use one OS, you'll have no trouble switching to another. And, each OS works with speech recognition. To open a pull-down menu with your voice, you can say a command like *File*, *Click File*, or *File menu*.

S TEP-BY-STEP ▷ 1.2

1. Choose the word **File** on the menu bar to display the menu. As you move your mouse pointer down the File menu, different options will highlight, and in some cases, spring open. The menus that pop out are called submenus.

2. You have several ways to close these pull-down menus. Try each of these options:
   a. Click outside the menu list.
   b. Choose **File** again and press **Esc** in Windows.
   c. With **File** displayed on the menu bar, click or drag your mouse to another menu heading.
   d. Select any option from the **File** pull-down menu.

3. Now that you know how menus work, select the **File** menu and choose **Exit** in Windows, as shown in Figure 1-4A. On the Mac, select the **Application** menu (in this case Explorer) and choose **Quit**, as shown in Figure 1-4B.

FIGURE 1-4A
The Windows File menu

FIGURE 1-4B
The Macintosh Application menu

Changing Windows

Net windows come in many shapes and sizes. You can change the size of many of them, but not all. Most application windows can be maximized (enlarged to fill the screen), minimized (reduced to a button on the taskbar or the dock), or closed. The buttons to control these operations are usually located in a corner of your Web browser window. The Windows buttons are shown in Figure 1-5A. The Macintosh buttons are shown in Figure 1-5B.

Clicking the Minimize button shrinks a window. A minimized window can be found on the taskbar (Windows) or dock (Mac OS), out of the way, as shown in Figures 1-6A and 1-6B. The taskbar and dock are toolbars that display running applications (or tasks). Clicking a taskbar button or icon restores the application to its previous size.

The Maximize button makes a window fill the whole screen. The Close button exits the program or window.

Net Concept

A ***network*** is a group of computers that can communicate or "talk" to each other through connections or links. The Internet is a massive communications network linking computers around the world. When you connect to a network (or Net), you can access the available information.

FIGURE 1-5A
Windows Minimize, Maximize, and Close buttons

FIGURE 1-5B
Mac OS Close, Minimize, and Maximize buttons

FIGURE 1-6A
Windows taskbar with minimized applications

Minimized application

FIGURE 1-6B
Mac OS dock with a minimized window

Minimized application

INTERNET MILESTONE

ARPANET

The forerunner of today's Internet was a 1960s project called ARPANET, the Advanced Research Projects Agency Network, which was established for military and scientific use. Its main purpose was to maintain communications in case of a nuclear war or a natural disaster that might destroy large sections of the communications systems. The theory was that if any part of the network went down, the ARPANET could automatically reroute or rechannel information instantaneously through different computers and communications channels, keeping at least part of the network "alive."

This theory was tested during the Gulf War in the 1990s. Despite precision bombing of key communication centers by the American and coalition forces, the Iraqis were able to maintain some communications, thanks to an ARPANET-style computer network.

Today's Internet has inherited many of the survivalist technologies from ARPANET. These technologies help make the current Internet very durable.

1. Launch your Web browser. Click the **Minimize** button.

2. On the taskbar or dock, click the button or icon to restore the browser application window to its normal size.

3. Click the **Maximize** button to make the window fill the screen.

4. Click the **Maximize** button again to restore the window to its original size. (Note: In Windows this button is now called **Restore**. It will restore your window to normal.)

5. You can resize a window by dragging the border and corners. Move your pointer to the bottom right-hand corner of your browser window, as shown in Figures 1-7A and 1-7B.

6. Click and drag the corner in and out to resize the window horizontally or vertically, or both.

7. When you are finished, click the **Maximize** button to restore the window to its original size or use your speech software to make the change. Leave your browser open for the next Step-by-Step.

Net Tip

You can change the shape of your browser window using voice commands, such as *Minimize Internet Explorer* or *Click Minimize*.

FIGURE 1-7A
Click and drag the lower corner in and out in Windows

FIGURE 1-7B
Click and drag the lower corner in and out in Mac OS

Scrolling Around Windows

Scroll bars let you move the contents of a window to bring items into view. Clicking and dragging the small rectangles along the bottom or side of open windows or clicking the arrows at the end of each scroll bar allows you to view the entire contents of a Web page. If an entire Web page fits in a window, the scroll bars will automatically turn themselves off or disappear. Scroll bars are shown in Figures 1-8A and 1-8B.

Clicking the arrow buttons scrolls the page a little bit at a time. Clicking in the scroll bar pages down one full screen at a time. Using click and drag on the floating bar is a good way to skim quickly through a Web page.

Net Tip

Click and drag means to click and hold down your mouse button and drag the mouse pointer to another location.

FIGURE 1-8A

A window with scroll bars

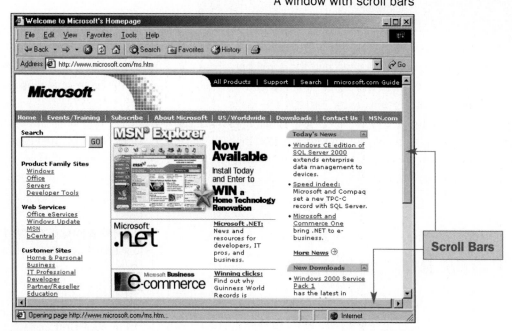

FIGURE 1-8B

A Mac window with scroll bars

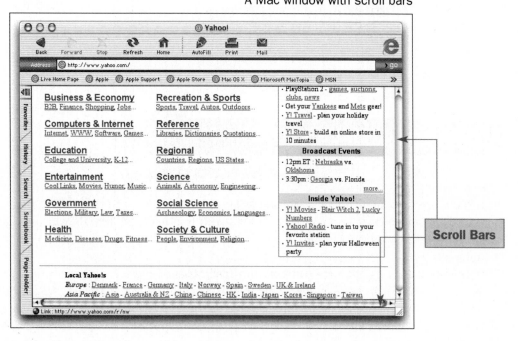

1. If you are at a Web page and the scroll bars are visible, click the up or down (or left or right) arrow points. How far did the page scroll? (Note: If you don't see scroll bars along the sides of your browser window, then make your browser window smaller and the scroll bars will appear.)

2. Try clicking just above the down arrow. How far did the page scroll this time?

3. Now click and drag the rectangular box, or "floating bar," in the scroll bar. What happened this time? Leave your Web browser open for the next Step-by-Step.

Saving and Creating Files and Folders

Your computer's hard drive is like a filing cabinet. It is a place to stash the documents and files that you find on the Internet. *Files* are storage places for data. Data include information that is processed or analyzed by your computer. Files can contain text, images, and even voice and video data.

Net Concept

Drives are physical storage places for your files and folders. They act like a file cabinet. With the Internet, you can even save your files and create folders on a hard drive on a computer halfway around the world!

INTERNET MILESTONE

THE BROWSER WARS

Netscape Communications Corp. and Microsoft have developed today's two most commonly used browsers: Netscape Navigator and Microsoft Internet Explorer. They have waged war on each other for years, each trying to dominate cyberspace (a word often used to describe the Internet).

They compete by adding significant new features and browser support for their products. Microsoft started the browser wars with its release of Internet Explorer in 1995. At the time, it was significantly behind Netscape, which controlled over 80 percent of the browser market. To cut into that lead, Microsoft added innovations, like *active server pages*. These are Web pages that allow you to change their size and appearance, much as you have done in this section. You can resize pictures and move things around, just like you can on your own computer files. Active server pages make life on the Net more exciting than ever.

If you want to know where our online lives are heading, keep your eye on Microsoft and Netscape. Netscape is now owned by AOL, or America Online, the largest provider of Internet connections in the world. The competition is sure to continue.

Files are saved in *folders*, which act like file folders in a file drawer. They are also called *directories*. Folders are a good way to organize your Internet discoveries. They can hold Web page files, homework assignments, applications, pictures, and other files.

Typical folder views in Windows are pictured in Figure 1-9A. Typical folder views in Macintosh are shown in Figure 1-9B.

FIGURE 1-9A

Windows list, icon, and thumbnail views

FIGURE 1-9B

Macintosh list, icon, and columns views

1. Open **My Documents** on the desktop in Windows. In Mac OS, choose the **Go** menu and select **Documents** from the **Favorites** submenu. (Note: You may be required to create your folder somewhere other than this documents folder.)

2. Select **File > New > Folder** in Windows or choose **File > New Folder** on your Macintosh.

3. Name your folder using your name. An example is shown in Figures 1-10A and 1-10B. Press **Enter** when you are finished entering the name.

4. Double-click your new folder to open it. Leave your browser open for the next Step-by-Step.

FIGURE 1-10A
John Smith names his folder with his name in Windows

FIGURE 1-10B
John Smith names his folder on a Macintosh

Downloading Web Pages

Folders can help you keep track of any Web pages or pictures that you find and wish to download from the Internet. When you download, you copy a file from one computer on the Internet to your personal computer. Let's download a Web page now.

1. Open any Web page of interest to you. After it finishes loading, select **File > Save As**.

2. Key **homepage.html** as the filename. Make sure the document type or format is HTML.

3. Find the folder you created in Step-by-Step 1.5. If you are using Windows, display the **Save in** drop-down list, select **My Documents** from the list, and find your folder (see Figure 1-11A). Then, open your folder. If you are using Mac OS, select **Documents** from the pull-down menu below where you just finished typing. Click the blue down arrow to the right of the pull-down menu to show the columns view (see Figure 1-11B). Click your folder in the far-left column.

4. Click **Save** to save the Web page to your folder. Remain in this screen for the next Step-by-Step.

 Net Concept

The Internet is the world's largest network, where computers from all over the world can share information. Today's Internet is made up of a backbone of high-speed communications systems that carry computer data. Servers at universities and businesses around the world are tied into this backbone.

FIGURE 1-11A

A Save Web page dialog box in Windows

FIGURE 1-11B

A Save Web page dialog box in Mac OS

Downloading Graphics

Downloading a Web page wasn't too hard now, was it? You can download all types of files from the Internet, including graphics, audio files, and even video files, with equal ease. Once you click save, you should be back at your home page in your browser ready to download again. Now let's download a picture.

STEP-BY-STEP ▷ 1.7

1. Find an image on your home page or search for another page that contains graphics.

2. Right-click on a graphic if you are using a Windows browser. If you are using a Macintosh browser, point to the image, click, and hold down the mouse button. A menu pops up.

3. From the menu that appears, select the command to save or download the picture or image. The command varies between Internet

Explorer and Netscape browsers in Windows and Macintosh. Look for a command such as **Save Picture As, Download Image to Disk,** or **Save This Image As**. After you choose the command, a Save dialog box will appear.

4. In the Save dialog box, key **mypicture.gif** or **mypicture.jpg** depending on whether you see the letters JPG or GIF as the name of the file type. Save the file to your folder. Leave your Web browser open for the next Step-by-Step.

Moving Files

Congratulations! You have just downloaded your first Web page and graphic from the Internet. Now let's move those files into a new Downloads folder.

STEP-BY-STEP ▷ 1.8

1. Click **File > Open**. (Choose **Browse** in Windows.)

2. In the Open dialog box, locate your folder again. Double-click its icon to open it.

3. Create a new folder inside your folder. This time, name the folder **Downloads**. (Review Step-by-Step 1.4 if you have forgotton how to create a folder.)

4. Your folder should now contain the **Downloads** folder, **homepage.html**, and **mypicture.gif** (or

mypicture.jpg). Click and drag **homepage.html** to the **Downloads** folder.

5. Click and drag **mypicture.gif** (or **mypicture.jpg**) to the **Downloads** folder.

6. Double-click the **Downloads** folder to open it and view your files.

7. Return to your main Web browser window. Leave your Web browser open for the next Step-by-Step.

Deleting Files

Great! You've managed to organize your files. But what happens when you get lots of files in your folders? Do you keep old files hanging around and cluttering up your folders? Of course not. Extra files are confusing and take up valuable hard drive space. We are finished with the files we downloaded in the previous exercises and won't use them again. Instead of having them clutter up your hard drive, let's delete them.

STEP-BY-STEP ▷ 1.9

1. Open your **Download** folder.

2. Select the **homepage.html** file you downloaded in Step-by-Step 1.6.

3. To delete a file, you can do one of the following. Pick the method that works best for you:
   a. Click and drag the file to the **Recycle Bin** (Windows) or **Trash Can** (Macintosh).
   b. Click the file once and press the **Delete** key in Windows or hold the **Apple** key next to the spacebar and press **Delete** in Macintosh.
   c. Click the **Delete** icon on the folder's toolbar.

4. Select the graphic you downloaded in Step-by-Step 1.7 and delete it.

5. Return to your Web browser's main screen and keep it open for the next Step-by-Step.

Net Concept

The term **network** is not limited to computers. In the business world, networking not only refers to the process of connecting computers but can also refer to the process of making friends and meeting new people who may share information with you and your company in the future.

INTERNET MILESTONE

FTP

Knowing how files and folders (directories) are organized on your personal computer is very helpful when you are on the Net. Net computers use a similar folder/file system to organize files on their hard drives. To copy from one Net computer's drives and folders to another, you'll use a service called *File Transfer Protocol (FTP)*.

FTP allows you to move files from place to place on the Internet. It is older than the Web and goes back to the earliest days of the Internet's existence. In the old days, you used text commands to move files, including:

Get—to get a file from another computer.
Send—to send a file to another computer.
Dir or ls—to list a directory of files on the FTP site.
Dele or Del—to delete a file or folder (called a directory).

A typical text command for FTP might be: *open ftp.netscape.com*
                                         get johnsmith/file.doc

Today, you can drag and drop the files from one computer to another by clicking and dragging the files you want with your mouse. Underneath all this user-friendly GUI ease a modern version of FTP is making the transfer for you.

Copying and Pasting Web Information

A **server-client network** is a network sharing information distributed by servers. This is the type of network on which the Internet system is based. It is kind of like going to a fancy restaurant. You, the customer (or **client**), look at the menu and give your order to the waiter. The waiter takes the order to the chef (the server), who prepares meals for everyone who has ordered. The waiter then brings the meal back and serves the meal to you, the (by now) hungry client.

Net Concept

A **server** is a high-speed computer that stores information to be shared and provides it to requesting clients.

The copy and paste tools can be very helpful when you are trying to capture information served to you by Web servers. With your Web browser's client tools, you can select text and images from a Web page, copy it to a virtual clipboard, and paste it to your document. For this activity, make sure you have a browser and a word-processing program accessible. You can use WordPad or Notepad in Windows or TextEdit on the Macintosh.

S TEP-BY-STEP ▷ 1.10

1. Open your word processor.

2. Launch your Web browser. Your home page should appear.

3. In the Web browser, move the mouse pointer to the beginning of the text you would like to copy. Any text will do.

4. Click and drag across the sentence or paragraph. Move your cursor down a couple of lines if you want to select more than one line. Release the mouse button. A section of the text should be highlighted, as shown in Figure 1-12A in Netscape Navigator or Figure 1-12B in Internet Explorer.

FIGURE 1-12A
Selecting text using Netscape

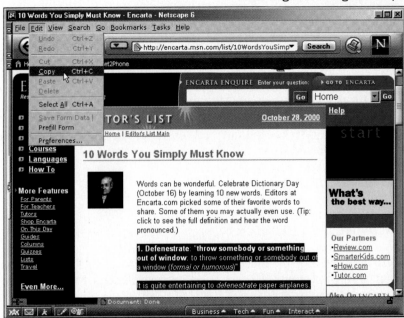

FIGURE 1-12B
Selecting text using Internet Explorer

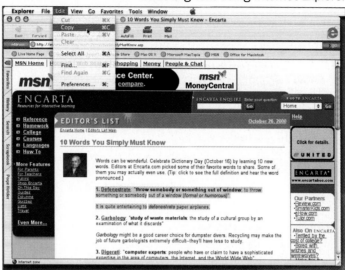

5. Select the **Edit** menu. Choose **Copy** to copy the selected text.

6. Switch to your word processor. You may do this by clicking its button on the taskbar or dock or by saying **Switch to <name of program>** if you are using speech software.

7. Inside your word processor document, choose the **Edit** menu and choose **Paste**. The text you selected in Step 5 should appear.

8. Switch back to your browser. Find an image on the home page that you would like to copy.

9. Right-click on the image to display the short-cut menu.

10. From this menu, choose either **Copy** or **Copy Image**, as shown in Figures 1-13A and 1-13B. (The name of the command varies depending on your browser or OS.)

FIGURE 1-13A
Copy image in Netscape

FIGURE 1-13B
Copy image in Internet Explorer

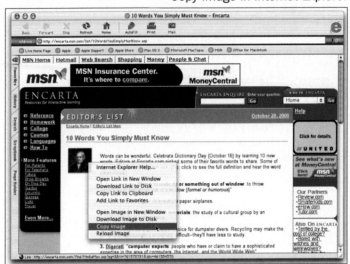

11. Switch to your word processor again.

12. Click just below the text you pasted. Choose **Edit > Paste**. The document should look similar to those in Figures 1-14A and 1-14B.

13. Close your Web browser and shut down if you are finished for today.

Net Concept

Some networks are called *peer-to-peer networks*, which means that every computer on the network has access to the resources on every other computer, including drives, files, and folders.

FIGURE 1-14A
Pasted text and image in WordPad

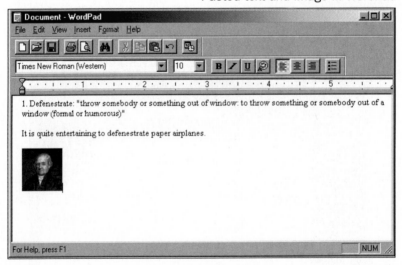

FIGURE 1-14B
Pasted text and image in TextEdit

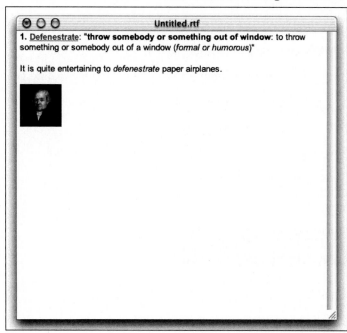

NET ETHICS

USING THE WORDS OF OTHERS

The Internet provides easy access to the ideas of others. As you saw in Step-by-Step 1.10, the Internet gives you the ability to copy and paste text and pictures into your document in an instant. However, just because this information is easy to copy, do not assume that you can present it to others as your own.

If you use the ideas of others in your writing, you should include a reference detailing where the information came from. Why do you think it is unethical to present the ideas of others as your own? What harm could result from doing this?

Summary

In this lesson, you learned:

- You can access pull-down menus and toolbars to control your browser.
- Today's browsers work in a similar manner on Windows, Macintosh, and Linux computers.
- You can scroll and resize windows to show more information on the Web.
- You can switch applications using the taskbar or dock.
- You can save a Web page or image using the File > Save As command.
- You can copy and paste Web information.

NET TERMS REVIEW

Define the following terms:

Active server pages	File Transfer Protocol (FTP)	Newbies
Client	Folder	Operating system (OS)
Dialog box	Graphical User Interface (GUI)	Peer-to-peer networks
Directory	Hypertext links	Server
Drives	Icons	Server-client network
File	Network	Speech recognition

LESSON 1 REVIEW QUESTIONS

TRUE/FALSE

Circle T if the statement is true or F if the statement is false.

T F   1. The Internet is one of the world's smallest networks.

T F   2. FTP moves files from servers to clients.

T F   3. Experienced Web users are called "newbies."

T F   4. Internet technologies have been around since the 1960s.

T F   5. The minimize button closes an application that is open.

FILL IN THE BLANK

Complete the following sentences by writing the correct word or words in the blanks provided.

1. The commands to copy and paste are found on the _____ menu.

2. A folder is also called a(n) _____.

3. Going online and exploring the Net is also known as _____.

4. _____ are like file cabinets that hold lots of files and folders.

5. A(n) _____ is a set of icons that provide one-click access to frequently used menu items.

WRITTEN QUESTIONS

Write a brief answer to the following questions.

1. What is the Internet and how does it work?

2. Describe how you can change the shape of a window using the click-and-drag method.

3. What tools would you use to move information from a Web page into your word-processing document? How do they work?

4. List the steps to create a new folder.

5. Explain how to copy an image from the Web.

LESSON 1 PROJECTS

SCANS

PROJECT 1-1

Create Your Own Personal Network

You just started working at GreatApplications, Inc., a software company in Atlanta, Georgia. The first day on the job is always difficult and exciting. You quickly discover that to do your job effectively you must depend on a number of other people. You may need a report from the marketing department, statistics from research and development, a spreadsheet from the accounting department, or help from network support.

You realize that you need to build a personal network of your own, made up of a list of friends, peers, colleagues, and business associates that can help you get your job done. Ultimately, a network of people will help you be a success at GreatApplications, Inc.

Build a network of school and business colleagues that can help you now and in the future. Interview at least five people and fill out a *Personal Network Contact Card* for each person. You must have a very diverse range of skills and interests in your group; it's ok to interview people you don't know.

Personal Network Contact Card

Name of contact

Personal Web page address: http://

Phone number

E-mail address

Interests

Skills

Computer experience

Comments (How could this person be helpful to me in my career?)

TEAMWORK PROJECT 1-2

Expanding Your Contacts

Form a peer group of three or four people. Do not form a group with your friends. Team up with people that you perhaps have never talked to before. Interview each other. Find out each person's skills, interests, and computer experience. Ask each of your new contacts, "How can we work together?" Create *Personal Network Contact Cards* for the newest members of your growing peer-to-peer network!

WEB PROJECT 1-3

Writing About Technology

Who should control online information? With what you know about the Internet at this point, write a 100- to 200-word answer to each of the following questions.

1. In your opinion, is it good or bad that so much personal information is available to everyone over the Net? Give reasons to support your decision.

2. How much control should the government have over Internet content? Should anyone have control over it? Support your position.

3. To what extent do computers and the Net have an impact on your life now? In what ways do you think that will change in the next 5 years? 10 years?

CRITICAL THINKING

ACTIVITY 1-1

Interpersonal Networking Online

Prepare a 100- to 250-word answer to the following. Think about your network of friends. What does each contribute to make your life better or easier? What do you contribute to each of them? In what ways do you think networking (computers and people) helps the business world or the government to run better? How can the Internet keep you in closer contact with your personal network of friends or future business contacts?

ACTIVITY 1-2

Organizing Online Data

Prepare a 100- to 250-word answer to the following. There are billions and billions of files in cyberspace. How difficult would it be to find something on the Net if every file was in one folder instead of separated and organized into folders broken down into many categories? What methods do you use to keep your computer organized? In what ways are they effective?

You have probably created hundreds, perhaps thousands, of files. On a sheet of paper, design a folder structure and organization that can help organize the files you have already saved and the many files you will save to your computer's hard drive in the future.

THROUGH THE LOOKING GLASS: A BROWSER PRIMER

OBJECTIVES

Upon completion of this lesson, you should be able to:

- Use a variety of browser tools.
- Use the address box to enter Internet addresses or URLs.
- View your history option.
- Move back and forth between pages you've visited.
- Visit Internet search portals.
- Add and organize your favorites/bookmarks.

⏱ Estimated time: 1.5 hours

NET TERMS

Address/Location box

Bookmark

Broadband

Cookie

Favorites

History folder

Mosaic

National Center for Supercomputer Applications (NCSA)

Search portal

Uniform Resource Locator (URL)

User-friendly

Long Ago in Cyberville

Not so long ago, the Internet was limited to scientists and military personnel who used difficult text-based commands to navigate from computer to computer. Back then, the Internet was not a *user-friendly* place to visit and only someone who really knew what he or she was doing could use it.

In 1993, the world's first well-known browser, *Mosaic*, was developed at the *National Center for Supercomputing Applications (NCSA)* by students and professors at the University of Illinois in Urbana-Champaign. The NCSA put a graphical user interface on the World Wide Web. Pictures could be viewed in the browser and linked to different pages using hyperlinks.

Net Tip

Hyperlinking is kind of like hyperspace on Star Wars. Choose a link, and suddenly you are transported from one place to another. You can jump from a Web page in your hometown to a computer in Hong Kong, Paris, or Kenya in the blink of an eye.

Introduce Yourself to Your Web Browser's Tools

In the previous lesson, we introduced you to your operating system and gave you a quick glance at your browser. Now we will go a little more in depth and help you become more familiar with the powerful tools contained in your browser. To get the most of the Internet, you must know how to use all the Web tools at your disposal.

There have been many different browser interfaces over the past decade. Every year, new innovations and greater creativity are added to the browser interface. You may have an old or a new Internet browser. In the activity that follows, you will compare your browser with the two shown in Figures 2-1A and 2-1B. The first shows a version of Microsoft's Internet Explorer for the Microsoft Network (MSN) users. The second figure shows a version of the Netscape Navigator.

S TEP-BY-STEP ▷ 2.1

1. Open your browser and compare the tools that your browser has with the samples shown in Figures 2-1A and 2-1B.

2. Mark all of the tools marked by the letters in Figures 2-1A and 2-1B with the tools listed in Table 2-1. When you feel like you can label all the tools by name on a quiz (hint-hint), move on to Step-by-Step 2.2.

3. Notice the similarities and slight differences between Netscape Navigator (Figure 2-1B) and Internet Explorer (Figure 2-1A). Which browser do you prefer and why?

4. Since its introduction in the 1990s, the browser interface has been constantly changing. Compare the two innovative browsers shown in Figures 2-1A and 2-1B with the more traditional browser shown in Figure 1-1. What changes do you see between the innovative and the traditional browser interfaces?

5. Compare the browsers shown in Figures 2-1A and 2-1B with your browser. Would you classify your browser as a traditional or an innovative browser? Which do you prefer?

TABLE 2-1
Identify these browser tools

LETTER		LETTER	
Forward button		Address box	
Back button		Scroll bar	
Close button		Home button	
Search tool		Title bar	

FIGURE 2-1A
Internet Explorer window

FIGURE 2-1B
Netscape Navigator window

MOSAIC

You've probably noticed by now that the Netscape Navigator and Internet Explorer browsers are very much alike. There's a reason for the similarities. Both browsers have their roots in an old software browser called *Mosaic.* Born at the National Center for Supercomputer Applications (NCSA), Mosaic became the "killer application" that made the World Wide Web popular. It is commonly believed that without Mosaic, the average person would never have heard of the World Wide Web or the Internet.

Mosaic was important in other ways. First, Marc Andreessen, the co-founder of Netscape, was a programmer on the original Mosaic software. Many of the other Mosaic programmers went to work for Netscape in 1994. Second, Mosaic never really died. A company called Spry bought the rights to the original Mosaic software. They in turn sold Mosaic to Microsoft, which used it as the basis for the original Internet Explorer.

Mosaic's place in history is secure, even if its place on your desktop has been relinquished to much more powerful browsing tools.

"Address Please" — Entering Internet Addresses

Probably the most important part of your Web browser is the *Address* or *Web Location box* shown in Figures 2-2A and 2-2B. This is where you enter the *Uniform Resource Locator* (**URL**)—the Web address of the Internet site you want to visit. Every URL is unique and is used to differentiate one Web page from billions of others.

FIGURE 2-2A

The Address/Web Location box in Explorer

FIGURES 2-2B

The Address/Web Location box in Navigator

STEP-BY-STEP ▷ 2.2

1. Launch your browser. If you need to connect to your Internet service provider, do so now.

2. Click once in the **Address** box. The URL in the box should be highlighted at this point. If it isn't highlighted, select all of the text with your mouse and press **Delete** to remove the address in the box.

3. In the empty box, enter the following address: **www.yahoo.com**.

4. Choose the **Go** or **Search** button to the right of the Address box or press the **Enter** key.

5. Yahoo! is an Internet search portal. Use the scroll bar take a quick look at the list of topics available at Yahoo! We're going to come back to Yahoo! in a later lesson.

6. Another way to enter a Web page address is the **File** menu. Select **File** and then **Open** (in Internet Explorer) or **Open Web Location** (in Netscape). The Open dialog box appears, as shown in Figures 2-3A and 2-3B.

7. Enter the address **www.excite.com**. Excite, like Yahoo!, is an Internet search portal.

8. Press the **Enter** key or choose **OK**. Leave your browser open for the next Step-by-Step.

Net Tip

The URL that was already in this box was the address of your home page. Your home page is the first page that automatically loads when you open your browser or create a new window.

FIGURE 2-3A
The Open dialog
box in Internet Explorer

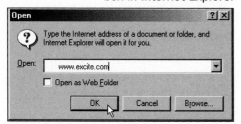

FIGURE 2-3B
The Open Web Location dialog
box in Netscape Navigator

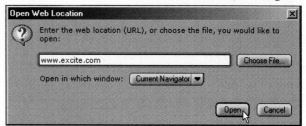

INTERNET MILESTONE

THE YAHOO! SEARCH PORTAL

Yahoo! was the first and remains a very popular *search portal*. A search portal maintains a directory of other Web sites. The brainchild of David Filo and Jerry Yang, two Ph.D. candidates in Electrical Engineering at Stanford University in 1994, Yahoo! quickly became a model for other search portals on the Internet.

David and Jerry wanted a way to keep track of their favorite sites on the Internet. This easy to use search portal has become a popular starting point for nearly everyone looking for information on the Internet.

The Toolbar: One-Click Commands

The toolbar gives you one-click access to the commands you'll use most. The Netscape Navigator and Internet Explorer toolbars are organized a little differently, as shown in Figures 2-4A through 2-4D. The most important buttons, including Back, Forward, Home, Stop, Refresh/Reload, Search/Find, and Print, are all easily accessible no matter which browser you use.

FIGURE 2-4A
An Internet Explorer toolbar

FIGURE 2-4B
Another Internet Explorer toolbar

FIGURE 2-4C
A Netscape Navigator toolbar

FIGURE 2-4D
A Mac Internet Explorer toolbar

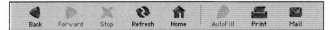

Using the Back and Forward buttons is a good way to move quickly between your most recently visited Web pages.

STEP-BY-STEP ▷ 2.3

1. With your Web browser open, visit **Yahoo!**

2. Now go to **Excite**.

3. At the Excite main page, choose any hyperlink.

4. Click the **Back** button (see Figure 2-5) to go back to the Excite main page.

FIGURE 2-5
The Back button

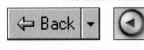

5. Click the **Forward** button (see Figure 2-6) to move to the previous page.

6. Click the **Back** button twice to move back to the Yahoo! main page. Leave your browser open for the next Step-by-Step.

FIGURE 2-6
The Forward button

A Refreshing Stop Home

The Home button (shown in Figure 2-7) is handy when you want to quickly jump to the home page. The Stop button (see Figure 2-8) lets you stop a Web page before it loads completely. You can use this tool if a Web page is loading too slowly or if you have changed your mind and want to go somewhere else.

The Refresh/Reload button (see Figure 2-9) loads your current Web page again. You can use this option if you have stopped a page in the middle of loading it, if a Web page doesn't load properly, or if you want to update a page to see if any changes have been made since you first brought the page up.

FIGURE 2-7
The Home button

 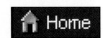

FIGURE 2-8
The Stop button

FIGURE 2-9
The Refresh/Reload button

STEP-BY-STEP ▷ 2.4

1. Enter the Web address **www.quicktime.com** and press **Enter**.

2. As soon as the Web site starts to load (but before it's finished), click the Stop button. The page may have some text on it, but most of the graphics will probably not be loaded completely.

3. Click the **Refresh/Reload** button to update and finish loading the page.

4. Press your **Home** button to return to your home page. Leave your browser open for the next Step-by-Step.

INTERNET MILESTONE

BROADBAND SPEEDS THINGS UP

The Net has never been more popular than it is today. This popularity once led to traffic jams and tie-ups on the Information Superhighway. Connections were slow, and a flood of users suddenly logging on would slow down the system in local areas. To limit user access, customers were charged for every minute they spent online.

Today, with a ***broadband*** high-speed connection, you can stay online for an unlimited amount of time for a set fee. Broadband has made it easier to get your Net work done. With broadband, multimedia Web pages, music, and videos download quickly.

Using the History Folder

In Step-by-Step 2.3, you learned how to use the Back and Forward buttons. The Back button is helpful to view a page that is a few steps back. But what if you want to view a page that is a few *hundred* steps back or one that you opened a few days back? Luckily, your browser keeps track of the most recent URLs you have visited in a ***History folder***.

The History folder is different in each browser, but each one shows the name of the pages you have visited and the URLs of those pages. This should be enough to help you find what you're looking for, even if your History folder contains hundreds of pages.

S TEP-BY-STEP ▷ 2.5

1. Choose the **History** button in Internet Explorer or select **Tasks**, **Tools**, and then **History** in Netscape.

2. Scroll through the list and find Yahoo! (see Figures 2-10A, 2-10B, and 2-10C).

3. Select the **Yahoo!** link to open that page in your browser window. Keep your Web browser open for the next Step-by-Step.

FIGURE 2-10A
History in Internet Explorer

FIGURE 2-10B
History in Netscape

FIGURE 2-10C
History in Mac Internet Explorer

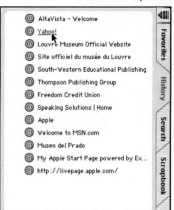

Adding Favorites/Bookmarks

Throughout your Internet travels, you'll want to return to many sites you've visited. Your browser makes this easy for you by creating *favorites* (in Internet Explorer) or *bookmarks* (in Netscape Navigator) for your favorite places. A bookmark or favorite is a little file that keeps track of the titles and URLs of the Web pages you want to visit frequently.

In the next Step-by-Step, we will bookmark a few additional search portals that we will make good use of in Unit 3. Search portals, such as Yahoo!, Excite, and AltaVista, are Web sites that maintain a directory database of other Web sites. You can enter in key words on these pages, and they will return many Web sites related to your topic.

Net Concept

Lynx was the first Web browser. Gopher is a primitive menu system that allows you to find files. Veronica and Jughead were early Net search tools. Pegasus and Eudora are e-mail programs. WebCrawler is a search engine. Who thought of all these weird names? Do you know any other strange Internet names?

STEP-BY-STEP ▷ 2.6

1. In the Address box, key **www.yahoo.com**.

2. In Internet Explorer, choose the **Favorites** menu. In Netscape Navigator, select the **Bookmarks** menu.

3. Select **Add to Favorites** (Internet Explorer) or **Add Current Page** (Netscape Navigator), as demonstrated in Figures 2-11A and 2-11B.

4. Click **OK** to add Yahoo!'s address to your Favorites/Bookmarks list.

5. Let's add an URL for another Web portal. In the Address box, key **www.altavista.com.**

6. AltaVista is one of the most powerful search portals on the Internet. Add AltaVista to your favorites by repeating Steps 2-4.

7. Now let's see how those favorites work when we want to go back to a page. Click the **Home** button to return to your home page.

8. Choose the **Favorites** or **Bookmarks** menu.

9. Move your pointer down the menu until Yahoo! is highlighted. Choose **Yahoo!**

10. Notice that you are now at Yahoo!'s Web page and the Address box displays Yahoo!'s URL. Try again with AltaVista. Leave your browser on your screen for the next Step-by-Step.

FIGURE 2-11A
Add to Favorites in Internet Explorer

FIGURE 2-11B
Add to Bookmarks in Netscape

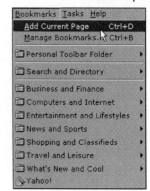

Cleaning House: Organizing Your Favorites

The more favorites you add, the more cluttered your favorites list is going to become. You need a way to organize the Favorites list so that you can quickly find exactly what you need, when you need it.

Let's start with the first two favorites/bookmarks you added. Both are links to search portal Web sites. A logical folder to put these in could be called *Search Portals*.

STEP-BY-STEP ▷ 2.7

1. Choose the **Favorites** or **Bookmarks** menu.

2. Select **Organize Favorites** or **Manage Bookmarks**.

3. In Explorer for Windows, click the **Create Folder** button (see Figure 2-12A). In Explorer for the Mac, select **Favorites** > **Organize Favorites** > **New Folder**. The Favorites tab will pop out from the left side of the browser window, as shown in Figure 2-12B. In Netscape, choose **File** > **New** > **New Folder** (see Figure 2-12C).

4. Name the new folder **Search Portals**.

5. Drag the **Yahoo!** icon to the **Search Portals** folder.

6. Drag the **AltaVista** icon to the **Search Portals** folder.

Net Concept

If you're doing research for e-business class, you may want to bookmark sites and then move them into a folder called *Business*. For sites related to your favorite football team, a folder called *Sports* or *Football* will do nicely. The most important thing to remember is to organize your folder system so that it makes sense to you.

7. Locate and add additional search portals to your folder, such as:

MSN:	www.msn.com
AOL:	www.aol.com
Google:	www.google.com
Ask:	www.ask.com

8. Close your Web browser and shut down your computer if you are done for today.

FIGURE 2-12A
Organizing Favorites in
Explorer for Windows

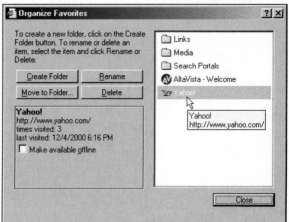

FIGURE 2-12B
Organizing Favorites in
Explorer for Mac

FIGURE 2-12C
Managing Bookmarks in Netscape

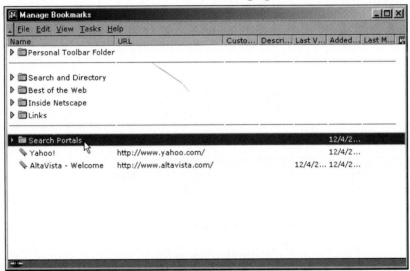

INTERNET MILESTONE

GOOD COOKIES, BAD COOKIES

You may be aware that every time you visit a Web site, a *cookie* can be saved to your hard drive. A cookie is information created by Web sites enabling them to collect information about you. It provides a way for the Web server to keep track of your habits and preferences and, with the cooperation of your Web browser, to store the information on your own hard drive.

Data from cookies can be added to the database of personal information of the company providing the cookie. This information can help the company adjust its advertising campaigns or even send you information or junk mail about things you might be interested in. Some cookie-like programs are powerful enough to read every file on your hard drive and scan every software program on your system.

Check the list of files on your hard drive. Do you have a *cookies.txt* file?

Summary

In this lesson you learned:

■ You can navigate using the toolbar buttons.

■ You enter a Web site's URL in the Address or Location box.

■ You can bookmark your favorite Web pages.

■ You can keep track of where you have been on the Web using the History feature.

■ You can access search portals.

NET TERMS REVIEW

Define the following terms:

Address/Location box
Bookmark
Broadband
Cookie
Favorites

History folder
Mosaic
National Center for
 Supercomputer Applications
 (NCSA)

Search portal
Uniform Resource Locator
 (URL)
User-friendly

LESSON 2 REVIEW QUESTIONS

TRUE/FALSE

Circle T if the statement is true or F if the statement is false.

T F 1. Cookies track your actions online.

T F 2. In Netscape, users save and categorize Web pages with the Favorites tool.

T F 3. Yahoo! and AltaVista are examples of search portals.

T F 4. The Refresh/Reload buttons are used to stop a page from loading.

T F 5. Toolbar buttons let you easily navigate back and forth between Web pages.

FILL IN THE BLANK

Label the parts of the browser window shown in Figure 2-13 by filling in the boxes.

FIGURE 2-13

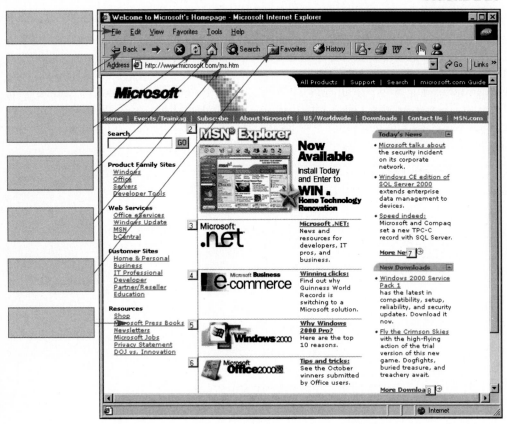

WRITTEN QUESTIONS

Write a brief answer to the following questions.

1. How can you locate and open a specific Web page by its URL with a Web browser?

2. What is the purpose of the Reload or Refresh tools?

3. How can the History feature help you?

4. What do bookmarks or favorites do for you and how can they be organized?

5. What differences are there between Internet Explorer and Netscape?

SCANS

PROJECT 2-1

Organizing Your Bookmarks

As you settle into your job at GreatApplications, Inc., you learn that much of your time will be spent doing research on the Internet. Because you will be visiting so many sites, you know how important it will be to keep track of sites you want to revisit.

Starting with an Internet search portal, find 25 Web sites of interest to you and bookmark them or make them favorites. However, this task isn't as simple as randomly clicking 25 links. You must organize your 25 Web pages into no more than five topics or categories. You can only have five URLs or Web sites in each category. Here is an example:

	SEARCH PORTALS	URL
1	AltaVista	www.altavista.com
2	Excite	www.excite.com
3	Yahoo!	www.yahoo.com
4	MSN	www.msn.com
5	Ask Jeeves	www.ask.com

Use what you have learned so far to organize your bookmarks or favorites. Use the following charts to organize your five categories. Then, transfer your work to your Web browser.

FIRST CATEGORY	
	URL
1	
2	
3	
4	
5	

SECOND CATEGORY

	URL
1	
2	
3	
4	
5	

THIRD CATEGORY

	URL
1	
2	
3	
4	
5	

FOURTH CATEGORY

	URL
1	
2	
3	
4	
5	

FIFTH CATEGORY	
	URL
1	
2	
3	
4	
5	

TEAMWORK PROJECT 2-2

Tackling Bookmarks With the Team

Sometimes when you work alone, you get stuck, fall into a cyber rut, and can't locate the best sites for each category you are researching. Teamwork can improve and greatly expand your selection of titles and Web addresses.

In teams of three or four, look at the lists you created in Project 2-1. Put together a combined team list that includes only the best URLs or Web addresses in each category. Make a copy for each member of the team.

WEB PROJECT 2-3

Writing With Technology

With what you know about the Net and Web browsers, write a 50- to 100-word answer to four of the following questions.

1. How is the organization of your favorites or bookmarks like the organization of the files and folders on your computer's hard drive?

2. In your opinion, which is the best Web browser? Why?

3. Explain, step-by-step, the process of finding a Web site or a specific Web page on the World Wide Web.

4. Try several Web search portals. Which provides you with the best information? What are the strengths and weaknesses of the search portal you chose?

5. Many people say they can't live without the Net. However, most people on the planet have never seen or used the Net. How important do you think the Web is in the personal life of the average individual?

ACTIVITY 2-1

Online Invasion of Privacy

Do companies have the right to put something on your hard drive without your knowledge? Do they have the right to scan or search your hard drive? Is this an invasion of privacy? If you requested a file from a server on the Web, should you be obligated to provide some kind of information back to the sender? What rules govern this type of information gathering? Is your hard drive like your home and should it be invaded only with a search warrant from a court? Or is your hard drive just another part of the Internet, open for all who have the technology to scan and read your computer's data? Prepare a 100- to 250-word answer to these questions.

ACTIVITY 2-2

Do You Have a Cookie Habit?

Check your History folder. (If you don't have much history yet, check a friend's History folder.) Do your Web travels show any patterns that reveal your (or your friend's) interests or habits? Why might such information be of interest to companies operating sites on the Web? What benefits may cookies have for the sender? Prepare a 100- to 250-word answer to these questions.

A Favorite Vacation Destination

A favorites list sure makes it easy to organize your favorite sites, even vacation sites. If you could go anywhere on vacation, where would you go? If you want to learn more about your favorite vacation destination, what kinds of information might you find on the Web? What folders would you need to keep track of the sites so you can find them when you plan that vacation? Prepare a 100- to 250-word answer to these questions.

WWWHAT? UNDERSTANDING NET ADDRESSES

OBJECTIVES

Upon completion of this lesson, you should be able to:

■ Identify and use hyperlinks.

■ Explain how hypertext links work in HTML.

■ Describe Internet addresses.

■ Discuss domain names.

■ Identify top-level, second-level, and country domain names.

■ Describe Internet protocol (IP) numbers.

⏱ Estimated time: 1.5 hours

NET TERMS

Cybersquatters

Domain name

Domain Name Server (DNS)

Host computers

Hyperlink (links)

Hypertext Markup Language (HTML)

Hypertext Transfer Protocol (HTTP)

Internet Corporation for Assigned Names and Numbers (ICANN)

Internet Network Information Center (InterNIC)

Internet protocol (IP)

Protocol

Second-level domain name

Top-level domain name (TLD)

Web servers

Hyper About Hyperlinks

The world has become hyper — hyperlinked, that is. ***Hyperlinks (links)*** make the Web popular by giving it an easy point-and-click interface. Hyperlinks allow you to point your mouse at words or pictures, click once, and jump to another page. And, it's getting so you don't even need a mouse. With speech recognition software, you can speak the links and zip all around the Net.

This lesson will show you how hyperlinks actually work. This is important to know, because you will probably be on the Web a great deal during your career and in school.

Net Concept

A *hyperlink* is a link to another Web page or Internet resource. The link is displayed as text or as an image. On Web pages, a hypertext link is usually displayed as underlined text. This text is often a different color.

S TEP-BY-STEP ▷ 3.1

1. Launch your Internet browser.

2. Select **Yahoo**! from your favorites list.

3. Move your mouse pointer slowly over the different hyperlinks and along the hyperlinked images. When your pointer turns into a pointing finger, as shown in Figure 3-1, you've found a hyperlink.

4. Move the pointer slowly over any hyperlink. This time, look at the status bar at the bottom of your browser window. It will display the address or URL where the hyperlink will take you.

5. Move your pointer slowly over another hyperlink. This time, choose an image such as the e-mail icon, a shopping link, or a hyperlinked graphic. Notice once again the new URL in the status bar.

6. Choose a hyperlink on the page and click it once. Your browser will take you to the new address. Leave your Web browser open for the next Step-by-Step.

FIGURE 3-1
Locating hyperlinks in Internet Explorer

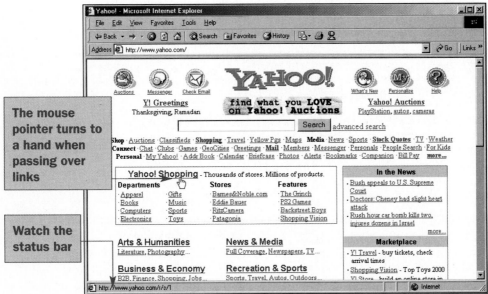

The mouse pointer turns to a hand when passing over links

Watch the status bar

How Hyperlinks Work

Because of its popularity, the Internet is attracting big business. Web addresses or URLs seem to be the hottest thing in advertising. You find URLs in advertisements in your favorite magazine, on TV, and even on the radio. However, most people who use the Web do not understand how URLs work.

URLs are like street addresses for the Web. A street address helps the postal service deliver mail by narrowing the search for the recipient to a country, state, city, particular area (using the ZIP code), certain street, and finally, to a specific location on a street. A mailing address has as many as six parts: (1) name, (2) street address, (3) city, (4) state, (5) ZIP code, and (6) country code, if the mail comes from overseas, as illustrated below.

> (1) *John Doe*
> (2) *1234 Anywhere Street*
> (3) *Santa Claus,*(4) *CA* (5) *09876* (6) *USA*

As you learned in Lesson 2, Internet addresses are known as URLs, which stands for Uniform Resource Locators. URLs locate resources on the Web the same way the postal person locates your home. URLs serve the same purpose as street addresses—they organize computers on the Internet so that no two have the same address and so they can all be located.

Here is a sample URL. Each part of the URL is numbered and then explained below.

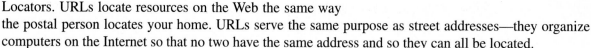

(1)www.somewhere.edu(2)/thisis/thepath/toa/(3)file.html

(1) *www.somewhere.edu* The first part of an URL identifies the **Web server** where the Web page is located. Web servers are **host computers** on the Internet that allow others to access their drives, folders, and files. They accept requests from Web browsers to transmit HTML pages and other files.

(2) */thisis/thepath/toa/* The second part lists the folders that need to be opened to locate the exact file being requested. The slashes (/) represent folders. Information on the Web's host servers are organized in folders just like those found on your computer.

(3) *file.html* The last part of an URL is the actual filename of the Web resource you are trying to find. Many times, the Web resource will be an HTML file ending with ".html" or ".htm."

INTERNET MILESTONE

INTERNET MILESTONE — PROTOCOLS

Internet protocols allow online computers to share information. One of the most common of these is **Hypertext Transfer Protocol (HTTP)**. HTTP is the communications protocol used to communicate to servers on the World Wide Web. Its primary function is to establish a connection with a server and transmit HTML pages to the client browser.

The *http://* part of the URL identifies the protocol that the computers use to talk to each other. A **protocol** is a communications system used to transfer data over networks. It is like a language that computers can speak and understand. Addresses of Web sites begin with an *http://* prefix. Other protocols include FTP (File Transfer Protocol), which begins with a *ftp://* prefix, and newsgroups (an e-mail-like service for groups), which begins with a *news://* prefix.

S TEP-BY-STEP ▷ 3.2

1. Analyze the address below. Explain to another person the four parts of this URL.

   http://www.disney.com/mickey/friends/ pluto.html

2. Make a list of three URLs that you have seen in advertisements, either in magazines, on the radio, or on television (for example, www.disney.com).

   a. _____

   b. _____

   c. _____

3. Visit the three URLs you listed in Step 2. Click on links that you find on those pages. This should open folders and allow new filenames to appear as you locate new resources on this Web site. Write the names of the folders' filenames that appear. The URLs will be much longer (for example, *www.disney.com/mickey/ mousefile.html*).

   a. _____

   b. _____

   c. _____

   Leave your Web browser open for the next Step-by-Step.

Creating Hypertext Links

Hidden HTML tags make hyperlinks or links work. Links hide inside Web pages where most people never see them. They are written similar to this:

<a href="http://www.disney.com">Click to link to Disney's Web site </a>

Hypertext links are created with the hypertext reference tag that begins with an angle bracket such as this: *<a href=*. This link appears on the screen as:

Click to link to Disney's Web site

Knowing how URLs work is essential to understanding how links work. You can view these hidden tags by choosing View on your browser's menu bar and then selecting the Source command to reveal them.

S TEP-BY-STEP ▷ 3.3

1. Visit any one of the URLs you listed in the previous Step-by-Step.

2. After the page loads, click the **View** menu and choose **Source** (or **Document Source** or a similar command), as shown in Figure 3-2.

3. The hidden Web page document will appear. All of the funny-looking writing (see Figure 3-3) tells Web browsers how Web pages are meant to work. Scan this document looking for HTML hypertext links. You can use the **Find** feature to look for three hypertext reference (HREF) tags.

4. Record the three hyperlink reference tags you locate using the following as an example: *<a href=http://www.google.com>The Google Search Portal</a>*.

<a href=http://_____>_____</a>

<a href=http://_____>_____</a>

<a href=http://_____>_____</a>

Keep your Web browser open for the next Step-by-Step.

FIGURE 3-2
Choose the **View** menu, then **Source**

FIGURE 3-3
Locating hyperlink HTML tags

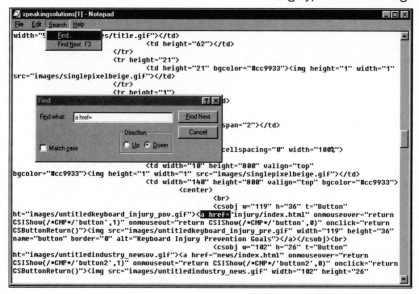

Domain Names and IP Numbers

URLs contain **domain names**. A domain name is like the ZIP code used by the U.S. Postal Service to find your home among the millions of homes around the world. Domain names help locate specific computers from the millions and millions of Web servers on the Internet. Take these popular domain names:

abc.com
apple.com
microsoft.com

 Net Concept

Like Web servers, Internet computer servers are assigned numbers. These numbers look like this: 158.91.46.101. IP numbers are written as four sets of numbers with dots or periods between them. The numbers in each set can go as high as 254, or as low as one. Every Internet server is assigned its own unique number.

But hold on a second! Computers use numbers to communicate—not words. So, how does this work?

A domain name like *www.abc.com* points specifically to a computer with a number called an *IP* or *Internet protocol* number that actually may be something like 158.91.6.46. No other computer on the Internet can use that same number.

When you want to visit the Disney Web site, you enter in the domain name *www.disney.com*, and a special *Domain Name Server (DNS)* looks up the name and matches it with its assigned number. Then, off you go, winding your way through numbered cyberspace to the correct Web server owned by ABC with a number like 158.91.6.46.

S TEP-BY-STEP ▷ 3.4

1. Let's see who owns which names on the Web and find their IP numbers. Enter the following URL:

   http://www.networksolutions.com

2. Click the **WHOIS Lookup** link, as shown in Figure 3-4.

3. The chart below lists a number of domain names. Enter each domain name in the site's search box, as shown in Figure 3-5. Click the **Search** button. A window similar to that shown in Figure 3-6 should open.

4. Enter the owner's name and IP numbers for each domain name in the chart. Remain in this screen for the next Step-by-Step.

 Net Concept

People have a hard time remembering IP numbers! Let's face it, it's a lot easier to remember Microsoft.com than it is to remember a number like 158.91.6.46. Luckily, domain names are converted to IP numbers by special DNS servers that match names to their assigned IP numbers and whisk your request along its path to the resources you are looking for.

DOMAIN NAME	OWNER	IP NUMBERS
disney.com		
nbc.com		
cbs.com		
fox.com		
espn.com		

FIGURE 3-4
Network Solutions' Web site

FIGURE 3-5
Network Solutions WHOIS page

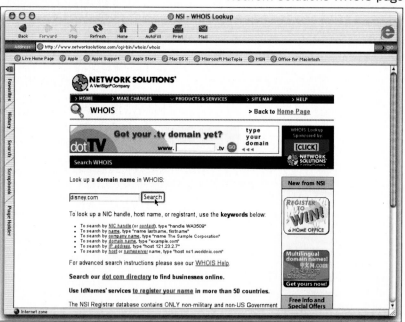

FIGURE 3-6

Locate the owner and IP number

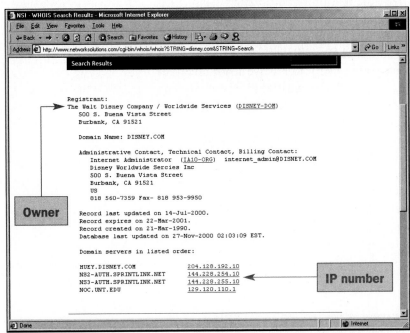

Top-level Domain Names

Imagine the fantastic number of businesses that must be on the Web now! What do you think would happen if two or three businesses wanted to use the same URL? What if both the fast-food chain McDonald's and the McDonald's Boot Repair Shop in Lubbock, Texas, want to use the URL *www.mcdonalds.com* and have them assigned to computers with different IP numbers, like 123.345.678.9 and 158.91.6.47?

Who should have rights to use the McDonald's domain name? Well, all that is decided by international organizations.

 Net Concept

The *www* in *www.mcdonalds.com* indicates that this is a host server on the World Wide Web. The second item to the right—*mcdonalds*—is the second-level domain name, which is the part of the URL that's registered by a company or individual. The last item—*com*—is the top-level domain (TLD).

InterNIC, or *Internet Network Information Center*, was the organization first assigned to register Internet domain names to their rightful owners. This was performed under a U.S. government contract. The honor of this task now falls to *ICANN*, the non-profit corporation established to assume responsibility for the domain name system. ICANN maintains and adds top-level domain names for the Internet. Understanding TLDs will help you identify the type of information you're likely to receive from a certain site. For example, TLDs tell you what kind of entity owns that domain. The first top-level domain names to appear on the Net were:

.com	Commercial institutions or businesses
.edu	Educational institutions
.gov	Government sites
.mil	Military sites
.net	Network gateways
.org	Organizations
.int	International organizations

These top-level domain names are like ZIP codes that help domain name servers quickly find the correct computer.

STEP-BY-STEP ▷ 3.5

1. Visit ICANN online at **www.icann.org** and answer the following questions.

   ICANN is an acronym. The full name of the organization is the _____ _____ for _____ _____ and _____.

   According to the information on its Web site, what is the purpose of ICANN?

   _____

   _____

   _____

   Search the ICANN site for information about IANA. What is this organization and what is it responsible for?

   _____

   _____

   _____

   Search the ICANN site for information about ccTLDs. What are ccTLDs?

   _____

   _____

   _____

Lesson ③ WWWhat? Understanding Net Addresses

2. Go to your favorite Web search portal and find an organization to match four of the six Internet top-level domain names listed in the chart below. For example, networksolutions.com would fit into the .com category.

TLDS	SECOND-LEVEL DOMAIN NAME CONTAINING THE SPECIFIED TLD	NAME OF THE ORGANIZATION THAT OWNS THIS SECOND-LEVEL DOMAIN NAME
.com	Networksolutions.com	Network Solutions
.edu		
.gov		
.mil		
.net		
.org		
.int		

3. In a November 2000 meeting in Cairo, Egypt, ICANN added new TLDs to the Internet. These names include *.museum, .biz, .info, .name, .pro, .aero, and .coop.* Each TLD describes the type of organization that might buy and use one of these top-level domain names. In the chart on the next page, enter a description of the type of organization you think might use these new top-level domain names.

4. Check and see how correct your guesses were by looking at the correct answers on page 61 in the lesson.

 Net Concept

Internet users are very familiar with the *www* that appears at the beginning of many URLs. However, organizations can decide not to require the *www*. Organizations can make their domain name successful without using this prefix. For example, the URL *apple.com* will access the same information as www.apple.com.

NEW TLDS CREATED IN 2000	DESCRIBE THE TYPE OF ORGANIZATION THAT MIGHT BE INTERESTED IN USING THIS TLD
.mil	Military organizations such as United States Army or the Canadian Air Force
.museum	
.biz	
.info	
.name	
.pro	
.aero	
.coop	

5. New top-level domains can be added by ICANN at any time. For example, the top-level domain names *.kids* or *.web* are popular suggestions.

Think of five top-level domain names that you would like to see added to the World Wide Web. List them in the chart below:

YOUR TLD SUGGESTIONS	DESCRIBE THE TYPE OF ORGANIZATION THAT MIGHT BE INTERESTED IN USING THIS TLD

 Net Concept

Second-level domain names are also popular to use with country codes. For example, a complete set of state second-level codes exist for the United States, such as .ca.us for California or .ut.us for Utah.

6. Country names are another set of top-level domain names that are used frequently. Some of them are obvious, such as *.us* for the United States or *.ca* for Canada. A typical URL using a country domain name could be: *http://shs.sugarville.ut.us*. This address could represent a high school (SHS) in Sugarville, Utah, in the United States. Guess the countries that have been assigned the top-level country domain names listed in the following chart.

TOP-LEVEL COUNTRY DOMAIN NAME	COUNTRY IT REPRESENTS
.va (Hint: Europe)	Vatican City (Rome)
.cl (Hint: South America)	
.gb (Hint: Europe)	
.gr (Hint: Europe)	
.kw (Hint: Middle East)	
.ru (Hint: Europe and Asia)	
.yu (Hint: Eastern Europe)	
.mx (Hint: North America)	
.fr (Hint: Europe)	
.ke (Hint: Africa)	
.jp (Hint: Asia)	

 Net Concept

Anyone can register a second-level domain name—businesses, organizations, or individuals. However, to get your own second-level domain name, you must pay a registration fee to a company like Network Solutions that will then register your name with the ICANN database for you. Although ICANN keeps track of registered domain names, you can't actually register at their site.

NET ETHICS — ONE DOMAIN, TWO DOMAINS, THREE DOMAINS, MORE

Domain names must be unique. In other words, there can be only one *www.disney.com* on the Internet planet. Only one *www.abc.com* can exist in cyberspace. Only one *www.cbs.com* can be found. But what if Mary Disney registers a domain name *www.disney.com*? Can she hold onto that name, even if the Walt Disney Co. seems to be a more logical owner?

Many people have deliberately registered domain names that major companies are likely to want. These people are called ***cybersquatters***. They register domain names for a few hundred dollars and try and sell the names later to other companies for several thousand or even millions of dollars.

Is this ethical? For example, should Mary Disney be able to keep her domain name if she wants to—especially since she got it first? Who should argue copyright disputes regarding domain names on the Net? What if Mary Disney is a travel agent who specializes in tours to Disney World? Should she be able to use the Disney name to promote her business? If she pays $100 for the name, can she sell the domain name *www.disney.com* to anyone she likes for $10,000, $100,000, or a $1 million or more?

Because some top-level domains, such as *.com*, were beginning to fill up, ICANN came up with more top-level domain names like *.biz* and *.pro* to decongest the Internet and make it more difficult for cybersquatters to hold Web addresses for ransom. But soon, these will start filling up too.

Summary

In this lesson, you learned:

- You can identify and use hyperlinks.

- You can identify the different parts of a Web address.

- You can understand how domain names and IP numbers work together.

- You can explain the difference between top-level, second-level, and country domain names.

- You can explain the role of various organizations and how they maintain the Internet's domain name structure.

NET TERMS REVIEW

Define the following terms:

Cybersquatters	HTTP	Protocol
DNS	Hyperlink (links)	Second-level domain name
Domain name	ICANN	TLD
Host computers	InterNIC	Web servers
HTML	IP	

LESSON 3 REVIEW QUESTIONS

TRUE/FALSE

Circle T if the statement is true or F if the statement is false.

T F 1. An example of a top-level domain name is *www*.

T F 2. Web addresses are similar to a postal address.

T F 3. Cybersquatters are people who register domain names so that they can sell them for thousands of dollars to large companies.

T F 4. Domain names are a group of numbers like 158.91.6.46.

T F 5. Entering *www.disney.com* will point you to a server with an IP number like 46.

IDENTIFICATION

Using the following Web address, identify the parts of an URL.

(1)*www.somewhere.edu/*(2)*thesis/apath/toa/*(3)*file.html*

1. _____

2. _____

3. _____

WRITTEN QUESTIONS

Write a brief answer to the following questions.

1. What are TLDs? Name as many examples as you can.

2. Explain the purpose of a top-level domain name.

3. How does a hyperlink work?

4. What is the difference between a domain name and an IP address?

5. Describe how you can find out who owns a specific domain name.

LESSON 3 PROJECTS

SCANS

TEAMWORK PROJECT 3-1

Start an URL Collection

Your first project at GreatApplications, Inc., is a little homework on what other companies are doing on the Internet. You first need to collect some Web addresses. Using the resources you have (at home, in the media, or in your library's periodical section), collect a list of URLs. You will need to find addresses in several different categories to get a broad view of the information available. Try to find URLs for companies in each category on the chart that follows.

Instead of finding all the URLs for the chart yourself, get together with your team and divide up the topics among team members. Team members should note the two most interesting sites they find for their assigned topic and view these sites with the team.

CATEGORY	DOMAIN NAME	COMPANY NAME	IP NUMBER
Automotive			
Technology/computers			
News/information			
Home shopping			
Food/beverage			
Entertainment			

SCANS

WEB PROJECT 3-2

Top-Level Domain Names for Other Countries

The international office of GreatApplications, Inc., has written you an e-mail asking for the top-level domain names of the countries listed below. Search http://www.icans.org or other online sources for the top-level domain names for these countries.

1. Brazil = _____
2. Kyrgzstan = _____
3. Nigeria = _____
4. Zambia = _____

CRITICAL THINKING

ACTIVITY 3-1

Thinking and Writing About Technology — The Impact of the Web

With what you know about business and the Internet, prepare a 100-word answer to four of the following questions.

1. How important is it for a business to have an Internet domain name? Why you think it is or is not important?

2. Is the Internet really a tool for business or is it mainly for entertainment? Give examples to support your answer.

3. How do you think the Web is changing the way we work? Give examples.

4. How has the Web changed the way we interact with one another? Is the change good or bad? Give examples.

5. Think about your address. What information does the different parts of your home address supply? Why is this information needed? How is the information conveyed by your home address similar to the kind of information conveyed in the URL for a Web site?

Answers to Step-by-Step 3.5, step 3.

.museum	Museums
.biz	Businesses and commercial institutions
.info	Informative sites
.name	Personal sites
.pro	Professional (doctors, lawyers, etc.) sites
.aero	Aerospace sites
.coop	Cooperative sites

YOUR DREAM BROWSER

Your Personal Browser

What if you were told that you couldn't have any pictures or decorations in your room or office? Your space would not be as personal, would it? Your office, room, and living areas don't seem personal until you make them that way.

Before graphical user interfaces, or GUIs, programs were impossible to customize. To perform any simple computer task, you had to memorize keyboard commands. There were no button bars or menus. However, as more and more people began to use computers, they demanded simpler, more personalized interfaces. User-friendly programs were born.

An interface is the way you interact with a computer program — how you tell it what to do. The interface includes toolbars, pull-down menus, title bars, and dialog boxes. Since you are the one who is going to sit in front of your browser day after day, you may want to personalize it a little to make it yours.

Before we get started, remember that your browser may be different from those pictured here. You may need to experiment to make the types of changes that have been described. In this lesson, the concepts are more important than the individual steps. Investigate how to make these concepts work with your browser.

Toggling the Toolbar and Status Bar

With top-quality software, you can customize your browser interface to fit your needs and likes. For example, you can change the way your browser displays hypertext links or you can turn off the toolbar and status bar. To increase the size of your browser window, try the optional settings described below with your browser.

STEP-BY-STEP ▷ 4.1

Reclaiming "Real Estate" in Internet Explorer

(Note: Netscape users should skip to the next section, called *Reclaiming "Real Estate" in Netscape.*)

1. In Internet Explorer for Windows, select **View** on the menu bar and then choose the **Full Screen** option, as shown in Figure 4-1A. In Internet Explorer for Macintosh, choose the **Collapse Toolbar** button above the **Favorites** tab (see Figure 4-1B). Presto! The toolbar shrinks, the menus disappear (in Windows), and the address and links toolbars vanish, giving you maximum screen "real estate" in which to view the Web. All you should see are navigation buttons.

FIGURE 4-1A
Full Screen option
on Windows
Internet Explorer's
View menu

FIGURE 4-1B
Collapse
Toolbar button
in Explorer for
Macintosh

Net Concept

Many of the commands on menus, such as those on the Toolbars submenu, are toggles. A *toggle* is a control that allows you to alternate between two options. It is like a light switch. In this case, the options are on or off.

2. Click the **Full Screen** (Windows) or **Collapse Toolbar** (Macintosh) option again to restore your previous settings. (Windows users can also restore the browser to normal by clicking the **Restore** button, as identified in Figure 4-2A.)

FIGURE 4-2B
Collapsed Toolbar navigation buttons in Explorer for Macintosh

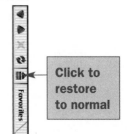

FIGURE 4-2A
Full Screen navigation buttons in Explorer for Windows

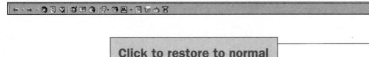

Click to restore to normal

3. To manipulate toolbars, Windows users should select the **Toolbars** option on the **View** menu to display a submenu, similar to the one shown in Figure 4-3A. Macintosh users may see the toolbars listed immediately, as shown in Figure 4-3B. (Note: A check mark indicates that the toolbar option is on. If no check mark appears next to the option, then the toolbar is off.)

FIGURE 4-3A
Toolbar toggles in Internet Explorer for Windows

4. Click each option on the Toolbars submenu to turn each toolbar off.

5. Restore your toolbar options to the original settings by reversing the process and then skip to the Changing Font Options section on page 66 to continue with the lesson.

FIGURE 4-3B
Toolbar toggles in Internet Explorer for Macintosh

Net Tip

The Maximize button is also a toggle. When the window is full size, or maximized, clicking the Maximize button makes the window smaller. Choose the Maximize button again, and the window returns to full size. This toggle allows you to alternate between two options: full size and reduced size.

Reclaiming "Real Estate" in Netscape

1. You can collapse a toolbar by clicking the button on the left side of the toolbar, as shown in Figure 4-4. Select the button now. This doesn't turn the toolbar off—it simply moves it out of the way.

FIGURE 4-4
Collapsing toolbars
in Netscape

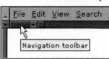

FIGURE 4-5
Expanding toolbars
in Netscape

2. Click the collapse button again to expand the toolbar to full size, as shown in Figure 4-5.

3. To turn toolbars on and off, select the **View** menu and choose **Toolbars,** as shown in Figure 4-6.

FIGURE 4-6
Managing your personal toolbar

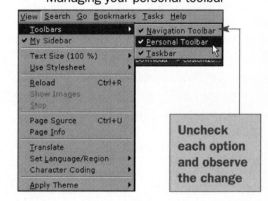

4. Click each option on the Toolbars submenu to turn it off.

Uncheck each option and observe the change

5. Restore your toolbar options to normal by reversing the process and then skip to the Changing Font Options section to continue with the lesson.

Changing Font Options

Most Web pages use your browser's defaults to display fonts, background colors, and hyperlinks. You can personalize the settings on your browser to suit your tastes. However, some Web pages will overwrite your settings by specifying certain fonts or color schemes.

Follow the directions for the browser you are using. If these steps do not fit your browser, use the Help feature to learn how to accomplish these tasks.

Net Tip

IE is short for Internet Explorer!

Net Tip

A list of choices that you can scroll through to make a selection is called a *list box*.

STEP-BY-STEP ▷ 4.2

Changing Font Options in Internet Explorer

(Note: Netscape users should skip to the next section, called *Changing Font Options in Netscape*.)

1. Select the **View** menu.

2. In Windows, choose **Text Size** and select **Medium** from the submenu, as shown in Figure 4-7A. On a Macintosh, select **Text Zoom** and then **100%**, as shown in Figure 4-7B.

3. Now, repeat steps 1 and 2, only this time select the largest setting. What happened to your Web page?

4. Select **View, > Text Size > Medium** (in Windows) or **View > Text Zoom > 100%** (in Macintosh) to restore the font size to normal.

5. In Windows, select **Tools > Internet Options**. On the Macintosh, select **Edit > Preferences**.

6. In Windows, select the **General** tab and click the **Fonts** button. On the Macintosh, select **Language/Fonts**.

7. In Windows, scroll down the list of fonts in the Web page fonts list box, as shown in Figure 4-8A. In Macintosh, select the down arrow next to the **Proportional** list box to display font choices, as shown in Figure 4-8B.

FIGURE 4-7B
Changing font size in Internet Explorer for Macintosh

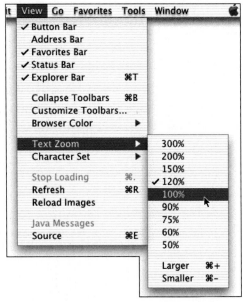

FIGURE 4-7A
Changing font size in Internet Explorer for Windows

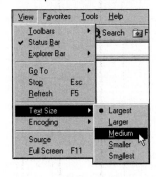

8. Select any font from the list, as shown in Figures 4-8A and 4-8B.

9. Click **OK** to apply your font choice.

10. Restore your font options to normal by reworking the steps and then skip to the Changing Colors section on page 69 to continue with the lesson.

FIGURE 4-8A
Changing fonts in Internet
Explorer for Windows

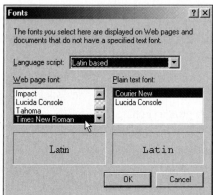

Net Concept

Just as wheelchair ramps provide accessibility to public buildings, *accessibility options* make the Web accessible to those with visual impairments. Changing the size of a font on a Web page can provide accessibility to the partially blind. Technology also exists to allow Web pages to be read to the blind, the very young, or the illiterate. These *text-to-speech (TTS)* technologies are making the World Wide Web accessible to millions.

FIGURE 4-8B
Changing fonts in Internet Explorer for Mac

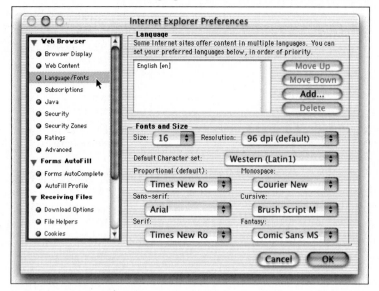

Changing Font Options in Netscape

1. Select **View > Text Size > Larger** to increase the font size (see Figure 4-9).

2. Try different options on the Text Size submenu and view the impact of the changes on your Web browser display.

3. Select **View > Text Size > 100%** to return the font size to normal.

4. Select **Edit** and then **Preferences**.

5. Select the **Fonts** option beneath Appearance, as shown in Figure 4-10.

6. In the Variable Width Font list box, select a font.

7. Select a font size from the **Size** list box.

8. Choose the **OK** button to apply the settings and view the impact of the changes you have made.

9. Restore your browser's font options to normal and then skip to the Changing Font Options section on page 64 to continue with the lesson.

10. Restore your font options to normal by reversing the steps and then skip to the Changing Colors section on page 70 to continue with the lesson.

FIGURE 4-9
Changing font size in Netscape

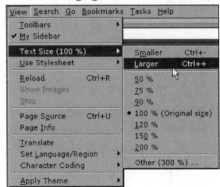

FIGURE 4-10
Changing fonts in Netscape

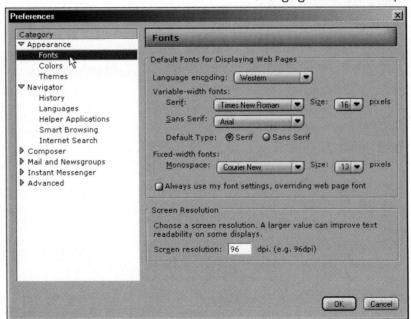

Changing Colors

You can change the color of many items in the browser window, including hyperlinks, fonts, and the background. These changes add interest and impact to Web pages.

S TEP-BY-STEP ▷ 4.3

Changing Color Options in Internet Explorer

(Note: Netscape users should skip to the next section, called Changing *Color Options in Netscape*.)

1. In Windows, select **Tools > Internet Options** and then click the **Colors** button. On the Macintosh, select **Edit > Preferences** and choose **Web Content**.

2. Select the color swatch button (see Figures 4-11A and 4-11B) next to each option to select a color. A *color swatch* is a special button that shows the currently selected color. (Note: In Windows, you must uncheck **Use Windows colors** to change the text and background options.)

3. Return to your browser and experience the changes that have taken place as a result of the selections you have made. Describe the changes here:

    _____

    _____

    _____

4. Repeat steps 1 and 2 to return your browser to its normal settings.

5. Close your browser and shut down your computer if you are done for today.

FIGURE 4-11A
Changing color schemes in Internet Explorer for Windows

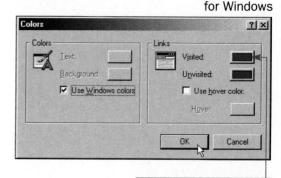

Color swatch button

Net Concept

Font sizes and styles affect the way a reader receives a message. For example, you will see many different font sizes and styles in this book. Why do you think some of these were selected? How does, say, bold type affect the message? If you were designing a Web page, what would you consider in selecting fonts, sizes, and styles for different parts of your message?

FIGURE 4-11B

Changing color schemes in Explorer for Macintosh

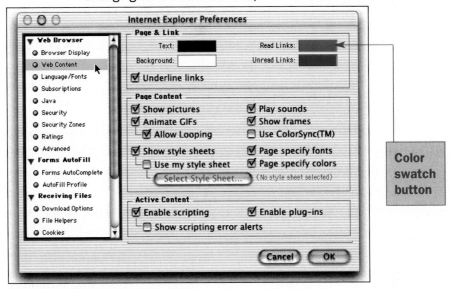

STEP-BY-STEP ⟹ 4.3 **CONTINUED**

Changing Color Options in Netscape

1. Select **Edit > Preferences.**

2. Choose **Colors** in the Appearance category, as shown in Figure 4-12.

FIGURE 4-12

Changing color schemes in Netscape

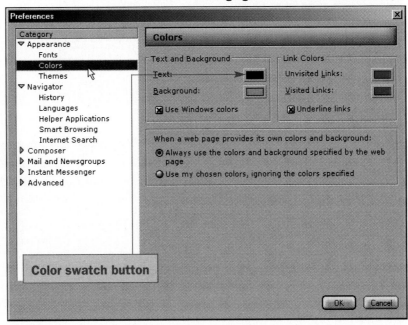

3. Choose a color swatch button next to each option. A color swatch, similar to that shown in Figure 4-13, displays color choices. Select any colors you like. (Note: In Windows, you must uncheck **Use Windows colors** to change the text and background options.)

4. Return to your browser and experience the changes that have taken place as a result of the selections you have made. Describe the changes here:

_____

_____

_____

5. Repeat steps 1, 2, and 3 to set your browser back to its normal settings.

6. Close your browser and shut down your computer if you are done for today.

 Net Concept

After you have visited a Web page, the hyperlink to that page will be colored with the *visited color*. Hyperlinks you haven't followed will display the *unvisited color*. It's a good idea to keep these colors different. The *Hover* option will highlight a hyperlink when your pointer is over it.

FIGURE 4-13
Typical color swatch

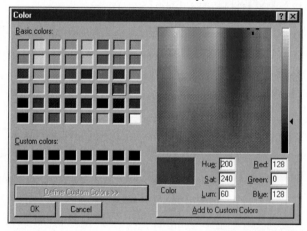

 Net Concept

Many Web page creators design backgrounds using graphic images rather than using typical color choices. This means that regardless of the changes you make, the Web page will appear exactly as intended by its creator. Graphics will be unaffected by the changes you are making in this section.

INTERNET MILESTONE

UNIX

All applications must be able to talk to an operating system, or OS. Without an OS, the computer hardware cannot interact with the software and the computer won't work.

One of the earliest and longest lasting operating systems is *Unix.* In 1965, Bell Labs was working with MIT and General Electric to write an OS for their large mainframe computers, called Multics. Bell Labs decided to leave the project; however, they still needed an OS and so they continued to work on one.

As sort of a pun on Multics, the new Bell Labs operating system was named Unix. Although it was slow to catch on outside of academic institutions, eventually businesses started using it. Unix went on to become the dominant network OS during the early days of the Internet. Unix remains a major force on the Net even today. In fact, Apple Computer integrated Unix into its next generation operating system, Mac OS X, to make it fast and powerful. The Linux OS is also based on Unix.

NET ETHICS

PUBLIC OR PRIVATE FUNDING

In the early days of the Internet, most Net services, connections, and software were considered free. They weren't really. Many of the early Internet services were developed by government grants to universities. The *National Science Foundation (NSF)* was a major force in the creation of the Net. Because of NSF grants of money, universities provided students with free e-mail and other Internet services. The first Internet GUI Web browser (Mosaic) was free, for example.

In 1995, businesses started to discover the Web, and many corporations found ways to make money on the Internet. E-commerce was born, and the Web went from being an academic information experiment to an essential business and profit-making tool.

Summary

In this lesson, you learned:

- You can customize your Web browser options and preferences.
- You can use Web browser toggle options.
- You can capture screen real estate.
- You can change font style options.
- You can change font colors.
- You can change the visited and unvisited link colors.
- There are many operating systems on the Web, such as Unix.
- You can access browser accessibility options.
- You can collapse and expand your toolbars.
- You can change the appearance of your Web site.

NET TERMS REVIEW

Define the following terms:

Accessibility options	NSF	Unix
Hover	TTS	Unvisited color
List box	Toggle	Visited color

LESSON 4 REVIEW QUESTIONS

TRUE/FALSE

Circle T if the statement is true or F if the statement is false.

T F 1. When you change your color options, it will change how every Web page is displayed.

T F 2. Unix is one of the newest operating systems on the Net today.

T F 3. You can change a color by clicking on a color swatch.

T F 4. A toggle switches between three options.

T F 5. Accessibility options are state-of-the-art, high-speed Internet connections.

FILL IN THE BLANK

Complete the following sentences by writing the correct word or words in the blanks provided.

1. As more people began to use computers, they demanded more personalized interfaces. Therefore, _____-_____ programs were born.

2. A(n) _____ is a control, like a light switch, that allows you to choose between two options.

3. _____ options make the Web accessible to those with visual impairments.

4. Without a(n) _____ _____, the computer hardware cannot interact with the software.

5. Both the _____ OS and the _____ OS are based on Unix.

WRITTEN QUESTIONS

Write a brief answer to the following questions.

1. If you start your browser and a navigation toolbar isn't on your screen, what can you do to get it back?

2. Explain step-by-step how to change a browser's font type to 11 pt. Arial.

3. Describe how to change your browser's font to red and your Web page background to blue.

4. Do you think the browser you are using is user-friendly? In what ways is it or isn't it? What would you change to make your browser more user-friendly for you?

5. How would you rate your browser's menu and toolbar organization? Is it easy to find the toolbar option you are looking for? What could be done to make it better?

LESSON 4 PROJECTS

WEB PROJECT 4-1

The Net Means Business

Noting your ability to gather and organize information, your boss has rewarded you with a new project: In next week's board meeting at GreatApplications, Inc., you are to give an evaluation of how companies are using the Internet to enhance their business online. Talk about pressure!

Surf the Net. Visit four business sites. Find out how top companies are using the Net. Explore as many pages on each site as possible. Evaluate the strengths and weaknesses of each site for next week's meeting. Use the evaluation forms that follow to help organize your research.

Company Name _____
Address _____

Site Organization   Poor ❑   Fair ❑   Good ❑   Excellent ❑
   Are categories well-defined? _____
_____

Site Information   Poor ❑   Fair ❑   Good ❑   Excellent ❑
   Does the site (overall) provide relevant and pertinent information? _____
_____

Page Organization   Poor ❑   Fair ❑   Good ❑   Excellent ❑
   Do the pages (in general) contain too much or too little information? _____
_____

Visual Aspects   Poor ❑   Fair ❑   Good ❑   Excellent ❑
   Are the graphics on the page helpful or distracting? _____
_____

   Personal Impression—As a consumer, would this site help or hinder your purchasing decision? What other feelings did you have about the site? Would you visit the site again? Why or why not?
_____
_____

Company Name _____
Address _____

Site Organization   Poor ❑   Fair ❑   Good ❑   Excellent ❑
   Are categories well-defined? _____
_____

Site Information   Poor ❑   Fair ❑   Good ❑   Excellent ❑
   Does the site (overall) provide relevant and pertinent information? _____
_____

Page Organization   Poor ❑   Fair ❑   Good ❑   Excellent ❑
   Do the pages (in general) contain too much or too little information? _____
_____

Visual Aspects   Poor ❑   Fair ❑   Good ❑   Excellent ❑
   Are the graphics on the page helpful or distracting? _____
_____

   Personal Impression—As a consumer, would this site help or hinder your purchasing decision? What other feelings did you have about the site? Would you visit the site again? Why or why not?
_____
_____

Company Name _____
Address _____

Site Organization   Poor ❏   Fair ❏   Good ❏   Excellent ❏
    Are categories well-defined? _____
_____

Site Information   Poor ❏   Fair ❏   Good ❏   Excellent ❏
    Does the site (overall) provide relevant and pertinent information? _____
_____

Page Organization   Poor ❏   Fair ❏   Good ❏   Excellent ❏
    Do the pages (in general) contain too much or too little information? _____
_____

Visual Aspects   Poor ❏   Fair ❏   Good ❏   Excellent ❏
    Are the graphics on the page helpful or distracting? _____
_____

    Personal Impression—As a consumer, would this site help or hinder your purchasing decision? What other feelings did you have about the site? Would you visit the site again? Why or why not?
_____
_____

Company Name _____
Address _____

Site Organization   Poor ❏   Fair ❏   Good ❏   Excellent ❏
    Are categories well-defined? _____
_____

Site Information   Poor ❏   Fair ❏   Good ❏   Excellent ❏
    Does the site (overall) provide relevant and pertinent information? _____

Page Organization   Poor ❏   Fair ❏   Good ❏   Excellent ❏
    Do the pages (in general) contain too much or too little information? _____
_____

Visual Aspects   Poor ❏   Fair ❏   Good ❏   Excellent ❏
    Are the graphics on the page helpful or distracting? _____
_____

    Personal Impression—As a consumer, would this site help or hinder your purchasing decision? What other feelings did you have about the site? Would you visit the site again? Why or why not?
_____
_____

TEAMWORK PROJECT 4-2

Voting Businesses Off the Web

After you finish your individual analysis of business Web sites in Project 4-1, meet with a team of three or four members. To keep things organized, nominate one person as the team leaders.

With an Internet browser running for all to see, review and analyze as a group the top company home pages collected by each team member in Project 4-1. Review all of the sites.

One by one, vote Web sites off the Web. Start with the worst sites and keep going until just one site survives. List the last site to survive below:

The Survivor _____

CRITICAL THINKING

ACTIVITY 4-1

To Make Money or Not to Make Money

Form two teams—one pro and one con—and debate the following questions:

Do private companies have a right to make a profit on the Internet, since it was essentially started with taxpayer dollars? Where do businesses' right to make money and and the rights of students, schools, and tax-paying citizens begin? What obligations, if any, should businesses have concerning Internet profits? Should the Internet be free to everyone at all times or all profit making all of the time?

ACTIVITY 4-2

Toggling Through Life

You learned that a toggle allows you to alternate between two options. Are there other examples of toggles in life? For example, the answers on a true/false exam are like toggles—each answer is either true or false. What other examples can you think of? List as many toggles as you can in 60 seconds.

BRINGING IT HOME: DOWNLOADING FILES

OBJECTIVES

Upon completion of this lesson, you should be able to:

- Find shareware programs.
- Explain why files are compressed on the Internet.
- Recognize common compression format extensions.
- Find information about decompressing files.
- Download and decompress files.
- Download and install FTP software.

⏱ Estimated time: 2 hours

NET TERMS

Algorithms

Compressed files

Download

Drivers

Executable files

File extensions

Leaseware

Mirror site

Patches

Self-extracting files

Shareware

Viruses

Get It, Try It, Buy It

The Internet has revolutionized the transfer of data from one place to another. Users can download many useful files from the Internet. For instance, the Internet has provided software companies with new ways to market, sell, and distribute their products as shareware or through online leasing programs called leaseware.

Shareware is software that anyone can download for free, try out for a certain period of time, and then purchase if they decide to continue using it. Shareware benefits the user because he or she enjoys the insurance of "try before you buy" to determine if the product is really worth buying.

You can also lease software, rather than buy it. With both shareware and leaseware, the software companies save money in two ways:

 Net Tip

Download means to transmit a file from one computer to another. Generally, download means receive and upload means transmit.

1. They don't have to spend a lot of money on expensive packaging and documentation. Everything is transmitted electronically over the Net.

2. Most major software programs are designed so that you have to access only the developer's Web page to automatically have your software updated.

Non-software businesses also benefit from the ability to transfer data online. For example, architects can trade drawings across the Internet with their clients and engineers working on the project. Salespeople on the road can dial into a company database and transmit the day's orders so they can be shipped immediately.

Finding Shareware

Shareware can be found all over the Net. All you have to do is enter the word *shareware* in any search tool, and you'll find over a thousand possibilities. You can use your search portal to locate a specific type of shareware.

Net Concept

There are many shareware compression programs. Each of these uses compression **algorithms,** or complex mathematical formulas, to make files smaller.

STEP-BY-STEP ▷ 5.1

1. Launch your browser.

2. *Shareware.com* is a very popular Net site maintained by CNet. It catalogs more than 250,000 shareware files on the Internet. Enter the address **www.shareware.com**.

3. In the search box, enter a search word such as *games*, *business*, or *compression*, as shown in Figure 5.1.

4. In the Choose from list box, choose your OS. For example, Windows users select Windows, as shown in Figure 5-1. If you are using a Mac, select Macintosh.

5. Choose **Search**.

6. View the files that appear and read the descriptions of the shareware. Scroll down the list so you can see the variety of shareware offerings.

7. Try some other search words and find new categories of shareware. Leave your Web browser open for the next Step-By-Step.

FIGURE 5-1

Search *Shareware.com* for shareware programs

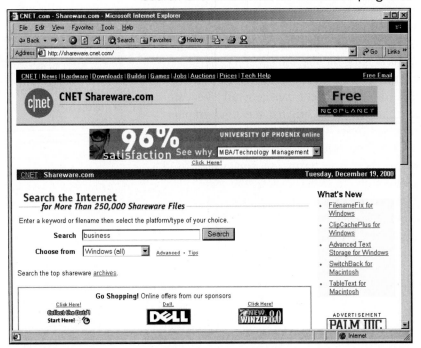

INTERNET MILESTONE

ONLINE SOFTWARE REPAIRS

Users benefit from being able to have the software on their computers updated over the Internet. Software code is very complex stuff. Often, software has bugs or problems that are not found until after the product has been delivered.

Software companies can provide updates and ***patches*** from their Web sites for users to download. Patches are fixes for software bugs. Imagine the cost of mailing disks to every one of the registered Windows users in the world to patch a bug. Instead, companies can use their Web sites to supply new files and graphics to an interface, fix a problem, or update a program.

Updating is especially important with virus protection programs. Because new ***viruses***—programs that are destructive to computers—are discovered every day, these protection programs allow you to download new virus detection files every month.

Software companies can also electronically distribute updated ***drivers***. Drivers are programs that allow hardware, like printers and sound cards, to communicate with your operating system. When you install a new hardware device on your computer, such as a scanner or CD-ROM drive, you must install its driver to run it. The operating system calls for the driver, which drives the device.

Compressing Files

Compressed files are compacted from their normal size to save space. File sizes are very important on the Internet, because the smaller the file, the faster it can transfer. No one likes to sit around for hours waiting for the newest shareware game to download. Text can generally be compressed to about 40 percent of its original size, and graphics files can be compressed from 20 percent to 90 percent.

Compressed files are often called archives, zip files, binhex files, or exe files. The terms are sometimes used interchangeably, although they aren't exactly the same. They often refer to a specific *file extension* that shows the type of compressed file. Extensions are usually three-letter endings after a dot that describe a file type or file category.

Net Concept

There are many compression techniques and software programs on the Net. WinZip, which can open zipped files, is a very popular compression program for Windows users. StuffIt Expander is a shareware program that can decompress both Macintosh and Windows files.

You'll notice that most of the files at the *Shareware.com* site end in three-letter extensions, as shown in Figures 5-2A and 5-2B. In Figure 5-2A, you will see *.exe* and *.zip* extensions for compressed Windows files. In Figure 5-2B, you will see compressed Macintosh files that end in *.hqx* and *.sit*.

FIGURE 5-2A
Compressed file examples for Windows

CNET : Shareware.com	Search Results for business		
Found: **233** Displaying: **76-100**		<Previous 1 2 3 4 5 6 7 8 9 10 Next>	
Re-sort by Filename		Platform/Type	File Date
directopps.zip Business Opportunities E Zine **Location:** winsite-win95 archive **Directory:** misc/ **Size:** 263K		Windows 95	05/29/2000
disdm21.exe A Business Organiser for Driving Instructers **Location:** winsite-win95 archive **Directory:** business/ **Size:** 642K		Windows 95	09/28/2000
disdm21.zip Business mgmnt prog. for Driving instructors **Location:** sim-win3 archive **Directory:** business/ **Size:** 623K		Windows 3.x	10/02/2000
dogfeetg.zip Dogfeetgames hoteldemo: Tourism business game **Location:** sim-win95 archive **Directory:** business/ **Size:** 172K		Windows 95	12/17/1999
dxl31.zip DESIGNEXPRESS LABELS v1.14 - The ultimate label program and utility desktop publisher. Professional designs, full Avery support, label sets, fonts, CD-R, Business Cards, Audio Tapes, more. **Location:** ad-asp-win3 archive **Directory:** ./ **Size:** 2.0MB		Windows 3.x	06/20/1997

FIGURE 5-2B
Compressed file examples for Macintosh

CNET Shareware.com	**Search Results for business**		
Found: **67** Displaying: **1-25**			\<Previous 1 2 3 Next\>
Re-sort by Filename		Platform/Type	File Date
ae-tracker.hqx		Mac	11/27/2000 *new*
Location: info-mac archive **Directory:** app/bus/ **Size:** 1.8MB			
amug-98-10.hqx		Mac	12/02/1998
Location: info-mac archive **Directory:** per/amug/ **Size:** 961.2K			
appwatcher-21.hqx		Mac	07/09/1999
Location: info-mac archive **Directory:** cfg/ **Size:** 229.9K			
appwatcher-21.hqx		Mac	07/09/1999
Location: info-mac archive **Directory:** cfg/ **Size:** 229.9K			
aqua-business-manager.hqx		Mac	10/07/2000
Location: info-mac archive **Directory:** app/bus/ **Size:** 5MB			
banking.lbr Small business checking system		Unspecified	08/05/1986
Location: oak-cpm-other archive **Directory:** dbaseii/ **Size:** 31.5K			

Decompressing Files

As you learned in Step-by-Step 5.1, files are compressed so that they can be downloaded more quickly. Some file types, like *.exe* files, are easy to decompress. Decompressing expands the files back to their original size. Compressed files are often Windows *executable files*. An executable file is a program file. It executes commands and runs the programming designed by the programmer of the executable file. In Windows, double-click on the file or choose **Start**, **Run**, and then **Browse**, find your file, and select OK, as shown in Figure 5-3. Your *.exe* file will launch an installation Wizard and install the program for you. Macintosh users should double-click to launch an executable file.

You can open certain compressed files on a Macintosh by double-clicking the downloaded file. A decompression utility, such as StuffIt Expander, will automatically decompress the file and expand it to full size.

FIGURE 5-3
Use the Run option to open an *.exe* file

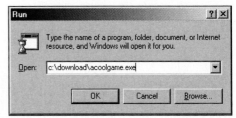

S TEP-BY-STEP ▷ 5.2

1. Visit **www.aladdinsys.com** and read how StuffIt works (see Figure 5-4). With the permission of your network administrator, you can download a trial copy of the software and give it a try. Be sure to download the correct version for your computer: Macintosh or Windows.

2. If you're a Windows user, you can also visit **www.winzip.com** and read the information about WinZip software (see Figure 5-5). With the permission of your network administrator, you can download an evaluation version and try it out! Leave your Web browser open for the next Step-By Step.

FIGURE 5-4
Read how StuffIt works

FIGURE 5-5
Read about WinZip

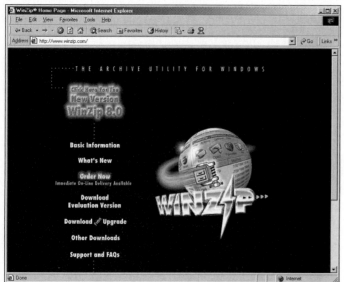

Net Concept

Compression File Types

It's good to be familiar with compression file types so that you will know which tool to use to expand them. Here are some file extensions that identify a few of the more common compression types:

For Windows:
Zip = *.zip*
Self-extracting file = *.exe*

For Macintosh:
StuffIt = *.sit*
Binhex = *.hqx*
MacBinary = *.bin*
Self-extracting archive = *.sea*
Windows *.exe* files and Macintosh *.sea* files are executable programs, not just files containing words and pictures. Because they do not require another program to decompress them, they are called **self-extracting files**. To decompress a Windows executable self-extracting file, select **Start**, **Run**, and then **Browse**, find your file, and select **OK**. To decompress a Macintosh self-extracting file, locate it and then double-click.

Downloading FTP Software

One of the primary methods for transferring files from one computer to another over the Internet is FTP. Browsers can handle most FTP tasks with simply a point and click. However, the FTP capability of a browser often is not efficient enough. Serious FTP users can download various FTP software programs from *www.tucows.com*.

Net Tip

Windows deliberately hides file extensions. To reveal them, click **Start**, **Settings**, and then **Control Panel** and open **Folder Options**. Click the **View** tab and remove the check from the Hide file extensions for known file types. (See Figure 5-6.)

FIGURE 5-6
Showing file extensions in Windows

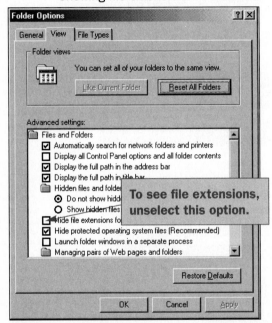

Net Concept

When software companies update your software online, they can scan your computer looking for illegal copies of their product.

STEP-BY-STEP ▷ 5.3

1. Enter the address **www.tucows.com** in your Web browser. The Tucows Web site will be displayed, as shown in Figure 5-7.

2. When Tucows prompts you, select your operating system from the menu provided.

3. From the pull-down menu select your country or, if you live in the United States, select a state near you (see Figure 5-8), and choose **GO**.

4. Choose a mirror site from the list. A *mirror site* is a site that has the same files as another Web site but is hosted by a different host server. You can download files faster from mirror sites because they are geographically distributed, taking the download pressure off the main site.

5. Choose the **Download Software** link.

FIGURE 5-7
Tucows Web site

FIGURE 5-8
Select your country and state

6. Under the Network Tools category, select the **FTP** link. Descriptions of various FTP software programs are listed, as shown in Figure 5-9. Scroll down and read the descriptions.

7. Get permission from your network administrator to download an FTP shareware program. Create a folder named **Download**. Review Step-by-Step 1.5 in Lesson 1 for instructions on how to create a folder. (Note: Save the file to this folder, so you can find and then delete the *.exe* or *.hqx* file after you finish installing the software, as in Figure 5-10.)

FIGURE 5-9
FTP software programs

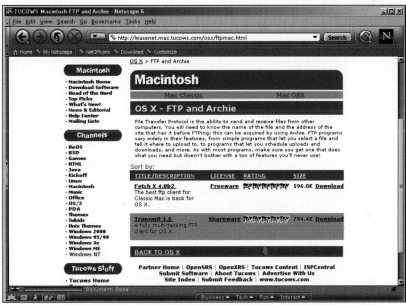

FIGURE 5-10
Downloading and saving FTP software

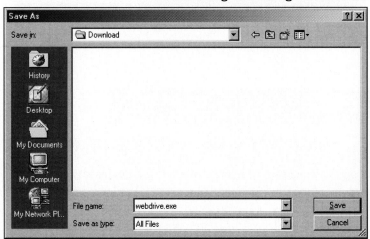

8. In Windows, you can watch the progress of your download on the status bar, as shown in Figure 5-11. You can do the same thing using the Internet Explorer Download Manager on Macintosh, as shown in Figure 5-12. After the program downloads, run it using the **Start, Run** option (in Windows) or double-click it with your mouse on either the Windows or the Macintosh platform. Follow the instructions as the program decompresses and installs. If you chose a file that needs special conversions, work with your network administrator or other team members to learn how to convert and open your downloaded file.

9. Exit any open programs and files if you are finished working today.

FIGURE 5-11
Download status bar in Windows

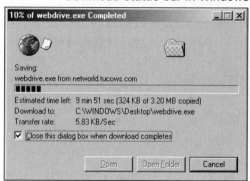

FIGURE 5-12
Internet Explorer Download Manager on Macintosh

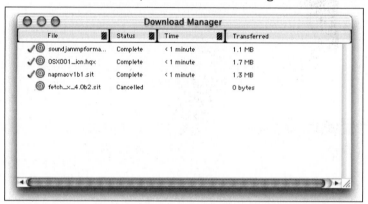

NET ETHICS

SHAREWARE AND LEASING DILEMMA

How many extra or pirated copies of a program do you think exist for every copy that has been purchased? That is an interesting question. When you download a shareware program, you are given a certain length of time to try the product before you buy it. However, many people never pay. This makes it hard on developers of shareware because they often depend on user revenue to continue to improve the program.

Summary

In this lesson you learned:

■ Shareware files can be found online.

■ Files can be compressed for transfer over the Internet.

■ There are common compression format extensions.

■ You can decompress files.

■ You can download and decompress files.

■ There are techniques to download and install FTP Software.

NET TERMS REVIEW

Define the following terms:

Algorithms	Executable files	Patches
Compressed files	File extensions	Self-extracting files
Download	Leaseware	Shareware
Drivers	Mirror site	Viruses

LESSON 5 REVIEW QUESTIONS

TRUE/FALSE

Circle T if this statement is true or F if the statement is false.

T F **1.** FTP stands for Front Top Publishing.

T F **2.** Compressed files are smaller than normal files.

T F **3.** A patch is something you move your mouse on.

T F **4.** Tucows is a place where you can download files.

T F **5.** Shareware is an expensive way to distribute software.

FILL IN THE BLANK

Complete the following sentences by writing the correct word or words in the blanks provided.

1. A(n) _____ site has the same exact files as a different or main Web site.

2. To use a scanner or printer you must first install a(n) _____.

3. Compressed files that do not need a program to expand are called ____-_____ ____.

4. Many files end with something like .exe or .zip. These endings are known as file _____.

5. _____ is software that you can "try before you buy."

WRITTEN QUESTIONS

Write a brief answer to the following questions.

1. Do you think the "try before you buy" philosophy is a good one? What are the advantages? What are the disadvantages?

2. What can software companies do to encourage people to pay for their shareware or leaseware?

3. What is the advantage of compressing and decompressing files? Are compressing and decompressing files more of a hassle than they are worth? Why or why not?

LESSON 5 PROJECTS

WEB PROJECT 5-1

Train Your Colleagues

Many of the new employees at GreatApplications, Inc., have very little actual computer experience. Since some of your team members have never used compression files before, you have been asked to conduct a training meeting on the things you learned in this lesson. You may need to become a little more familiar with the various steps for finding, downloading, and decompressing files. Explore Help files and Web sites for hints and help.

When you are comfortable with the process, write an outline to guide you through your presentation. You will need to help employees step-by-step through the process. Prepare any Help files and folders you need for your presentation.

Make your instructions clear and easy to follow. Teach the concept and then follow it up with reinforcement. Remember, the better you teach your colleagues now, the fewer problems they will have in the future.

TEAMWORK PROJECT 5-2

Build a Training Program as a Team

Meet with your team of three or four classmates and combine your presentations from Project 5-1 into one multimedia training program for new employees. Create the multimedia presentation on the basis of what your team has learned from each other about this important procedure.

CRITICAL THINKING

ACTIVITY 5-1

Is Compression Necessary?

Many Net users are aware that files on the Net are compressed or made smaller by special compression software. What would happen if none of the files on the Net were compressed? What would the impact be on the worldwide transfer of data?

ACTIVITY 5-2

One Cow, Tucows, Three Cows, More

Tucows uses a cow system to rate shareware: five cows for the best programs and one cow for the worst programs. If you're a shareware provider and got four and a half cows, would you want your product listed? What if you only got a cow and a half? Would you still want to be listed? What suggestions would you give shareware providers to help make their software the best five-cow program on the list?

REVIEW QUESTIONS

TRUE/FALSE

Circle T if this statement is true or F if the statement is false.

T F 1. GUI stands for Greater User Interaction.

T F 2. Graphics and pictures on a computer are often called icons.

T F 3. Marc Andreessen was the co-founder of Yahoo!

T F 4. Only the last URL visited can be found in the History folder.

T F 5. LYNX is a popular operating system for Web servers.

T F 6. IP is short for Internet protocol.

T F 7. The extension *.com* represents a second-level protocol name.

T F 8. A toggle switches between two options.

T F 9. UNIX is a powerful Web browser that rivals Netscape and Internet Explorer.

T F 10. You should pay for the shareware you use.

MATCHING

Match the description in Column 2 to its correct term in Column 1.

Column 1	**Column 2**
____ 1. Linux	**A.** High-speed Internet connection
____ 2. Algorithms	**B.** Software that allows Web surfing without a mouse
____ 3. Yahoo!	**C.** Popular Internet server OS
____ 4. Download	**D.** Fixes for software bugs
____ 5. Speech recognition	**E.** A window that the information be entered before the software can execute a command
____ 6. Protocol	**F.** To receive an online file onto your computer
____ 7. Broadband	**G.** Created the first GUI browser
____ 8. Patches	**H.** A search portal
____ 9. Dialog box	**I.** Mathematical formulas
____ 10. NCSA	**J.** A communications system that allows the smooth transfer of data over the Net

CROSS-CURRICULAR ACTIVITIES

Internet search portals are extremely powerful tools for conducting research on academic subjects. The humanities make up a broad range of subjects, including art, music, history, and literature, to name a few. Use various search portals to discover the broad range of information about some of these topics.

ART 1-1

Visit your favorite Internet search portal and search for the art section. List the many categories of art that can be found, such as Renaissance, impressionist, and neoclassical, in a word processing file. Save your file as **Art 1-1** in the saving folder that you created with your name in Step-by-Step 1.5.

ART 1-2

Choose one area of art and investigate it more thoroughly. Write a short 250-word report about this art category and explain why it is distinctive or different from other forms of art. Save your word processing file as **Art 1-2** in your saving folder.

ART 1-3

Download a Web page that describes the style of art you wrote about in Art 1-2. Save it to your personal saving folder. Rename the file **Art 1-3**.

MUSIC 1-1

Just as there are categories of art, there are categories of music. These categories are often called genres. Nearly every Internet search portal has a section on music. Visit the various genres of music that have been organized by a search portal. For example, you're certainly going to find rock, jazz, soul, and classical. List all the general categories of music that your search portal has organized in a word processing file. Save your file as **Music 1-1** in your saving folder.

MUSIC 1-2

Choose one of the categories of music and investigate it more thoroughly. Write a short 250-word report about this style of music and explain why it is distinctive or different from other forms of music. Save your word processing file as **Music 1-2** in your saving folder.

MUSIC 1-3

Download a Web page that describes the style of music you wrote about in Music 1-2. Save it to your personal saving folder. Rename the file **Music 1-3.**

CRITICAL THINKING

ACTIVITY 1-1

Do you think offering shareware online is a good way for small companies to make money? What kinds of shareware do you think would be most popular with Net surfers? What are some possible pitfalls to shareware? Record your thoughts in a 100- to 250-word essay. Save your file as **Activity 1-1** in your saving folder.

ACTIVITY 1-2

Certainly there is a great deal of piracy over the Internet. This fact brings up many thought-provoking and ethical issues. What do you think about people who deliberately steal and pirate copies of shareware? Would your attitude change if a person was pirating leaseware or making copies of software CDs of various commercial game programs? What can and should you do if you know that a friend of yours is deliberately pirating and copying software illegally? These are tough questions. Record your thoughts in a 100- to 250-word essay. Save your file as **Activity 1-2** in your saving folder.

ACTIVITY 1-3

Should everyone have personal access to the Internet any time they want it? What would be the impact if every single person on the planet had a broadband Internet connection and was connected constantly to the Internet? Do you think the positives would outweigh the negatives? Record your thoughts in a 100- to 250-word essay. Save your file as **Activity 1-3** in your saving folder.

SIMULATION

JOB 1-1

GreatApplications, Inc., needs to develop a shareware software library of various Internet and network related tools. Use what you know about shareware to research and make a list of possible shareware programs that employees would find helpful for their jobs. Save your list as **Job 1-1** in a word processing file and place it in your saving folder.

JOB 1-2

Think of second- and first-level domain name combinations that would be very marketable and powerful domain names for companies in the following industries. For example, *speakingsolutions.com* would be a great name for an speech recognition software company. Input your answers and then save your file as **Job 1-2** and place it in your saving folder.
1. A multimedia and graphic arts company.
2. A community bank.
3. A fishing supply company.
4. A cabinet construction and woodworking company.
5. A travel agency.

E-COMMUNICATION: ... ETC.

LESSON

6

GOODBYE SNAIL-MAIL: AN INTRO TO E-MAIL

OBJECTIVES

Upon completion of this lesson, you should be able to:

- Compose and send an e-mail message.
- Retrieve and read an e-mail message.
- Create folders and organize your mailbox.
- Send an attachment.
- Use the address book.

⏱ **Estimated time: 2 hours**

NET TERMS

Archive

Attachments

Blind copy (BC)

Courtesy copy (CC)

E-mail

Emoticons

Header

Inbox

Internet Service
Provider (ISP)

Post Office Protocol (POP)

Proprietary software

Rich Text Format (RTF)

Spam

Subject line

E-mail E-merges

E-mail is short for electronic mail. It includes memos, messages, and attachments transmitted over a network. Almost everyone on the Internet uses e-mail as a primary means of communication. With e-mail, you can communicate with anyone in the world within seconds. Even better, e-mail can be free.

Many businesses use e-mail as an essential communications system both within and outside the company. An advantage of e-mail in business is the ability to communicate the same message to one person or several hundred people at the same time.

Thanks to improved transfer and file compression methods, almost any type of file can be attached to an e-mail message. You can send a sound clip of your band, the latest picture scanned into your computer, or a word-processing document.

You can receive e-mail service through a proprietary system, through an Internet service provider for a fee, or free over the Internet on an advertisement-based e-mail provider.

Proprietary E-mail

Proprietary software is a program owned and controlled by a company or person. If your school or business maintains its own e-mail system, chances are it uses proprietary e-mail software, such as Microsoft Exchange, Novell GroupWise, or Lotus Notes. These e-mail systems allow a great deal of control for the system managers, but the trade-off is that they cost megabucks to purchase and maintain.

Net Tip

Internet Service Providers (ISPs) link their Web servers to the Net. An ISP is a business that physically connects its customers to the Internet.

Your school or business may, however, use a less expensive system built for the Internet. E-mail programs using the *POP* or *Post Office Protocol* can be set up virtually for free. Most of these run on Unix or Linux computers. Free or shareware POP e-mail compatible programs, like Outlook Express (see Figure 6-1), Netscape E-mail, and Eudora, offer all the user features found in e-mail systems costing thousands more.

FIGURE 6-1

Outlook Express can be used by proprietary and ISP providers

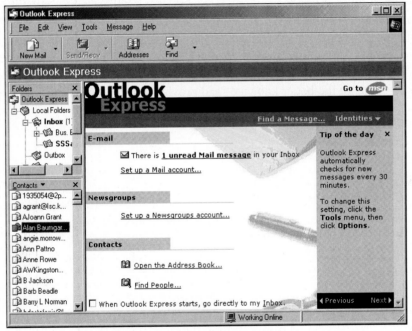

INTERNET MILESTONE

QWERTYIOP

In 1971, a computer engineer named Ray Tomlinson invented e-mail. The first test message was something like QWERTYIOP, letters found along the top line of the keyboard. Intended for communication among research scientists, university students, and military personnel, e-mail quickly gained popularity, causing great interest in a "new" thing called the Internet. E-mail preceded the World Wide Web by about 20 years and opened the door to chat and messaging technologies (see Lesson 7).

E-mail From an Internet Service Provider

Another alternative is to pay a small monthly fee to have an *Internet Service Provider (ISP)* provide e-mail service. America Online and Microsoft Network are the largest of these ISPs. There are ISPs of all shapes and sizes to choose from. The ISP provides all the software you need and maintains the system for you. Purchasing e-mail service through an ISP is very popular, because it is inexpensive and mostly trouble-free.

Free Advertisement-Based E-mail on the Web

Free e-mail can be obtained over the World Wide Web at any one of a hundred advertisement-based e-mail providers. This service is quite popular, particularly among students. You don't need any special software. At some of these free e-mail Web sites, you're also allowed to post a personal HTML Web page. To get all these goodies, all you need is a Web browser.

Advertising pays for this kind of e-mail service (see Figure 6-2). If you want to subscribe, you must provide certain personal information that is shared with advertisers. So, before you subscribe, read the information found in the *Net Ethics: Subscription Ethics and Free E-mail* special feature on p. 101.

A short list of some of the better known e-mail providers follows. You can find more providers by keying *free e-mail* in a search portal's search tool.

www.hotmail.com
www.juno.com
mail.yahoo.com
mail.excite.com

Net Concept

You will want an e-mail account that you can access from anywhere in the world with any Web browser. If you change jobs, change ISPs, change schools, or just go home for the holidays, you want an account that you can use by borrowing any nearby Web browser.

FIGURE 6-2

Excite was one of the first advertisement-based e-mail services

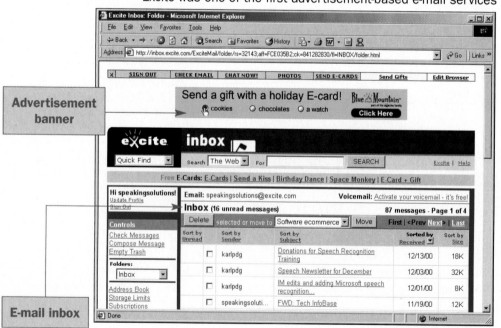

Compose and Send a New Message

An e-mail message, like a letter, contains several essential parts, as noted in Figure 6-3. The *header,* the first part, gives controlling information, such as who sent the e-mail, who it was mailed to, who should receive copies, and the subject.

The *subject line* in the header is the place to insert a brief description of the message. This description is very important, because it gives the receiver a hint about the contents. The *body* is the text you write.

E-mail may contain one or more attachments. *Attachments* are files linked to an e-mail message so they can travel to their destination together. Any type of file can be attached—database, spreadsheet, graphic, photograph, video, or program files.

Net Tip

An e-mail name can be almost anything you like, such as *author123@hotmail.com*. On corporate networks, however, names are typically assigned and made up of the first initial and last name or the first name and last initial, followed by the "at" (@) symbol. An example of this is *brown@corpview.com*.

FIGURE 6-3

Parts of an e-mail message

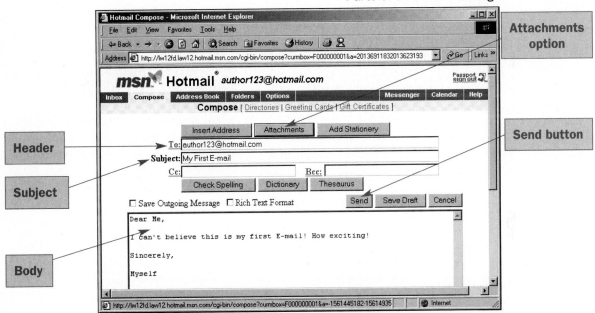

All e-mail programs are essentially the same. In this lesson, we'll use Hotmail, a free advertisement-based e-mail service, as an example. However, you may use another program or service provided by your network administrator. The steps will be nearly the same for any e-mail program you choose.

S TEP-BY-STEP ▷ 6.1

1. Start your Internet browser.

2. Go to **www.hotmail.com**. If you do not have a Hotmail account already, ask your system administrator if you can create one. Follow the instructions at Hotmail for setting up a new e-mail account.

3. After your account has been created, log in to Hotmail by entering your user name and password and choosing **Sign In**, as shown in Figure 6-4.

4. Select the **Compose** option (refer to Figure 6-3). (Note: This is often called New Mail or New Message in other e-mail programs.)

5. In the **To** box, key your e-mail address. If you are not using Hotmail, your network administrator can provide you with one.

6. In the **Subject** box, enter something like *My First E-mail*.

7. In the body text area, enter a short message to yourself. You may want to close with a traditional *Sincerely* or *Thank You*, or you may want to be more creative and use an ending that characterizes you, like *Later*.

8. When you are ready to send your message, click the **Send** button.

9. When you are finished, exit your e-mail program.

Net Tip

The sender's name and the subject line are the first things people see in their inbox. Be sure the subject line is clear and to the point.

FIGURE 6-4
Hotmail sign in

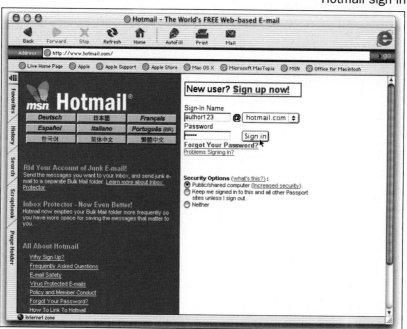

Read a Message

Although e-mail messages are delivered quickly, don't assume your friend in Paris is going to receive and reply to your e-mail in half a second. It can take anywhere from several minutes to a few hours to deliver your message. It all depends on how much traffic is going through the servers that carry your message to your intended receiver.

And even though e-mail is pretty reliable, e-mail servers can crash and burn, leaving people stuck without e-mail until the problem is corrected. Computers are only human, after all!

Let's retrieve the message you just wrote to yourself.

Net Tip

It is important to exit or to sign off of your e-mail program so that no one can read your e-mail after you have left your computer or use your e-mail account without your knowledge or permission.

NET ETHICS

SUBSCRIPTION ETHICS AND FREE E-MAIL

How much information should you provide to someone over the Internet? If you give out your name, address, and phone number to an advertisement-based e-mail system, chances are you will be "spammed" with junk mail and ads related to the interests you selected as you subscribed. *Spam* is what Netizens (or citizens of the Net) call unwanted and unsolicited advertising or other unwanted messages, such as political or social commentary.

The best free e-mail systems will not ask you for your personal phone number or home mailing address but will advertise to you only via your e-mail account. As you visit the Web site, you'll see active ads that you can click on or ignore.

Some e-mail systems create personal profiles. This information is then shared with other users, who can look you up in the address book. Do you want people to have this information about you?

The real scary option is to hook up with a free e-mail system that asks for your credit card number. They might explain that supplying your credit card number now eliminates the hassle of entering it later if you decide to buy something. This is a lame reason. Your credit card number should be given only to reputable companies for specific services.

1. Start your browser and sign on to Hotmail.

2. When you sign on, the first thing you will see is your inbox. (Note: If you don't see your inbox, click the **Inbox** link or button.) Unread messages in your Inbox will usually be highlighted for easy identification, as shown in Figure 6-5. Select the message you sent to yourself in the previous Step-by-Step.

3. Notice the header information of the opened e-mail. It will tell you who the information is from, when the message was sent, and other information about how the message was sent.

4. Respond to the message by clicking the **Reply** button. This will automatically fill in the **To** box and make a copy of the message you just read and place it in the new message.

5. When you are finished, be sure to exit your e-mail program. (Note: Check back tomorrow to read your reply.)

Net Concept

When you send a message, it goes to the mail server of your ISP where it gets in line behind all the messages that were posted first. Eventually, it will be sent to the recipient's mail server, where it will wait again until the person retrieves his or her mail.

FIGURE 6-5
Hotmail Inbox

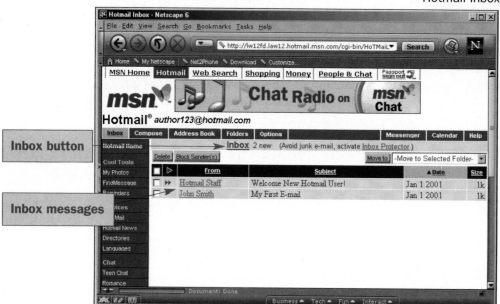

Create Folders to Organize Your Mail

In time, you will accumulate many messages. Multiply all the messages you send and receive by the number of other users on your network, and sooner or later your mail server is going to be very full. Be a thoughtful user and delete your mail when you are finished with the messages.

You may want to delete some messages after you have read them. Others, you'll want to store. You can use multiple folders to store the important messages you need to keep. The *Sent Messages* folder stores every message that you have sent, taking up room on the mail server. Go through this folder from time to time and delete the messages you don't want any more.

Now let's create new folders for storing the important messages that you want saved.

Net Concept

When you reply to an e-mail message, it is considered polite to include the information that you are responding to. The reason is clear. Some people send 40 or 50 e-mail messages every day and sometimes they forget specifically what it was they were talking to you about! Politeness dictates that you remind them of the previous communication.

STEP-BY-STEP ▷ 6.3

1. Launch your browser and sign on to Hotmail.

2. Choose the **Folders** button to display a list of your folders. See Figure 6-6.

3. In the Folders window, select **Create New**.

4. You may need a folder for a specific project you are working on, or you may want a folder for a specific person you correspond with regularly. In this example, key **Business Correspondence** in the New Folder Name field, as shown in Figure 6-7, and then click **OK**.

5. Return to your Inbox. Check the box next to the message you just sent to yourself.

6. Find the **Move to** button. From the pull-down menu next to it, select **Business Correspondence** and click the **Move to** option.

7. When you are finished, exit your e-mail program.

Net Concept

Saved messages are often stored long-term in an *archive* folder. Archived e-mail messages are often compressed to take up less space.

FIGURE 6-6
Hotmail folders

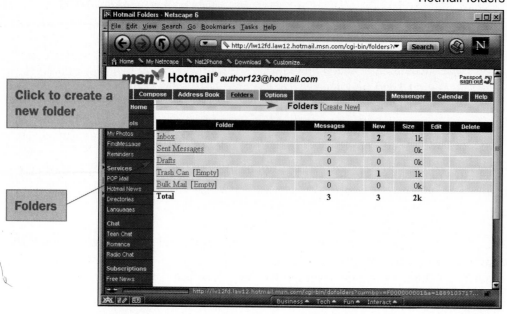

FIGURE 6-7
Creating a new folder in Hotmail

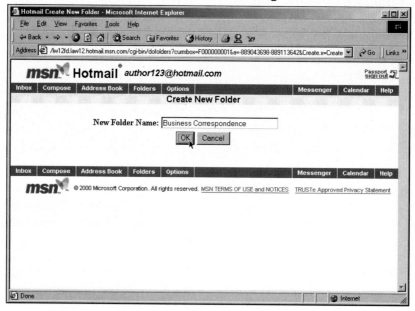

Send an Attachment

E-mail has definitely come a long way since its text-only days, when only words could be communicated over the Internet. Now you can send documents in a variety of formats.

Some types of files that you may send might not be readable by some e-mail and software programs. Whenever possible, it is best to use a very common format such as ***Rich Text Format*** (**RTF**). Rich Text Format is great to use for attachments because it can be read by nearly any word-processing program. The format also supports font styles, such as bold, italics, and underlines, and different fonts and colors.

In addition to RTF documents, you can also attach photographs, pictures, sound, and video clips or documents created in a variety of programs. With attachments, sharing information is as easy as clicking the mouse.

Net Tip

If you are using a proprietary e-mail system, moving files to folders is as easy as drag-and-drop. Simply drag an e-mail message to a folder, and it will automatically move there. Also, to delete messages, just select a message or mark it as directed and press the Delete option. The message will be moved to the trash folder.

STEP-BY-STEP 6.4

1. Open your word processor and create a short document, perhaps a note to a friend about a Web site you would pick as the best on the Web. Save the file as **My Pick**.
2. Launch your browser and sign on to Hotmail.
3. Select **Compose** to start a new e-mail.
4. Enter the address of a classmate in the **To** box.
5. In the **Subject** box, key **Attachment Exercise**.
6. Write a short note explaining the contents of your attachment.
7. Click the **Attachments** option. The Attachments window opens, as shown in Figure 6-8.

FIGURE 6-8
Attaching a file in Hotmail

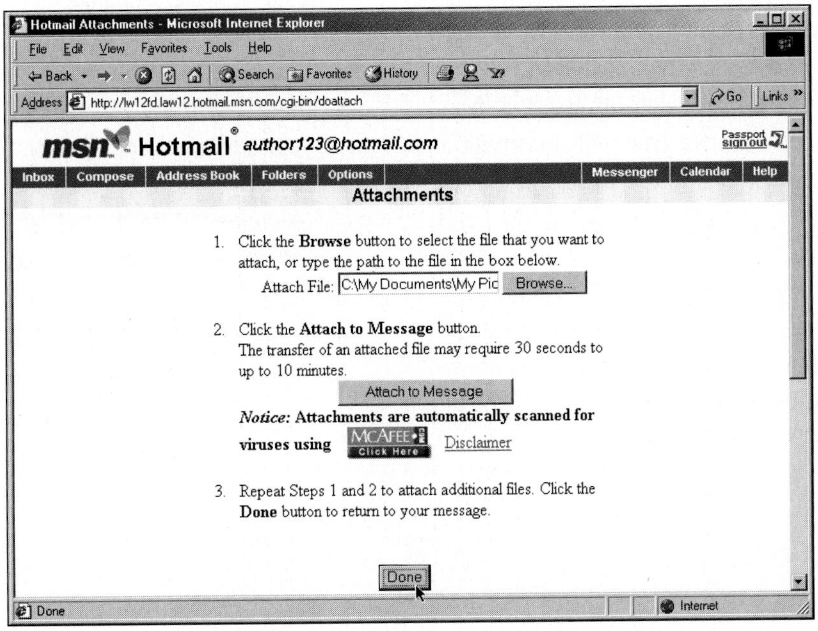

8. Choose the **Browse** button to locate your **My Pick** file and attach the message. Then choose **Done**.

9. Finally, choose **Send** to send your message and the attachment on its way. Keep your Web browser and e-mail account open for the next activity.

Using Your Address Book

Most e-mail programs and services have an address book feature to help you keep track of e-mail addresses. Using your address book, you can quickly select one or many recipients and their addresses will automatically be inserted in the *TO, CC,* or *BC* fields, as you indicate. Some address books allow you to keep track of phone numbers, street addresses, and other important information besides e-mail addresses.

 Net Concept

Many people are confused about the use of TO, CC, and BC. Use the TO option to send a message to the primary recipient(s). Send a *courtesy copy* to a secondary participant with the CC option. Use *blind copy* (BC) when you wish to send a copy to someone but you don't want anyone else to know that person has received a copy. How sneaky!

STEP-BY-STEP ➤ 6.5

1. Select the **Address Book** option to show your list of contacts if you have any.

2. Choose the **Create New** button to add a contact to your address book. Explore the different fields of the new page, as illustrated in Figure 6-9. Notice the types of information the address book allows you to store.

3. Using your personal contact cards from Lesson 1 Web Project 1-1 (remember those?), fill in the new contact information for each person you interviewed. When you finish filling in the information for a contact, choose **OK** to store it in the address book.

4. Make entries for the people you would like to correspond with so that you can communicate with them easily.

5. Compose a new mail message. Choose **Insert Address** to open a new window with your address book. Check the box next to the name of a person you want to send an e-mail to under the **To** column and select **OK**. Your receiver will appear in the **To** field.

6. Close your e-mail program and shut down your computer if you are done for today.

FIGURE 6-9

Create a new address book contact in Hotmail

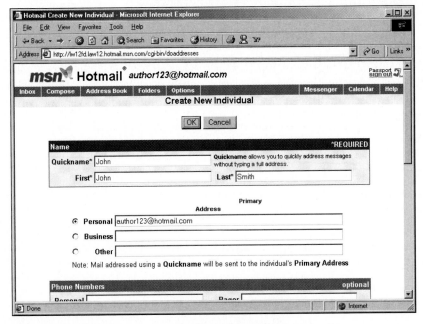

INTERNET MILESTONE

EMOTICONS

In the early days of e-mail, people were constantly searching for ways to interject emotion into their messages. Shouting was accomplished by using ALL CAPS. Somewhere along the way, somebody discovered that you could make sideways faces with characters on the keyboard. A smiling face was made by using a colon for eyes and a close parenthesis for a smile like this : -). A frowning face used the open parenthesis : -(. These creations became known as *emoticons*—icons that show emotion.

Many others soon followed. Here are some common ones:

:-<	sad
:-|	so-so
>:-(	mad
:-o	surprised
:-{	scared
;-)	wink
:-Q	nausea (tongue hanging out)
8-)	smile (user wears glasses)
:-D	wide smile
;-{)	smile (user has mustache)
:-{)}	smile (user has mustache and beard)
*<|:{)}	Santa Claus

Emoticons have gone to the next level. Many instant message programs have full-color emoticons. If you type a smiling emoticon, the program will automatically change it to a yellow smiley face. You can even select a smiley face from a pull-down menu!

SNAP, CRACKLE, POP SERVERS

POP is short for *Post Office Protocol*. POP1, POP2, and POP3 are examples of the many versions of this protocol. POP was developed in the Internet's early years to transmit e-mail from UNIX computers to UNIX users. POP specifies how exchanges of information are made between e-mail servers and e-mail clients.

Summary

In this lesson, you learned:

■ You can compose and send e-mail messages.

■ You can retrieve and read e-mail messages.

■ You can organize your mailbox by creating folders and moving messages.

■ You can send attachments.

■ You can use and organize an address book.

NET TERMS REVIEW

Define the following terms:

Archive	Emoticons	Proprietary software
Attachments	Header	RTF
BC	Inbox	Spam
CC	ISP	Subject line
E-mail	POP	

LESSON 6 REVIEW QUESTIONS

TRUE/FALSE

Circle T if this statement is true or F if the statement is false.

T F 1. Hotmail is an example of a proprietary e-mail system.

T F 2. E-mail is a fast and easy way to communicate over the Internet.

T F 3. You can use an address book to keep track of friends.

T F 4. You can attach a sound file to an e-mail message.

T F 5. There is no way to express emotion in an e-mail message.

IDENTIFICATION

Study Figure 6-10 and identify the different parts of an e-mail.

1. _____

2. _____

3. _____

4. _____

5. _____

FIGURE 6-10

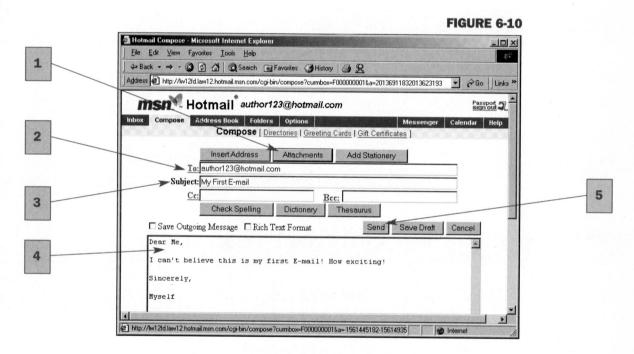

WRITTEN QUESTIONS

Write a brief answer to the following questions.

1. Describe the steps you would follow to write an e-mail message to a friend, with a copy to another friend. Assume that their addresses are already in your address book.

2. How would you go about attaching a file to your message?

E-COMMUNICATION: E-MAIL, ETC.

3. Create two new emoticons of your own, and state what they mean.

4. What limitations should be placed on e-mail in a corporate environment or in a school environment?

5. Describe how to add a new address to your address book.

LESSON 6 PROJECTS

WEB PROJECT 6-1

Preparation for Your Big Presentation

Your boss at GreatApplications, Inc., has asked you to send an e-mail to your team members, informing them that next Friday's meeting has been moved to this Monday. Panic! (Actually, just get used to it. Meeting times change all the time in business.) Remind all members of your team that they must come prepared to share the Web sites they found in Web Projects 4-1 and 4.2. Anyone who is not prepared will be demoted, sent to a Siberian mink farm, and deleted from the e-mail address book.

Write an e-mail to your colleagues about the change in schedule. Tell them to be prepared to give a five-minute presentation on their Web site findings. They will need to have visual examples of good and bad Web sites. They also need to reply to you with a summary of their presentation, so that it can be previewed in the meeting agenda.

TEAMWORK PROJECT 6-2

Tag Team E-Mail

E-mail systems vary in speed and efficiency. Some message systems take seconds to route messages. Other systems take hours, even days, to clear the e-mail. How fast is your e-mail system?

Test the responsiveness of your e-mail system. Divide up into teams of four or five people. Teammate #1 starts the chain by sending an e-mail message to Teammate #2 with a message, "Hi, this is [name of Teammate #1]. Please forward this message to the next member of the team." Teammate #2 uses the Forward feature, adds his or her name to the message, sends it to Teammate #3, and so on until the message reaches the last teammate. The last person must have the names of all the e-mail's previous senders to prove that the chain was complete. The first team to get the final forwarded message to the last teammate wins. This contest may take minutes, hours, or days.

111

CRITICAL THINKING

ACTIVITY 6-1

Your Comments on E-mail

With what you know about e-mail and e-mail systems, give a 100- to 250-word answer on a separate piece of paper to four of the following questions.

1. Many professional people receive hundreds of e-mail messages a day. How can busy people handle that amount of e-mail? How can they quickly identify messages they may want to read first?

2. Did you ever have an unwanted ad placed on your doorknob? Did your home mailbox ever fill up with junk mail that have nothing to do with you? Junk mail is an institution in our society, and with e-mail, it is now easier and cheaper to distribute junk advertising to more people. What can be done about spam? Is receiving advertising by e-mail of any benefit to you?

3. What impact has e-mail had on the postal system? Is there a future for traditional mail?

4. Why might you want to attach something to an e-mail? Assume that your best friend moved to another state. What would you like to send to him or her over the Internet?

5. Do you think you could get used to an electronic address book? What are some of the advantages over a traditional handwritten book of addresses? Are there any disadvantages?

ACTIVITY 6-2

Writing About Technology

Write a 250- to 500-word essay on e-mail's impact on the way we write and communicate. Is it improving our writing or is it having a negative impact on the way people communicate?

E-COMMUNICATION: E-MAIL, ETC.

INSTANT MESSAGING: REAL-TIME E-MAIL

OBJECTIVES

Upon completion of this lesson you should be able to:

- Create a buddy list.
- Send an instant message.
- Voice chat with a buddy.
- Send a real-time attachment.

⏱ Estimated time: 2 hours

NET TERMS

Chat

Chatter's jargon

Emulate

Instant Messenger (IM)

Instant messaging client

Internet Relay Chat

Telephony

John has Just Signed On

Instant Messages are live, interactive e-mail-like messages between two or more people online at the same time. As soon as one person hits the Send command, the message instantly appears on the other user's screen. The recipient can then reply, and both can have an online conversation (or *chat*) in real time.

To send and receive an instant message, you need to have an *instant messaging client (IM)*. An IM client is software that allows access to a specific network protocol used for chatting back and forth. Many different companies have their own version of an IM client. The most popular are AOL Instant Messenger by America Online (Figure 7-1A), MSN Messenger from Microsoft (Figure 7-1B), and Yahoo! Messenger by Yahoo! (Figure 7-1C).

Net Tip

Most IM clients are very similar. However, each uses its own standards, so you may have difficulty sending an instant message to a person with a different IM client than yours. Things will work more smoothly if all of your buddies are running the same client. You can download most IM clients for free, so this limitation should not be a major roadblock for you and your friends.

FIGURE 7-1A
AOL Instant Messenger

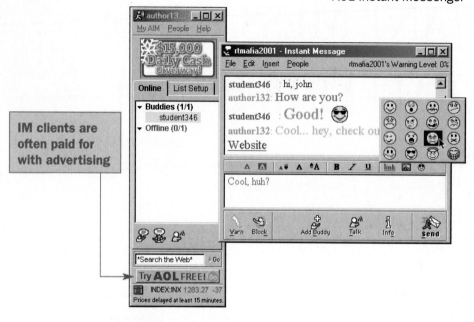

IM clients are often paid for with advertising

FIGURE 7-1B
MSN Messenger

FIGURE 7-1C
Yahoo! Messenger

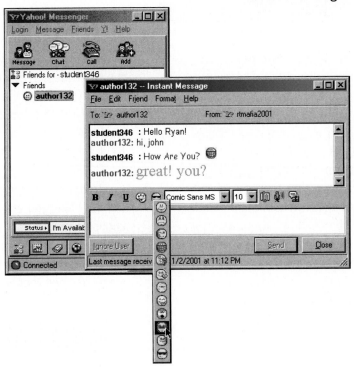

FIGURE 7-1C
Yahoo! Messenger

Sign In and Buddy Up

Instant messages are fun, but if you don't have anyone to send them to, there is no point. Let's sign in and find some buddies to talk with. In different programs, users on your list are referred to as either buddies or contacts.

In this example, we will use MSN Messenger. If you have a Hotmail account, these instructions will give you powerful new tools to work with. If you're using another instant messaging service, such as America Online or Yahoo!, you'll find these instructions very helpful because the basics are very similar.

 Net Concept

Did you know that there were 5.5 million users of IM in 2000? That number is expected to grow to 180 million users in 5 years. This makes IM a great venue for advertising! Most Internet messaging systems are paid for either through subscriptions or advertising. Be very careful which advertisements you click on. While most advertisements are legitimate, there may be some that are not appropriate.

 Net Concept

Protect yourself and *never ever* give out personal information to anyone you are chatting with, even if you believe they are your friends.

1. Launch MSN Messenger (or your particular IM client) by double-clicking the icon. Instructions for other IM clients will be similar to these steps. (Note: If you don't have an IM client, your system administrator can download one from *www.aol.com, messenger.msn.com, messenger.yahoo.com,* or another IM provider. Get permission before you download and install IM software.)

2. In the **Sign-in** name box, enter your Hotmail address (or the user name for the IM client you are using). Enter your Hotmail (or other IM client) password in the **Password** box, as shown in Figure 7-2. Then, click **OK**.

3. The first time you launch MSN Messenger, it will tell you that your contact list is empty. Select the **Add** button, as shown in Figure 7-3, to add a buddy.

4. Your messenger client will ask you how you would like to find a contact. Choose **By e-mail**

address or sign-in name, then click **Next**. In the next screen, enter the Hotmail address of one of your classmates and click **Next** and then click **Next** again. Now click **Finish**. If you would like to add another classmate, click **Next** and repeat this step.

5. Congratulations! You now have someone to talk to! When you are finished, remember to choose **sign out** from the File menu and exit the program. If you don't sign out before you exit, someone else will be able to read your e-mail and see your buddy list.

Net Tip

If you are sharing your computer with others, don't click the *Remember my name and password on this computer* option or else others will be able to read your e-mail and see your buddies.

FIGURE 7-2
MSN Messenger login

FIGURE 7-3
Add a contact

Send an Instant Message

Like e-mail, your instant messages are delivered quickly, but don't assume your friend in Madrid will receive and reply to your message in half a second. It can take anywhere from several seconds to several minutes to deliver your message, and then the other person may take a minute or two to write a response. It all depends on how much traffic is going through the servers that carry your message from you to your intended receiver and how fast your friend can enter text.

INTERNET MILESTONE

INTERNET RELAY CHAT

Internet Relay Chat, or **IRC**, was the first form of instant messaging. It remained an obscure Internet application and was popular among college students in the early days of the Internet. In 1985, Steve Case cofounded America Online, which popularized IRC by incorporating instant messaging as part of its Internet service client. Messaging allowed AOL members to communicate more interactively than with simple e-mail because they could instantly chat with other members online.

By 2001, over 600 million real-time conversations were being generated each day. New enhancements are being added all the time. For example, you can send and receive instant messages with AOL on your computer, TV, cell phone, and small hand-held personal digital assistants such as the PalmPilot.

117

1. Launch MSN Messenger from your desktop and sign in. (Choose it from the Start Menu in Windows or the Dock in Macintosh.)

2. In the window, you will see which of your contacts is currently signed in. Ask one of your buddies to sign in, and you will receive a message similar to the one shown in Figure 7-4.

3. When one of your buddies has signed in, you can either click the **Send** button and choose that user from the list or simply double-click the contact's name in the window.

4. You will soon see a window similar to the one shown in Figure 7-5. In the bottom box, enter a brief message and click **Send**.

5. When your buddy responds, simply enter another message and send it back! Now you're communicating!

6. When you are finished, remember to sign out and exit the program.

 Net Tip

You can send multiple messages before the other person responds.

 Net Concept

If you have more than one buddy on your list, you can three-way, four-way, or ten-way chat. To add another person to your instant messaging group, click the **Invite** button, choose **To Join This Conversation**, and then select the name of the buddy(s) you would like to add. Voila! Multiple buddy chat!

FIGURE 7-5
An Instant Message window

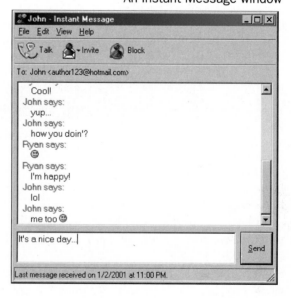

FIGURE 7-4
John has just signed in

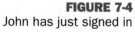

What Could Be More Fun? Voice Chat!

Instant messaging is becoming a more powerful tool with every passing day. Now, with a computer that has a microphone attached, you can actually talk over the Internet as simply as using a phone with technology. This is known as *telephony*. Internet telephony is a service that *emulates* or imitates a telephone on the Internet. You can use it to voice chat from PC to PC or even make calls from your PC to a phone at virtually no cost. Most instant messaging clients allow you to use voice chat by simply clicking a button.

STEP-BY-STEP 7.3

1. Launch MSN Messenger and sign in. (Note: You will need a microphone connected to your sound card to continue.)

2. Ask a buddy to come online and then send him or her a message.

3. Click the **Talk** button, as shown in Figure 7-6. (The first time you do this, you will see an Audio Tuning Wizard. Follow the instructions and then proceed to Step 4.)

4. When your buddy accepts your request, you can talk just as if you were on the phone with him or her.

5. Chat for a few minutes with your buddy. You can use the controls shown in Figure 7-7 to adjust the speaker volume and turn the microphone on and off.

6. When you are finished, click **Hang Up** to return to straight text messages.

7. Sign out and exit the program.

> **Net Tip**
>
> You can also send text messages along with your speech.

INTERNET MILESTONE

EMOTICONS (PART DEUX)

Remember in the last lesson how we mentioned something called emoticons? Well, instant messages are a great place to throw in a smile or frown. Most clients have colorful smiley face icons to make your instant messages even more interesting! Type :-) into a message and send it to see what happens! If you are using Yahoo! Messenger or AOL Instant Messenger, click the smiley face icon in the message to show a list of several emoticons you can send. You can see them in Figures 7-1A and 7-1C.

FIGURE 7-6
Activating Internet telephony

FIGURE 7-6
Activating Internet telephony

FIGURE 7-7
Voice chat in MSN Messenger

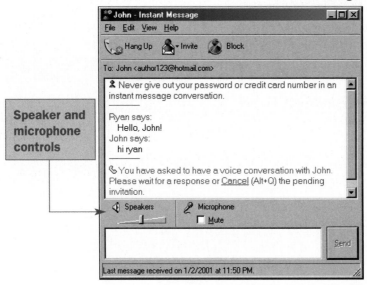

Attaching Files

Just like e-mail, you can send files along with the text of your instant messages in a few simple steps. You can send pictures, spreadsheets, answers to question number 3 on your math homework… oh, just kidding! You get the idea.

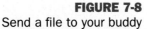

STEP-BY-STEP ▷ 7.4

1. Launch MSN Messenger and sign in.

2. Ask a buddy to come online and then send him or her a message.

3. To attach a file, go to the **File** menu and select **Send a file**, as shown in Figure 7-8.

4. Browse through your hard drive and find a file in your **My Documents** folder to send to your buddy. Select the file and click **Open**.

5. Your buddy will be asked to accept the file. If he or she does, the file is off and away, and by now, in your buddy's hands!

6. When you are finished, remember to sign out and exit the program.

FIGURE 7-8
Send a file to your buddy

CHATTER'S JARGON

Jargon is used all the time. For example, people use the abbreviation BTW to replace By the Way. TGIF has replaced Thank Goodness It's Friday in normal conversations. *Chatter's jargon* replaces words and phrases with letter combinations in chat rooms or in IM clients and also allows messages to be entered more quickly. Jargon allows you to cut down on your typing, reducing your risk of keyboard-related injuries. Chatter's jargon also allows you to cram more words into rapidly moving lines of text.

Ways to say I'm leaving for a second, but I'll be back soon:

AFK = Away from keyboard

BAK = Back at the keyboard

BRB = Be right back
Ways to say that you're finished chatting for the day:

B4N or BFN = Bye for now

CUL or CUL8R = See you later

LD = Later, dude

TLK2UL8R or TTYL = Talk to you later

TTFN = Ta-Ta for now
Phrases that cut down on your typing:

BTA = But then again...

BTW = By the way...

DITYIU = Did I tell you I'm upset?
Ways to tell people that you are laughing:

LOL = Laughing out loud

ROL = Rolling over laughing
Ways to say thank you:

THX = thanks

TIA = Thanks in advance

Summary

In this lesson, you learned:

- You can create a buddy list.

- It is simple and fun to send an instant message.

- You and your buddies can voice chat.

- Attachments can be added to messages.

NET TERMS REVIEW

Define the following terms:

Chat	Instant Messenger (IM)	Telephony
Chatter's jargon	Instant messaging client	
Emulate	Internet Relay Chat	

LESSON 7 REVIEW QUESTIONS

TRUE/FALSE

Circle T if the statement is true or F if the statement is false.

T F   1.   IM clients usually cost a lot of money to buy and use.

T F   2.   You can chat with only one person at a time with IM.

T F   3.   Instant messaging is slower than e-mail.

T F   4.   You can use an instant messaging client to talk as if you were using a telephone.

T F   5.   Instant messages allow you to use different fonts, colors, and emoticons.

FILL IN THE BLANK

Complete the following sentences by writing the correct word or words in the blanks provided.

1.   _____ are keystrokes or icons that express emotion.

2.   _____ is used to emulate a telephone over the Internet.

3.   Instant messaging was made popular by an online service called _____.

4. A file sent with an e-mail or instant message is called a(n) _____.

5. ROL is chatter's jargon for _____.

WRITTEN QUESTIONS

Write a brief answer to the following questions.

1. Describe the steps you would follow to add a friend to your buddy list.

2. How would you go about attaching a file to your instant message?

3. How would you set up a three-way chat with buddies?

4. Describe the steps to start voice chatting with a buddy.

5. How would you go about using your PC as a telephone?

LESSON 7 PROJECTS

SCANS

PROJECT 7-1

Collaborate With IM

Your IT (Information Technology) department at GreatApplications, Inc., has upgraded all of your computers with the latest version of IM. Your boss feels that this will help you work more efficiently. He wants you to put all of the members of your team on your buddy list ASAP so you all can collaborate on your next project.

With what you know, set up your buddy list with all of the members of your team so that you can get together for the next Teamwork Project (7-2).

PROJECT 7-2

Buddy Up

Now that you have everyone on your team on your buddy list and everyone has you listed, use IM to discuss how this technology can save time for employees on the job.

Designate one person to start the chat. Have that person start an instant message with one person, and then add the rest of the members of your team for your group collaboration. Once everybody is in, discuss the value of using this system to talk about a project or to meet a company deadline. Debate whether or not this is a good technology to use in a job environment or whether it is better suited for personal communication between friends. As a group, discuss its strengths and weaknesses live in your IM session.

After this experience, do you think that instant messaging helps professionals collaborate more, or is it simply a distraction that causes them to avoid getting their work done? On a separate sheet of paper, prepare a 100- to 250-word answer to this question.

CRITICAL THINKING

SCANS

ACTIVITY 7-1

Messaging versus Phoning

How do you think that voice chatting on a PC will affect telephone companies? Do you think that it would benefit them or cause them to collapse? Why? Prepare a 100- to 250-word answer to these questions.

SCANS

ACTIVITY 7-2

E-mail versus Instant Messaging

Some predict that Instant Messaging will soon pass e-mail as the way people communicate with their friends and business colleagues. Which do you think is a more effective communications tool: e-mail or instant messaging? Prepare a 100- to 250-word report that lists some advantages and disadvantages of each.

WHAT'S THE NEWS ABOUT NEWSGROUPS

OBJECTIVES

Upon completion of this lesson, you should be able to:

- Find a newsgroup of interest to you.
- Subscribe to a newsgroup.
- Read a newsgroup post.
- Learn how to post a newsgroup response.

🕐 **Estimated time: 3 hours**

NET TERMS

Call for Votes (CFV)

Flame

Newsgroup

Post

Request for Discussion (RFD)

Spam

Subscribe

Thread

Unsubscribe

Usenet

Newsgroups A-Plenty

 Net Concept

*N*ewsgroups, despite the name, are not electronic newspapers. They are collections of messages on the Internet about a particular subject. People *subscribe* to, or join, newsgroups on their favorite subjects so they can meet and talk electronically with other people interested in the same subjects. They can also *unsubscribe*, or quit receiving a newsgroup, if they grow tired of it.

A newsgroup is a special kind of e-mail system that allows many users to have conversations on topics of personal interest. The first newsgroup ever created was called SF-Lovers. No, it wasn't an online dating service; it was a forum for geeky scientists to talk about their one true love: science fiction novels.

Chances are there is a newsgroup that fits your particular interest. Are you a fan of the TV show Star Trek? As you learn to access newsgroups, try *alt.tv.startrek*. Do you follow the Chicago Bulls closely? Look in *alt.sports.basketball.nba.chicago-bulls*. Are you into investing? Then *misc.invest.mutual-funds* or *misc.invest.stocks* might be for you. If, by some strange quirk in the universe, you can't find a newsgroup about your special interests, you can start one up.

But newsgroups aren't just for entertainment. For example, users in the *comp.cad.autocad* newsgroup can *post*, which means to upload or send, questions about their favorite drafting software, AutoCAD. More often than not, someone in the group has an answer to these technical AutoCAD questions. There are other software newsgroups, like the Microsoft Office and speech recognition newsgroups.

Searching for a Newsgroup

You can use a proprietary software package (like Outlook Express or the Discussions part of Netscape) or your Web browser to read and post newsgroup messages anytime anywhere.

STEP-BY-STEP ▷ 8.1

1. Open your Internet browser.

2. Enter the Web address **groups.google.com**. Google offers access to free online news and keeps track of the most popular newsgroups on the Web. Study Figure 8-1.

3. Newsgroups have been divided into several categories or classes. Each category has a prefix or a three- or four-letter abbreviation. Find the prefix for each of the categories in the table below (the first answer is given for you).

4. Using the Search Groups option, enter a subject that interests you and choose **Search**, as shown in Figure 8.1. You can use almost anything, like *History*, *Boston Bruins*, *Los Angeles Lakers*, *Investing*, or *Crocodiles*, or you can choose a topic of your own. (Note: The results

of the search for Crocodiles are shown in Figure 8-2. The various discussion forums, such as **rec.pets.herp**, are listed at the top of the window. Below that, you see a list of messages in various forums that contain your topic. Choose one of the discussion forums that most closely matches your interest.)

5. Now you will see all of the messages in your specific forum. To subscribe to or join this forum, select the **Subscribe** link. (Note: You might have to scroll down to find the Subscribe link. You may first need to sign up for Google's free service to subscribe, but you can read and post messages without signing up. If you do sign up, be sure and log out of the site when you are finished or someone else may be able to access your postings.) Keep your browser open for the next Step-by-Step.

NEWSGROUP	CATEGORY PREFIX
Alternative topics or subjects	alt
Computer related	
Business	
Educational	
Miscellaneous	
Usenet news	
Recreation	
Science and technology	
Social issues	
Current issues and debates	

FIGURE 8-1
Viewing Google's Newsgroup Web site

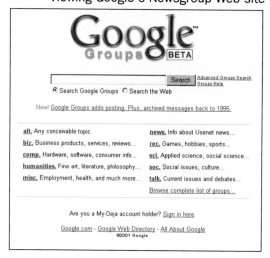

FIGURE 8-2
Searching Google's Newsgroup Web site

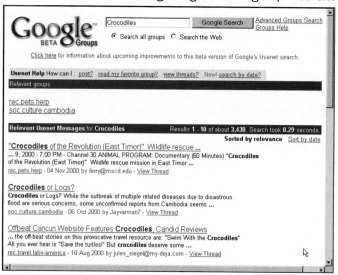

NET ETHICS

ANONYMITY

Although newsgroups can be a lot of fun, they are an open forum for all sorts of people. Anonymity when posting a message allows for freedom of speech that common courtesy might otherwise prevent. And, there is also a concern that someone might misuse the information you share with them over the Net. This poses several ethical questions. Should you exercise extreme caution when sharing personal information with a newsgroup? Many would advise that you should never give out personal information in a newsgroup setting. What does this precaution say about Internet society? At what point should people be held responsible for the things they send and receive online?

Reading Newsgroup Posts

Newsgroups can be overwhelming because of the sheer number of **posts** (or messages uploaded or sent) made every day. Most users quickly browse through the list of postings, looking for topics that interest them. Sometimes, the user will pose the question or remark that encourages a lot of responses.

When several users post responses to an earlier post, they have started a **thread**. A thread consists of several posts related to the same topic. Figure 8-3 shows a thread related to the Los Angeles Lakers. Let's find some posts of interest to you.

FIGURE 8-3
A newsgroup message and thread

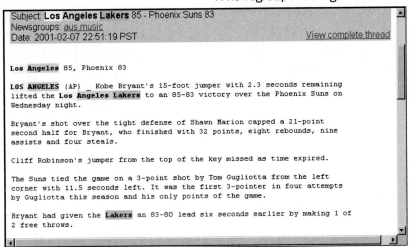

INTERNET MILESTONE

USENET

Usenet, which comes from USEr NETwork, is a giant public access network on the Internet. Once maintained entirely by volunteers, it provides users with newsgroup services.

Usenet was invented in 1979 by students at Duke University and was originally used to exchange information with students at the University of North Carolina. In 1981, another college student, Mark Horton, and a high school student, Matt Glickman, improved Usenet's capabilities to handle larger volumes of postings. There are now tens of thousands of newsgroups.

1. Return to **groups.google.com**.

2. Search for your topic of interest, then enter your forum or group by selecting the link.

3. Browse through the list. When you find something of interest, choose it to view the thread, as seen in Figure 8-3. Threads start with the original posting at the top and are followed by responses as they are posted. It is generally a good idea to read all the related posts to get the entire context or whole story.

4. In your opinion, do the participants in the thread you visited follow the rules outlined in the feature titled Net Ethics — Newsgroup Niceties? Explain each answer with examples from the thread. If you need more space, write your answers on a separate piece of paper.

1. Do the participants stick to the topic? Yes/No Example: _____

2. Are the participants brief in their replies? Yes/No Example: _____

3. Are the participants considerate? Yes/No Example: _____

4. Do the participants quote key points of original messages so that latecomers can follow the discussion? Yes/No Example:

   _____

5. Do some participants continually repeat themselves? Yes/No Example:

   _____

5. Keep your browser open for the next Step-by-Step.

Posting a Response

Newsgroups have a netiquette, or rules of behavior, all their own. You learned earlier about SHOUTING with all caps. Generally, people ARE NOT VERY HAPPY IF YOU DO A LOT OF THIS IN NEWSGROUPS.

Usenet groups are also very opposed to any type of advertising in their newsgroups. It's kind of like an invasion of privacy. *Spam* is unsolicited and unwanted advertising and other garbage on the Internet. Spamming can occur in newsgroups as well as through e-mail.

Before posting a message, be sure to read through several of the posts. Get a feel for what kinds of discussions go on in the newsgroup. Posting messages can be tricky. To prepare, be sure to read a group for about a week before jumping in. If you decide to respond to a posting, think about whether your post will benefit the group or not. If not, you may want to e-mail the person whose message you are responding to rather than wasting the valuable time of all the newsgroup's members.

 Net Concept

A negative response to spam and other inappropriate comments on the Internet is called a *flame*. A flame is an emotional electronic rebuke that newsgroup members post to discourage spam and inappropriate messages.

STEP-BY-STEP ▷ 8.3

1. Find a message that you want to respond to and choose the **Post Reply** option.

2. On the next screen, enter your e-mail address and then enter a subject for your response.

3. Type your message. Be short and to the point in the body of the message.

4. When you are finished, select the **Submit** message option to post your response.

5. Close your browser if you are finished for today.

Net Concept

Remember, it is important to be specific in your subject line. Because of the number of postings in most newsgroups, most people never read more than a few messages. If you want someone to respond to your post, make the subject line count.

NET ETHICS

NEWSGROUP NICETIES

Newsgroup users should follow a code of conduct called newsgroup netiquette. The guidelines for good newsgroup netiquette follow:

1. Read a newsgroup for a few days before you start participating in the threads. This will help you get into the culture of the group before you jump in.
2. Stick to the topic of the group.
3. Be brief.
4. Be considerate. Remember that your postings may be read by thousands of group participants.
5. If you're responding to a message, quote the key point of the original message, so others can more easily follow along.
6. Don't repeat yourself.
7. Use descriptive titles for your postings.

INTERNET MILESTONE

THE FREEDOM TO CREATE NEW NEWSGROUPS

What happens if you really can't find a newsgroup to fit your interests? You can create one! But before you try to form your newsgroup, take a look at *news.announce.newsgroups*. You will see just what it takes to create a newsgroup.

To start a new group, you must submit a charter describing the goals of your newsgroup. Then, a *Request for Discussion (RFD)* is issued. For a few weeks, the new group can discuss any potential problems and try to garner support. This is kind of a trial period to see how popular the new group will be.

After the RFD period, a *Call For Votes (CFV)*, will be issued. Users vote on whether to continue the newsgroup or not.

Summary

In this lesson, you learned:

- There are a variety of newsgroups.
- You can read newsgroup postings.
- Responses to newsgroups can be posted.
- New users should analyze newsgroup netiquette.

NET TERMS REVIEW

Define the following terms:

CFV	RFD	Unsubscribe
Flame	Spam	Usenet
Newsgroup	Subscribe	
Post	Thread	

LESSON 8 REVIEW QUESTIONS

TRUE/FALSE

Circle T if the statement is true or F if the statement is false.

T F 1. Newsgroups are an electronic version of a newspaper.

T F 2. Newsgroups are a great way to discuss topics with many other people.

T F 3. Anyone can start a newsgroup.

T F 4. Sadly, it is impossible to stop receiving a newsgroup after you have subscribed to it.

T F 5. You should SHOUT most of the time in your posts.

FILL IN THE BLANK

Complete the following sentences by writing the correct word or words in the blanks provided.

1. RFD stands for _____ _____ _____.

2. _____ is the category for computer-related discussions.

3. A message and the many responses to it are known as a(n) _____.

4. CFV stands for _____ _____ _____.

5. You are _____ IF YOU TYPE IN ALL CAPS.

WRITTEN QUESTIONS

Write a brief answer to the following questions.

1. List three don'ts concerning newsgroups.

2. Choose a topic of interest to you and describe how you would go about finding a newsgroup on this topic.

3. How could you find help with a homework problem using a newsgroup?

4. Why do you think newsgroups go through the RFD and CFV processes?

5. Describe how you would post a response to a newsgroup message.

LESSON 8 PROJECTS

SCANS

PROJECT 8-1

Newsgroups as Sources for New Product Ideas

GreatApplications, Inc., has just marketed a new product designed for the speech recognition market. The first version wasn't successful in the marketplace. Evidently, the product lacked features. Still, the company is determined to establish itself in the speech recognition market with a useful voice program.

Often, users in newsgroups will have ideas about how voice software can be improved. Of course, some of these ideas stem from frustration, but many are good, and your company is going to learn from some of them. Try to identify five complaints the users have with their speech software and the companies that sell them.

List of Complaints

1.

2.

3.

4.

5.

PROJECT 8-2

Consensus Recommendations

Bring your results together with your team. Prepare a team report that summarizes everyone's findings. Have a recorder keep track of the discussion. Have one member report on the results and another team member keep the discussion moving. A final team member should provide snacks to keep the group motivated. On the basis of the information your team gathered from the speech recognition newsgroup discussions, what needs should your company's new product fulfill? What pitfalls should they watch out for in developing this new product?

PROJECT 8-3

Writing About Technology

Using what you learned in Project 8-1, write a brief response to each of these questions:

1. Do you think newsgroups are a viable tool for planning in business?

2. What can businesses accomplish through newsgroups?

3. What limitations or drawbacks do they have for business?

4. Can a newsgroup help a business increase sales? How?

CRITICAL THINKING

ACTIVITY 8-1

Censorship?

Recently in the news, some content providers decided to ban certain newsgroups whose content was patently offensive. However, many people felt that this was a violation of their First Amendment rights. Should there be censorship in newsgroups? Who should decide what gets through? Prepare a 100- to 250-word answer to these questions.

ACTIVITY 8-2

Name That Group

From browsing through the list of newsgroups, what kinds of groups did you see? What could you determine about the discussion topics from the group names? Prepare a 100- to 250-word answer to these questions.

ACTIVITY 8-3

TLD versus Newsgroup Names

How do the newsgroup categories listed in Step-by-Step 8.1 relate to the top-level domain names discussed in Lesson 3? In what ways are they similar and in what ways are they different? Prepare a 100- to 250-word answer to these questions.

E-communication: E-mail, Instant Messaging, and Newsgroups

REVIEW QUESTIONS

TRUE/FALSE

Circle T if this statement is true or F if the statement is false.

T F 1. The first e-mail may have been a simple test message containing the letters QWERTYIOP.

T F 2. The subject line is the last and least important part of an e-mail or newsgroup message.

T F 3. E-mail travels at the speed of light and always arrives to the recipient in a matter of seconds!

T F 4. Your inbox stores messages sent to you.

T F 5. IM is chatter's jargon that replaces the word IMmediately in online chats.

T F 6. IRC is an acronym meaning Internet relay chat.

T F 7. Normally, users will sign on to an IM client with a sign-in name and a password.

T F 8. IM chats are limited to three participants.

T F 9. A newsgroup is a specialized type of e-mail that allows groups of people to share information on topics of common interest.

T F 10. BIZ. is a top-level domain name whereas .BIZ is a Usenet category.

MATCHING

Match the correct term in Column 1 to its description in Column 2.

Column 1	Column 2
___ 1. :-o	**A.** Sad
___ 2. ;-)	**B.** So-so
___ 3. :-<	**C.** Mad
___ 4. >:-(	**D.** Surprised
___ 5. :-{)}	**E.** Scared
___ 6. :-l	**F.** Wink
___ 7. 8-)	**G.** Santa Claus
___ 8. :-{)	**H.** Smile (user has a mustache and a beard)
___ 9. :-{	**I.** Smile (user has a mustache)
___ 10. *<l:{)}	**J.** Smile (user wears glasses)

Match the correct term in Column 1 to its description in Column 2.

Column 1	Column 2
___ 1. AFK	**A.** By the way
___ 2. TTFN	**B.** Bye for now
___ 3. BTW	**C.** Did I tell you I'm upset?
___ 4. TIA	**D.** Ta-ta for now
___ 5. ROL	**E.** But then again
___ 6. DITYIU	**F.** Away from keyboard
___ 7. THX	**G.** Back at keyboard
___ 8. BTA	**H.** Thanks in advance
___ 9. BAK	**I.** Rolling over laughing
___ 10. B4N	**J.** Thanks

138

Newsgroups, e-mail, and instant messaging can help with your homework. You can send e-mail assignments to your teacher, ask your friend for advice with an assignment using your instant messenger client, or visit a newsgroup to see what is going on in your most difficult subject. Apply what you know about these tools to help you with the following school assignments.

HOMEWORK 1

Go to your e-mail address book and add the names of people you know that can help you with your homework in any of your classes.

HOMEWORK 2

Create a special IM buddy list of online friends that you know have the same classes as you. Pick a time that most of the members of your group can go online and conduct an online chat to do your homework remotely as a group.

LANGUAGE ARTS 2-1

Visit *groups.google.com* and create a list of newsgroups related to the Language Arts subjects that you are studying in school. For example, if you are studying a particular author, find newsgroups related to that author. If you are studying writing and grammar, there are plenty of newsgroups that cover these topics as well. Save your list as **Language Arts 2-1** in your saving folder.

MATH 2-1

Visit *groups.google.com* and create a list of newsgroups related to the level of Math that you are studying in school. List five possible newsgroups that would be helpful with your homework. Save your list as **Math 2-1** in your saving folder.

HISTORY 2-1

Visit *groups.google.com* and create a list of five newsgroups related to the History topics you are studying in school. Save your list as **History 2-1** in your saving folder.

SCIENCE 2-1

Visit *groups.google.com* and create a list of five newsgroups related to the Science subjects that you are studying at school. Save your list as **Science 2-1** in your saving folder.

FOREIGN LANGUAGE 2-1

Visit *groups.google.com* and create a list of newsgroups related to the Foreign Language classes that you are taking at school. Save your list as **Foreign Language 2-1** in your saving folder.

CRITICAL THINKING

ACTIVITY 2-1

In the old days, a letter sent as first-class mail was the number one most profitable item delivered by the United States Postal Service. However, with so many people using e-mail, cell phones, and instant messaging, letter writing is on the decline.

Is there any danger of the post office going out of business? What must the post office do to compete? What new kinds of things can they still deliver and make a profit? What other ideas to you have to keep the postal service around for another hundred years? Record your thoughts in a 100- to 250-word essay. Save your file as **Activity 2-1** in your saving folder.

ACTIVITY 2-2

Just like the post office has to change, so must your local phone carrier. Just a few short years ago, most of the traffic over the telephone system consisted of voice conversations. Today, most of the traffic over phone lines is data streaming to and from the Internet. People can use their Internet connections to make long distance phone calls virtually for free. The computer becomes a phone with unlimited access to everybody else on the Internet without the long-distance charges.

With wireless Internet connections and improved telephony, how can your local phone company stay in business? What kind of services can they offer that will make them important in the next decade? Record your thoughts in a 100- to 250-word essay. Save your file as **Activity 2-2** in your saving folder.

ACTIVITY 2-3

Do you think that instant messaging is a good tool to use on the job? Do you think it will help employees perform better or interrupt their work? How do you think IM clients should be used in a business setting? Record your thoughts in a 100- to 250-word essay. Save your file as **Activity 2-3** in your saving folder.

JOB 2-1

Visit the corporate Web site for a large corporation that you know something about. See if they have an e-mail address that you can use to receive information and vital statistics about this company and what it does. Write an e-mail message to the company. Copy and paste any replies you receive as **Job 2-1** in a word processing file and place it in your saving folder.

JOB 2-2

Many corporations hire their employees over the Internet. Visit several business Web sites and see if you can find an e-mail address that prospective employees can use to communicate directly with the employment offices or human resources hiring departments. Write five such e-mail addresses down next to their companies and save the list in your saving folder as **Job 2-2** in a word processing file.

FINDING A NEEDLE IN THE GLOBAL HAYSTACK

"I THINK I CAN!" THE LITTLE SEARCH ENGINE THAT COULD

Finding the Haystack: Keyword Searches

Finding the information you need on the Net can be as difficult as finding the proverbial "needle in the haystack." A *query* is like asking a question. It's a method of filtering data to find information that meets specific search criteria. In Lesson 2, you learned that you can narrow your search using search portals, such as Yahoo! and AltaVista. To make such a search possible, these portals use software called *search engines* that allow you to look for information based on some criterion, such as a keyword.

Search engines catalog the Web, organizing information so that it is easier to find. Some search engines offer indices, so you can search by category. Many search engines also catalog pictures, video, music, and other multimedia clips on the Web. Often, the terms search portal and search engine are used interchangeably.

A *keyword* can be any word you choose. A keyword search can produce a list of hundreds of thousands, if not millions, of *hits.* You can see this for yourself every time you use the keyword search. Search engines locate documents and other sources of information that contain the keywords you've entered. A *hit* can mean a couple of things. Every time someone goes to a Web page, it counts as a hit. Site owners often count the number of hits on their site to judge its effectiveness in attracting users. In this lesson, hits are the number of items found in response to a search query. For example, if your query results in a list of 25 items that meet your search criteria, then the query resulted in 25 hits. Let's try some searches.

STEP-BY-STEP ▷ 9.1

1. Launch your browser and go to www.google.com. Key the word Science in the search window and press Enter or click Google Search, as shown in Figure 9-1. Note the number of hits you received (see Figure 9-2).

2. When inquiring about a broad topic like science, a keyword search may result in simply too many hits to be helpful. To prove this point, try a keyword search again by entering the word History. Note the number of hits. Keep your browser open for the next Step-by-Step.

INTERNET MILESTONE

THE LIFE OF A WEBMASTER

Webmasters are the guardians of cyberspace. Webmasters are people who create, organize, and manage Web sites. Most Webmasters got into the Webmaster business because it was fun. Since then, sites have become more and more complex.

There are two kinds of Webmasters: those who focus on hardware, software, and protocols, and those who focus on the content that a site provides. Every Webmaster must know the basics of the hardware that link computers to the Net, the software the Internet uses, and the specialized languages and programming commands required to make the Web work. HTML, Java, JavaScript, CGI, and FLASH are all familiar terms to Webmasters. Qualified Webmasters for major companies command respectable salaries, but the hours are long and much of the work must be done at night when users are less likely to be on the Net.

FIGURE 9-1
Using a keyword search in Google

FIGURE 9-2
Our Google search provides millions of hits

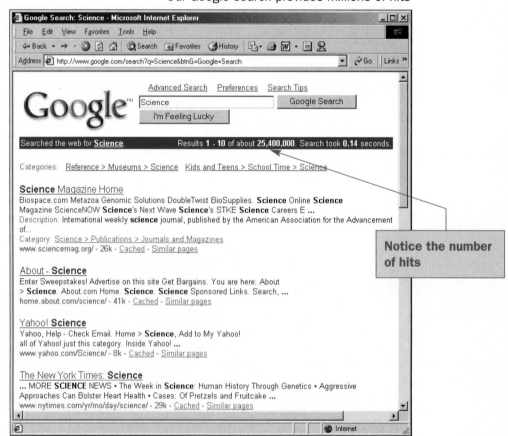

Finding a Needle In a Haystack: Natural Language and Phrase Searches

Information overload has become a huge Internet problem. People feel overwhelmed by the sheer amount of information available online, which leads to a feeling of overload. In this section, we will discuss two techniques that can help you narrow a search so you can find that needle in the cyber-haystack.

Phrase searching means searching for exact sequences of words in a query by enclosing the words in quotation marks. *Natural language searching* is a search method in which the query is expressed in English, French, or any other spoken language, usually in the form of a question. An example of a natural language search is *Why is the sky blue?*

Phrase searching and natural language searching are among the easiest and most powerful techniques at your disposal.

STEP-BY-STEP ▷ 9.2

1. First, let's explore phrase searching. Go to **www.altavista.com** and key the words **food poisoning** in the search box. Note the number of hits.

2. Try the search again, but this time, enclose the words **food poisoning** in quotation marks, as illustrated in Figure 9-3. Note the number of hits.

3. Now we will perform a natural language search. Go to **www.askjeeves.com**. In the search box, enter **Who won the Cy Young Award in 2000?** and choose **Ask**, as illustrated in Figure 9-4. (The Cy Young Award is given to the most valuable pitcher in Major League Baseball.)

4. Note the number of hits, or pages that match your question. Skim through the displayed summaries to see if you can figure out who won the Cy Young Award in 2000.

5. Using three of the search engines you bookmarked in earlier lessons, make a note of how many hits each query for the Cy Young Award returned.

   Search Engine 1: _____
   Number of hits _____

   Search Engine 2: _____
   Number of hits _____

   Search Engine 3: _____
   Number of hits _____

   Leave your browser open for the next Step-by-Step.

 Net Concept

By default, most search engines look for all pages containing the words you key in. Unfortunately, this method can identify many pages unrelated to the topic you're researching. Phrase searching is a good way to limit a search very quickly.

147

FIGURE 9-3

Using phrase searching in AltaVista

FIGURE 9-4

Using natural language when searching at *AskJeeves.com*

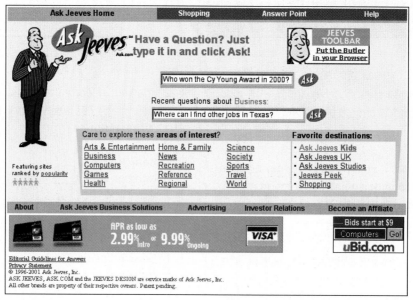

Pinning Things Down Even Further!

If you had to look at thousands of pages at random to find one or two containing useful information, you wouldn't use the Internet much. Learning how to limit or pin down your searches is essential to tapping into the Internet's wealth. Search engines allow you to limit your search by using keywords and *operators*. Operators are symbols or special words used to perform computer operations.

The real benefit of using operators lies in combining them properly to refine your searches. As you learn more about each operator, try refining your searches by combining operators. Watch how your hit list shrinks to only a few of the most applicable pages.

AND/OR

The AND operator instructs the search engine to search for all documents containing one keyword AND another keyword. For example, if you enter the words *cats AND dogs* the search engine will look for all documents containing these keywords. Some search engines use the + symbol as an operator. The + symbol acts just like the AND operator.

Most search engines do not require you to keep the operator in all caps. However, it may be helpful for you to do this to keep your search words separated from the operators.

The OR operator instructs the search engine to search for documents containing either keyword you specified. If you enter *cats OR dogs* in the search box, all documents containing either word will appear.

Let's try out these operators.

Net Concept

Many search engines use **Boolean logic**, invented by George Boole, a nineteenth century mathematician. The system uses operators to manipulate data, based on a simple yes or no ranking system. Just like add (+), subtract (-), multiply (*), and divide (/) are the primary operators of arithmetic, AND, OR, and NOT are the primary **Boolean operators**.

STEP-BY-STEP ▷ 9.4

1. Launch your browser. Using your bookmarks (Netscape) or favorites (Internet Explorer), go to Yahoo! at **www.yahoo.com**.

2. You had a chance to look through Yahoo!'s directory system earlier. This time, let Yahoo! do the searching. Yahoo! searches for site categories first. Enter **dogs** into the search box and click the **Search** button. Yahoo! will display all the categories with the word dogs in them.

3. Let's refine our search by adding the AND operator. Click the **Back** button to return to the search box. Enter **dogs AND breeds**, as shown in Figure 9-5. Click the **Search** button and note your hits or results.

4. Generally, the OR operator will expand a search to include more pages. It can be very helpful when used in combination with the AND operator. Go to **www.webcrawler.com** and enter **dogs AND labradors OR retrievers** in the search box. Click the **Search** button to view your results, as illustrated in Figure 9-6. Note the number of hits you receive.

5. To find out more about how these operators change the results, observe and record the results, or the number of hits, you get from the following searches:

   dogs _____

   dogs AND labrador _____

   dogs AND retriever _____

   labrador _____

   retriever _____

   labrador OR retriever _____

   Leave your browser open for the next Step-by-Step.

Net Tip

Be careful. Search engines default to an AND search, so entering *dogs breeds* will bring up all documents with the keyword *dogs* and the keyword *breeds*.

149

FIGURE 9-5
Using the AND operator in Yahoo!

FIGURE 9-6
Combining the AND and OR operators in WebCrawler

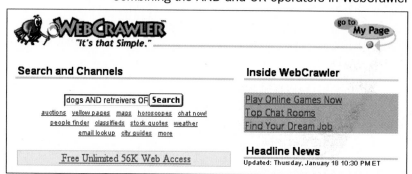

Don't Bother with Some Haystacks: NOT/-

Sometimes it's easier to narrow a search by specifying what you are *not* looking for. The NOT operator excludes documents containing a keyword you specify. Some search engines use the minus (-) symbol as the operator, which works the same way as the NOT operator. Be sure to check the instructions for using operators on each search engine. Some, for example, require you to include AND with the NOT operator (as in *Simpsons AND NOT Homer*).

INTERNET MILESTONE

BOOLEAN OPERATORS AND BINARY SYSTEMS

Boolean operators can be combined to create very powerful queries. They operate on a simple system of *binary* numbers. Binary code uses only 1s and 0s (where 1 is "yes" or "on" and 0 is "no" or "off").

For example, a search for cars AND NOT (trucks OR rental) can be turned into this set of yes or no questions: Does the page have the word *car* on it, yes or no? From the list of yes answers, do any of the pages have the words *trucks* or *rental* on them, yes or no? If the answer is yes to the first question and no to the second question, then that page is returned as a hit. Simple.

1. Go to **www.hotbot.com**. In the **Look for** list box, choose **Boolean phrase** from the pull-down menu.

2. In the Search box, enter **carbon monoxide AND symptoms** and then choose the **Search** button. Note the number of hits returned: _____

3. Now add **NOT com** to the end of **carbon monoxide AND symptoms** search phrase, as shown in Figure 9-7, and click the **Search** button. This refinement will eliminate the .com domains, which are mainly businesses advertising carbon monoxide detectors. Therefore, the number of hits is reduced significantly.

Many of the remaining sites are educational organizations that will (hopefully) contain more useful information. Leave your browser open for the next Step-by-Step.

Net Concept

Searching is a process of trial and error. Entering different combinations can lead to drastically different results. It is better to spend a little extra time narrowing down your search than following every hit you get.

FIGURE 9-7
Combining the AND and NOT operators in HotBot

Look In Nearby Haystacks: NEAR/ADJ

The NEAR/ADJ operators are used by more advanced search engines. These operators look for keywords within a certain proximity to another keyword.

For example, if you were to use the NEAR operator in the search *tornadoes NEAR Texas*, it would usually find hits in which the two words are within 25 words of each other. You can change the proximity to within five words by using NEAR/5. Most search engines don't check for word order, so tornadoes could be within five words before or after Texas.

The ADJ operator stands for adjacent. This operator will return only documents in which, say, George is adjacent to Washington. ADJ is more strict than NEAR and will return fewer hits. Let's try these operators.

STEP-BY-STEP ▷ 9.6

1. In your browser, go to **www.lycos.com**.

2. Enter **volleyball NEAR indoor** to find sites about indoor volleyball, as shown in Figure 9-8. How many hits do you have?

3. Look at the list of hits. Some contain information about outdoor volleyball. Add the NOT operator to eliminate those sites. Enter **volleyball NEAR indoor NOT outdoor**. This trims your list even more. Now how many hits are there?

4. Now try the search with the ADJ operator. Enter **volleyball ADJ indoor**. Note the number of hits now.

5. Add the NOT operator to eliminate references to outdoor volleyball. Try **volleyball ADJ indoor NOT outdoor**, as illustrated in Figure 9-9. Note the hits now.

FIGURE 9-8
Using the NEAR operator in Lycos

FIGURE 9-9
Combining the ADJ and NOT operators in Lycos

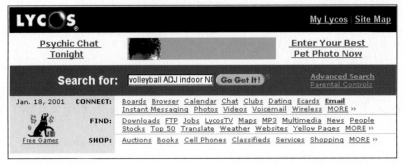

Parentheses with Power

The use of parentheses in Internet searches is similar to their use in mathematics. In math applications, parentheses are used to identify those operations that should be performed before other operations.

Here are some math expressions using parentheses. Notice how different the results can be depending on the placement of the parentheses.

2*(4+8/2)=16
2*4+8/2=12
(2*4+8)/2=8

Parentheses can be used to filter all sorts of lists and can be combined with most search operators.

STEP-BY-STEP ▷ 9.7

1. In your browser, go to **www.excite.com**.

2. Enter **cars** in the search box and click **Search**. Note the number of hits.

3. Click the **Back** button.

4. Enter **cars AND NOT (truck OR rental)** in the search box and click **Search**, as shown in Figure 9-10.

5. Note the number of resulting hits.

FIGURE 9-10
Using parentheses with the NOT and OR operators in Excite

NET ETHICS

WHAT A WEBMASTER KNOWS

Webmasters are in charge of computers for schools, businesses, and governmental organizations. As a result, they have access to all sorts of confidential files and sensitive information. On some sites, the Webmasters also maintain the e-mail system. If they want to, they can read all the mail sent to and from their Internet e-mail servers.

What kind of person do you want to be your Webmaster? What can organizations do to safeguard confidentiality?

Using Real-Names Searches

America Online created real-name keyword searches to make it very easy for its customers to find its most popular sites. For example, if you are an AOL member, you can type a keyword like Rosie into AOL's software to locate information about Rosie O'Donnell. A possible limitation of this type of searching is that you may be taken to only one site. You may not be given a list of additional sites that discuss the famous talk-show comedian. Still, this type of searching makes popular commercial sites easy for fans to locate.

Some Internet companies, like RealNames, applied this same principle to the Internet. Essentially, companies pay for the right to have certain keywords go directly to their sites. This eliminates the need for potential customers to remember long and difficult URLs. Table 9-1 lists some popular examples.

TABLE 9-1
Real name search words and URLs

IF YOU ENTER	... YOU WILL GO TO A WEB SITE WITH AN URL LIKE THIS
hp	http://welcome.hp.com/country/us/eng/welcome.htm
The Gap	http://www.gap.com/asp/home.html?wdid=0
RealNames	http://web.realnames.com/Eng/Eng_Corporate_RealNamesHomepage.asp
Panasonic DVD	http://www.panasonic.com/consumer_electronics/dvd/index.htm

Obviously, real-name keywords are a snap to remember compared with long Internet URLs. Some of the companies that signed on early with this easy navigation system include Panasonic DVD (Figure 9-11), Disney, Hewlett-Packard, Barnes & Noble, Nintendo, and Eddie Bauer.

FIGURE 9-11
Enter real names into your Internet Explorer address window

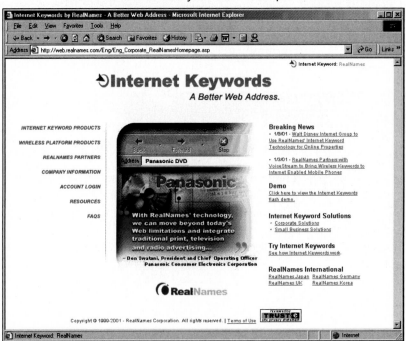

STEP-BY-STEP ▷ 9.8

1. Open your Web browser. (This exercise works best in Internet Explorer.)

2. In the Web address box of your browser, enter the following terms and see what appears!
   a. Apple Computer
   b. HP
   c. The Gap
   d. Panasonic DVD

3. Try three additional real-name combinations of your own choosing. Record them below along with a description of what happened and what appeared on your screen as a result. (Some of your attempts may work and some may not. Record the successes as well as the failures.)

What real name did you enter?	What happened?
1.	
2.	
3.	

INTERNET MILESTONE

SEARCHING BY VOICE

Real-name searches have important implications for the future of Internet searching and surfing. How much better would it be to simply say *Barnes & Noble* into a microphone and be taken immediately to *barnesandnoble.com*, the online bookstore?

Such technologies are now available to millions of Internet users. For instance, you can access Web pages with a cell phone by saying real names. You can also access voice pages by speaking into a microphone attached to your personal computer. All it takes is the correct Internet browser configured with speech recognition software.

155

Summary

In this lesson, you learned:

- You can refine a search with the AND/OR/+ operators.

- Searches can be refined with the NOT/-operators.

- The NEAR/ADJ operators can be used to refine a search.

- You can refine a search with the parentheses operator in a search request.

- Searches can be refined with natural language and phrase searching.

- Keyword and real name searching can be used to narrow searches.

NET TERMS REVIEW

Define the following terms:

Binary	Information overload	Phrase searching
Boolean logic	Keyword	Query
Boolean operators	Natural language searching	Search engine
Hits	Operators	Webmaster

LESSON 9 REVIEW QUESTIONS

TRUE/FALSE

Circle T if the statement is true or F if the statement is false.

T F 1. You can narrow searches by using Webmaster operators.

T F 2. The OR operator will return hits that contain all keywords.

T F 3. Phrase searching allows you to search by asking a question.

T F 4. Webmasters are in charge of Web content on a Web site.

T F 5. Hits occur when you punch a key on the keyboard.

FILL IN THE BLANK

Complete the following sentences by writing the correct word or words in the blanks provided.

1. The _____ Boolean operator shows sites with one keyword or the other.

2. The _____ Boolean operator shows only sites with both keywords.

3. Sites that are returned related to your keywords are called _____ .

4. The AskJeeves Web site lets you search for sites using _____ language searching.

5. A(n) _____ search uses keywords in quotation marks.

WRITTEN QUESTIONS

Write a brief answer to the following questions.

1. Give an example of a search query using each of the operators. Describe the strengths, weaknesses, and limitations of searching with each operator and what can be done (how the search can be revised) to overcome those limitations. When would you use these operators and when would they be ineffective?
   A. AND/+

   B. NOT/-

   C. OR

   D. NEAR/ADJ

   E. ( )

PROJECT 9-1

Fly-fishing for Computer Geeks

Since you have fast become the Internet guru at GreatApplications, Inc., the boss wants you to do some research for the company's forthcoming CD-ROM, "Fly-fishing for Computer Geeks." You need to find answers to the following questions:

1. How many Americans fish?
2. How many Americans fly fish?
3. How many women fly fish?
4. How fast is the sport of fly-fishing growing?

Knowing what you know about search engines, what do you think is the most efficient way to access this information? Perform the search and find answers to the questions. Take notes of the search queries that worked well and those that didn't work so well and save them for Project 9-2.

PROJECT 9-2

Fly-fishing as a Team Sport

After each member of your team has researched the four questions in Project 9-1 individually, work as a team to prepare an e-mail to your boss. In the e-mail, include the answers to the questions and the URLs of the five sites with the best information on fly-fishing. Briefly describe the kinds of information on fly-fishing each site contains.

CRITICAL THINKING

SCANS

ACTIVITY 9-1

Writing About Technology

How useful would the Web be without search engines? Prepare a 100- to 250-word report explaining various ways that small businesses can use search engines to help them succeed.

ACTIVITY 9-2

Snake Bites

What did you learn about how the AND/OR operators affect search results in Step-by-Step 9.4? Let's say you want to look up information about rattlesnake bites. How would you go about narrowing down the number of hits on this topic? Prepare a 100- to 250-word answer to these questions.

ACTIVITY 9-3

Not Again!

The Net is a virtual library at your fingertips. The problem is too much information. You have to find ways to focus your searches. Why do you think the NOT operator works so well? Prepare a 100- to 250-word answer to this question.

ACTIVITY 9-4

Future Filters

Now that you have been introduced to the most common operators, can you think of other ways you might want to filter information? List five useful ways to focus your hits.

1.

2.

3.

4.

5.

VIRTUAL LIBRARY: USING ONLINE RESOURCES

OBJECTIVES

Upon completion of this lesson, you should be able to:

- Research information from online knowledge sources.
- Locate online libraries.
- Use online encyclopedias.
- Visit online museums.
- Find e-mail and street addresses using search portals.

⏱ Estimated Time: 2.5 hours

NET TERMS

E-book

Mirror site

People finder

A Worldwide Knowledge Web

Traditional sources of knowledge, including museums, libraries, encyclopedias, and even phone books, have gone online.

You can take a virtual tour through many of the world's finest museums. You don't have to spend thousands of dollars getting there or worry about finding a place to park.

Online encyclopedias are also valuable sources of knowledge. The world is accumulating information at such a tremendous rate that printed materials can no longer stay up to date. Online encyclopedic resources can be updated as soon as new information and statistics become available.

As the world becomes digitalized, libraries are making more of their knowledge available online. You can check out a book at any time, since there are enough copies for everyone. And no books ever get lost. Books that have been digitized and put on the Internet in their complete form are known as *e-books*.

Net Tip

The Library of Congress in Washington D.C. contains more than 117 million books, images, and other multimedia contents. You can search the Web for interesting facts about the Library of Congress and the history of the United States.

Virtual Libraries

One day, most of the world's books will be available from virtual libraries via the Internet. The selection of titles and e-books at online libraries is growing steadily. For example, one online library features over 14,000 works, with authors as diverse as Shakespeare, Jane Austen, and Plato.

Let's find a few online libraries and take a look at the future of libraries.

Net Concept

Digitizing millions of printed books takes time and money. Most organizations responsible for putting content online are non-profit. They are working tirelessly with a lot of volunteer effort to accomplish a Herculean task.

STEP-BY-STEP ▷ 10.1

1. Go to your favorite search portal.

2. Key **Library of Congress** in the search box and press **Enter**.

3. Browse through and click the link that points to the Library of Congress Web page.

4. Choose **Search the Catalog,** as shown in Figure 10-1, to find your favorite book in the Library of Congress. You can search by title, author, or keyword, just as if you were at your local library. Select **Keyword** and key the name of your favorite author to see if his or her book is available at the Library of Congress.

5. Take a few minutes to browse through the other resources available at the Library Congress. Try to find something you don't already know about U.S. history.

6. Return to your favorite search tool and this time enter **libraries AND online**. (Note: You may need to be in the search engine's "advanced search" area to use Boolean operators.)

7. Browse through the hits until you find a public library. Look for the bigger libraries, such as the Internet Public Library, the Library of Virginia, or the Houston Public Library.

8. Search through the resources at the library you selected. For example, at the Internet Public Library lobby (Figure 10-2), you can visit the Online Texts link. You can search for an e-book by author or title or browse by Dewey decimal categories.

9. Try looking up your favorite author. If he or she isn't listed, look up a book you've read for an English class. Find several e-books to read!

10. Name three e-books you have found that you may like to read, along with the names of their authors.

   1. Title: _____

   Author: _____

   2. Title: _____

   Author: _____

   3. Title: _____

   Author: _____

Leave your Web browser open for the next Step-by-Step.

FIGURE 10-1
The Library of Congress

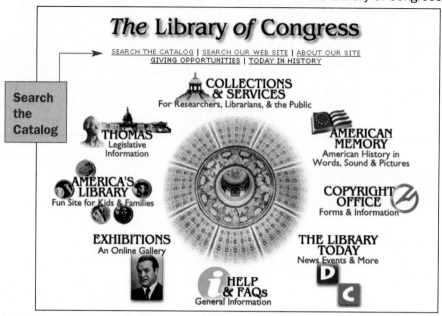

FIGURE 10-2
The Internet Public Library lobby

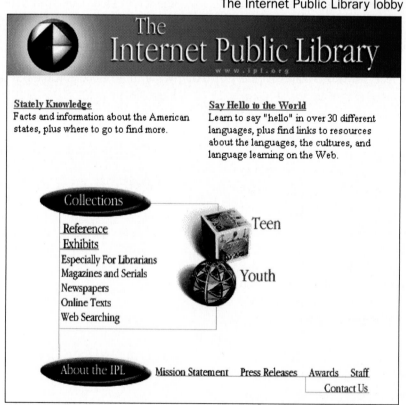

Virtual Encyclopedias

One of the biggest challenges in using the Internet as a research tool is that anyone can post anything. It used to be difficult to get a book or article published. Facts had to be meticulously checked and cross-checked. Claims had to be supported. But as more and more information becomes available, it becomes increasingly difficult to discern fact from fiction.

In this lesson, you will locate several online encyclopedias. You will then try to look up the same information in each of them and evaluate the quality of the information you find from each source.

Net Tip

If you intend to read an e-book, save the page to your computer. Exit your browser and read the book offline to avoid unnecessarily taking up valuable Internet access lines that your fellow netizen could use.

STEP-BY-STEP ▷ 10.2

1. Start your Web browser and go to your favorite search portal.

2. Find a list of online encyclopedias. If your search portal has categories, try looking under the reference or education sections. If not, simply enter **online encyclopedia** and choose **Search**.

3. Find articles about the country of Yemen, located near Saudi Arabia (see Figure 10-3).

4. Your first search may be unsuccessful or you may need more than one source. Use a search portal to find more information. Enter Yemen into several online encyclopedias. Search until you find three articles that tell you about the country, and list them below.

   Name of Article   Web Address or URL

   1.

   2.

   3.

5. Never assume that your first find is the most accurate. Always double-check your sources. Which source listed in Step 4 do you trust the most and why? Leave your Web browser open for the next Step-by-Step.

Net Concept

Many of the well-known CD-ROM and printed encyclopedias have online versions. While many of these offer a free trial period, most require a fee to access them. They include Britannica, World Book, and Grolier's. Use a search portal to find one you can use for free.

FIGURE 10-3
All about Yemen...according to Encarta Online

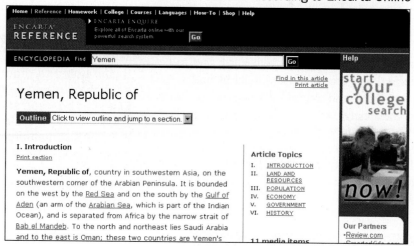

Virtual Museums

Virtual museums are popping up everywhere in cyberspace. The Louvre in France and the National Gallery of Art in Washington D.C. are two of the world's greatest museums. Millions visit every year. But billions more never have had the opportunity until now.

Of all the online reference sources, museums seem to offer the greatest variety of knowledge sources. From the Prado in Madrid to the Smithsonian Institution in Washington, D.C., museums around the world are opening their electronic doors. People who would never be able to physically visit the world's greatest museums can now tour their collections from the comfort of their personal computer.

INTERNET MILESTONE

GET A VIRTUAL DEGREE

Observing the growing power of the Internet in education, many universities and colleges have begun to offer classes and degrees online. It is now possible to earn your associate, bachelor, master, or Ph.D. degree from classes taken over the Internet.

Try searching for schools that offer classes over the Internet. Can you find a school that will let you graduate without physically attending a class? Can you obtain your college degree entirely over the Internet? How would you like to sit home every day and take e-classes over the Web? What keywords would you use to search for online schools and universities?

S TEP-BY-STEP ▷ 10.3

1. Let's start with the Louvre. Go to your favorite search portal and enter **Louvre** in a search tool. Follow a link from the list of hits to the museum.

2. Unless you speak French, follow the language links to English, and then choose the Virtual Tour.

3. Choose an exhibit and then a hall. Wait for the hall to load on the next page and then click the image anywhere and drag left or right to virtually view the paintings in the room, as shown in Figure 10-4. (Note: You may need to download Quicktime to view the exhibit.)

4. Which hall did you choose to visit?

5. Now search for the **National Gallery of Art** in Washington D.C.

6. Choose **Exhibitions** on the home page, and then **Virtual Exhibitions**.

7. Choose one of the virtual exhibitions. You can select Van Gogh, Calder, or many others.

(Note: You can view the exhibit in QuickTime or just in pictures. If you choose QuickTime, you can scroll through the rooms and view them as if you were actually at the museum.)

8. Find a painting or sculpture that interests you in one of the online exhibits. Click it to make it larger and see interesting information about the work, as shown in Figure 10-5.

9. Browse through and find more interesting information about the paintings on exhibit at the National Gallery of Art.

10. Use a different search portal to see if you can find other virtual museums. For example, try to locate the Smithsonian Institution or the Museo del Prado in Spain.

11. Of all the museums you have visited, which was your favorite?

12. Which was your favorite exhibit? Explain what you most liked about the exhibit and give a short description of its main features. Leave your browser open for the next Step-byStep.

INTERNET MILESTONE

PROJECT GUTENBERG

W ant to read *Alice in Wonderland*, *War of the Worlds*, or one of Shakespeare's plays for free? Well you can, and you can thank Project Gutenberg for it.

In 1971, Michael Hart was given $100 million worth of computer time on the mainframe computer at the University of Illinois. Wondering how to use this time effectively, he came up with Project Gutenberg, which, among other things, replicates e-books and makes them available for free on the net.

Project Gutenberg was the first major electronic publication and distribution project of its kind. Much of the philosophy of sharing found on the early Internet can be traced to this great project.

FIGURE 10-4
View the Mona Lisa at the Louvre

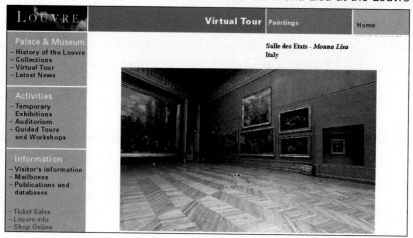

FIGURE 10-4
View the Mona Lisa at the Louvre

FIGURE 10-5
See Vincent Van Gogh at the National Gallery of Art

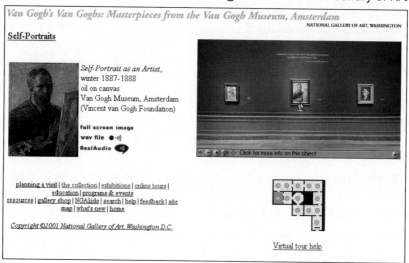

People Finders

Ever have a problem reading someone's phone number? How about someone who has moved away, but you don't remember where? A *people finder* is a feature provided by search services on the Internet that helps you find addresses and phone numbers. People finders can help you locate long-lost friends, search for people who attended your high school, or even find the e-mail address of the President of the United States.

Net Concept

Former Vice President Al Gore was a national leader in the fight to fund and expand the information superhighway and to make the Internet available to schools. In fact, he coined the phrase "information superhighway."

STEP-BY-STEP 10.4

1. Many search portals offer a people finder option. See if your favorite search portal has one by keying **people finder** in the search box and then pressing **Enter**. If your search portal doesn't have a people finder option, try Yahoo! or Lycos.

2. For your first search, fill in your own name and information about yourself. If the search doesn't find you at the city level, leave the city option blank and search only at the state level. If the search still doesn't find you, try entering one of your parents' names and city information.

3. Search for yourself on more than one people finder. You may find yourself at any number of previous addresses or you may not be listed at all, depending on which people finder you use.

4. For your second search, let's find the President of the United States. Enter the name of the current president in the people finder box (see Figure 10-6). Did you find the address to the White House?

5. Close your Web browser if you are finished for today.

FIGURE 10-6
Finding people on the Internet

U.S. PEOPLE PAGES

First Name: George W.

Last Name: (required) Bush

☐ Exact matches only.

City: Washington

State: D.C. ▾

☐ Include nearby areas.

[Find] Search Tips   Reverse Lookup

Use the PeoplePages to:
- Search for people nationwide
- Update your listing
- Save listings to your personal address book
- Get maps and driving directions
- Find neighbors

Plus much more!

NETIQUETTE

USE LOCAL MIRROR SITES

Sites that receive a lot of hits (get a lot of visitors) will often set up *mirror sites*. A mirror site is a copy of the original site that resides on a computer in another location. Mirror sites contain the same information as the master host site distributed to other computers to reduce network traffic to one host. This strategy accommodates more people.

Another advantage of setting up mirror sites is to speed up transmission to very slow Internet connections. If you are surfing the Internet in Florida, it is probably going to be faster for you to download the latest exhibit information from a museum's mirror sight in Washington, D.C., than from a host site in Paris, France.

It is considered good netiquette to select the mirror site closest to your geographical location whenever possible. Another good strategy is to pick a site that is "in the dark." That is, if it is daytime in North America and 2 a.m. in Australia, download from a mirror site in Australia when netizens down under are probably asleep.

PRETTY GOOD PRIVACY'S VIEW

Does anyone have the right to read your e-mail, your files, or your private publications? Phil Zimmerman, the creator of Pretty Good Privacy, Inc., doesn't think so. He made his now famous PGP (Pretty Good Privacy) encryption software available over the Net. In his view, every Net user has the right to electronic privacy.

However, the federal government has a different view. According to an official White House press release dated November 15, 1996, "encryption products, when used outside the United States, can jeopardize our foreign policy and national security interests. Moreover, such products, when used by international criminal organizations, can threaten the safety of US citizens here and abroad, as well as the safety of the citizens of other countries." In short, when PGP became available over the Net, anyone in any country could download and use it. Phil was charged with the crime of exporting encryption technology. The case stirred a great debate over personal privacy versus national security. Phil is now in the clear and has since started his own electronics security company, but the debate continues.

What do you think comes first, personal privacy or national security? Who is right: Phil, for protecting personal communications, or the government, who knows that foreign agents and drug dealers can use encryption software to menace our lives?

Summary

In this lesson, you learned:

- You can research online knowledge services.
- It is possible to locate online libraries.
- Encyclopedias can be located and researched online.
- You can find and tour virtual museums.
- E-mail and street addresses can be found online.

NET TERMS REVIEW

Define the following terms:

E-book   Mirror site   People finder

LESSON 10 REVIEW QUESTIONS

TRUE/FALSE

Circle T if the statement is true or F if the statement is false.

T F   1.   All virtual encyclopedias are free of charge.

T F   2.   You can search for books on the Internet, but you can't actually read them.

T F   3.   It is a good idea to use mirror sites only at night.

T F   4.   The Library of Congress contains almost 17 million different books.

T F   5.   George W. Bush coined the phrase, "the information superhighway."

FILL IN THE BLANK

Complete the following sentences by writing the correct word or words in the blanks provided.

1.   The Mona Lisa can be seen on the Virtual Tour of the _____ in Paris.

2.   A(n) _____ is an electronic version of a book or text.

3.   _____ _____ was responsible for first transferring books into an electronic form for sharing over the Net.

4. A(n) _____ _____ is an exact copy of an original Web site that helps distribute traffic away from the main host site.

5. _____ is a country located on the southern side of Saudi Arabia.

WRITTEN QUESTIONS

Write a brief answer to the following questions.

1. What are some benefits of online libraries?

2. In what ways was Project Gutenberg important?

3. Describe how you would search the Web to find out what four countries last hosted the Winter Olympics.

4. You are going to Seattle and you would like to look up an old friend with whom you have lost touch. What steps would you follow to find this person?

5. Describe how you might take a virtual tour of the Smithsonian.

LESSON 10 PROJECTS

PROJECT 10-1

Free Stuff

GreatApplications, Inc., needs a customized list of library, governmental, and other free research-oriented resources that employees can use when they are doing their business research. Compile a list of libraries, encyclopedias, and e-books that employees would find useful. Save this list of resources in an electronic file in your Resources folder. Include at least 25 resources on your list. Name it **Freestuff**.

PROJECT 10-2

Teaming up to Compile Useful Resources

As a team, combine your Freestuff resource lists into a master list of resources that employees in a company like GreatApplications, Inc., would find beneficial. Save this list of resources in your common folder. If one team member knows HTML, that person can create a Web page listing all of the URLs.

PROJECT 10-3

Writing About Technology

With what you have learned about PGP and the National Encryption Security debate, prepare a 100- to 250-word essay supporting one of the following opinions. Use your searching skills to find information that supports your point of view.

1. Encryption technology should only be in the hands of the government.

2. Encryption technology should be available to every Net user in the United States but shouldn't be given to anyone in a foreign country.

3. The Internet is an international tool, not subject to the laws of any one country. Therefore, encryption technology should be available to all.

4. Since the government funded the development of the Internet, it should control the use of encryption on the Net.

SCANS

ACTIVITY 10-1

Library Success

The Internet Public Library seems to embody the very reason the Internet was invented. The articles and links found in the library are maintained by experts in each field from around the world. Truly, this is a collaborative effort. In your opinion, does it work? How do you think the Internet Public Library will evolve in the future? Will it be a big success, a mild success, or a failed effort? Prepare a 100- to 250-word answer to these questions.

SCANS

ACTIVITY 10-2

Encyclopedia Success

How would you rate the online encyclopedias you found? Are they better or worse than their text-based counterparts? How about CD-ROM based encyclopedias? Can you find the information faster if you enter *What is the area of Yemen in* a search tool or from a CD-ROM? Prepare a 100- to 250-word answer to these questions.

ACTIVITY 10-3

Writers for Hire

Contrary to popular belief, most writers like to be paid for their work. Usually, they get a percentage of their book sales. If books are being made available on the Internet for free, will writers have any incentive to write? Prepare a 100- to 250-word answer to these questions.

ACTIVITY 10-4

Personal Privacy

Do you think most people will be happy to know that their name, address, and phone number are accessible to just about anyone in the world? Should you be able to get your name removed from those lists? How do you think the lists are created in the first place? Prepare a 100- to 250-word answer to these questions.

Finding the Needle in a Global Haystack

REVIEW QUESTIONS

TRUE/FALSE

Circle T if the statement is true or F if the statement is false.

T F 1. A query is like a question.

T F 2. Because of various legal restrictions, search engines can catalog text pages but not music and video.

T F 3. A keyword can be any word you choose!

T F 4. You may receive hits as a result of a query in a search engine.

T F 5. Webmasters create, organize, and manage Web sites.

T F 6. The Library of Congress is in New York City.

T F 7. Many great libraries are disappearing because they failed to move their content online.

T F 8. Virtual encyclopedias can be updated more quickly online than their printed counterparts.

T F 9. State laws prohibit taking classes over the Internet for college credit.

T F 10. Many major museums like the Louvre and the National Gallery of Art don't have Web sites because of the fear that people will no longer visit them if they can see the exhibits online.

MATCHING

Match the correct term in Column 2 to its description in Column 1.

Column 1   **Column 2**

___ 1. Searches for the exact sequence of words in a query.   **A.** Operators

___ 2. Instructs the search engine to search for documents   **B.** AND
containing either keyword you specify.

                                                                   C. NEAR

___ 3. Symbols or special words used to perform computer
operations.   **D.** Phrase searching

___ 4. Looks for keywords within five words of another keyword.   **E.** OR

___ 5. Instructs the search engine to search for all documents   **F.** Parentheses
containing both keywords you specify.

                                                                   G. NEAR/5

___ 6. Excludes documents containing a specific keyword.
                                                                   H. NOT

___ 7. Organizes groups of operators that must be performed
before other parts of the operation can be calculated.   **I.** ADJ

___ 8. Will return documents adjacent to another keyword.   **J.** Natural language searching
More strict than the NEAR operator.

___ 9. A search in which the query is expressed in a spoken
language in a normal manner.

___10. Looks for keywords in close proximity, usually within
25 words.

CROSS-CURRICULAR ACTIVITIES

Narrowing down searches and researching with the help of virtual online resources are critical academic and working life skills. For instance, it's impossible to think of doing a research paper without accessing these essential resources.

MATH 3-1

Having trouble in algebra class? No problem. Use your search skills to find software that can help you learn algebra but not trigonometry, geometry, calculus, or any other math discipline. Does such software exist? Enter the names of any software programs that you locate in a file named **Math 3-1.**

LANGUAGE ARTS 3-1

Visit a virtual library or encyclopedia and learn as much as you can about the late author Frank Baum. Prepare a short 250-word report on the famous author. Add a short description on his book *The Wizard of Oz*. Save the report as **Language Arts 3-1**.

HISTORY 3-1

Using your best search and virtual library skills, create a list of at least ten resources about the history of your specific state or province. Save your list as **History 3-1.**

HISTORY 3-2

Using the list of resources that you created in the previous exercise, write a short 250- to 500-word report on the earliest beginnings of your state or province. Save your report as **History 3-2**.

TECHNOLOGY 3-1

Using your keyword search and operator skills, find a personal computer that utilizes Microsoft Windows but not Macintosh OS. Find a computer that would be suitable to take to college and that would be powerful enough to be used for four years without a major upgrade. List your computer choice and its specifications in a document named **Technology 3-1**.

TECHNOLOGY 3-2

Reverse your search and find a computer that would be suitable to use in college that is not dependent on Microsoft Windows as its operating system. Save your computer choice and its specifications in a file named **Technology 3-2**.

CRITICAL THINKING

ACTIVITY 3-1

Which type of search system do you feel is the most helpful? Do you prefer natural language, keyword, or phrase searching? In a 150- to 250-word report, compare these search methods while describing how each system works. Save your file as **Activity 3-1**.

ACTIVITY 3-2

Of the many search engines that exist in cyberspace, which do you prefer using? Explain the rationale for your choice in a 150- to 250-word report. Save your file as **Activity 3-2**.

ACTIVITY 3-3

Compare the value of online museums with the value of online encyclopedias. When it comes to preparing a report on a specific topic such as the "history of aviation," which type of resource is most valuable? Which will help you complete a research task more quickly and thoroughly? Prepare a 150- to 250-word report comparing these two important resources and listing their strengths and weaknesses. Save your file as **Activity 3-3**.

SCANS

JOB 3-1

Using your considerable Boolean searching skills, find ten resources that would help a corporation answer corporate tax questions. Are there any resources that specifically provide tax advice and assistance for small businesses? Save your list as **Job 3-1**.

SCANS

JOB 3-2

Marketing and sales are critical to corporate success. Search online for ten resources that will help a marketing department plan its Internet and Web marketing strategy. To make it a little more interesting, pretend the company you are searching for sells a line of clothing aimed at young consumers. Save the list as **Job 3-2**.

EXPLORING THE NET FOR FACT AND FICTION

UNIT 4

Estimated Time for Unit 4: 11.5+ hours

EXPLORING ONLINE SCIENCE AND MATH

OBJECTIVES

Upon completion of this lesson you should be able to:

- Gather scientific information.
- Find weather-related sites for various locations.
- Visit and navigate NASA's home page.
- Locate biology-related sites.
- Dissect a virtual frog.
- Find math-related sites, puzzles, and games.
- View geometric shapes.

 Estimated time: 2.5 hours

NET TERMS

Black Thursday
Filters
Internet worm
Proxy server

Space-Out on the Internet

The Internet was originally invented by and for scientists to share information. It stands to reason that some of the richest online content is in the fields of math and science. You can explore everything from the most current subatomic particle tests at CERN in Switzerland to the latest pictures of far-off galaxies from the Hubble telescope.

By way of the Internet, people all over the world were able to participate in the Shoemaker-Levy comet collision with Jupiter. And now, you can pinpoint the exact location of the International Space Station.

Meteorology

Planning a picnic? Are you hoping that the ski season will start early this year? Wanting more information about Hurricane Jane? The Internet definitely has the weather covered.

You won't have to search very hard for sites about the weather. Start by looking on any of the search portals that use categories. Categories pull together the best resources, saving you the hassle of finding them individually. Most search portals have a category for weather.

STEP-BY-STEP 11.1

1. Open your browser and go to **www.weather.com**. The *weather.com* home page is shown in Figure 11-1.

2. Enter your ZIP code or your city in the appropriate box and click **Go**.

3. Look up and record the weather information for the following locations:

CITY/STATE	CLOUD COVER	TEMPERATURE	DEW POINT	WIND VELOCITY	RELATIVE HUMIDITY
Your Town					
New York, NY					
Atlanta, GA					
Dallas, TX					
Salt Lake City, UT					
Seattle, WA					
Los Angeles, CA					
Honolulu, HI					

FIGURE 11-1
Weather.com

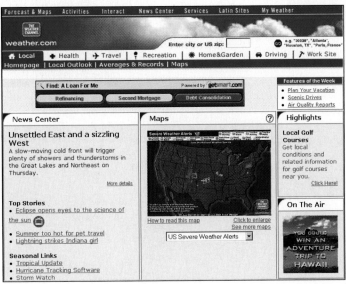

4. Under the **Local** tab, select **Maps**. Here you can view weather maps of the United States and other countries. Click **Map Type**, then **Satellite US National** (see Figure 11-2).

5. From the drop-down list below the map, choose the region where you live to show local cloud cover. This map is as up-to-date as the weather person's map on TV. But wait, there's more! You can view this weather map in full-motion.

6. Select the **show map in motion** hyperlink. After a second or two, the map will reload and, this time, it will be animated just like on TV. Many of the maps, like the one illustrated in Figure 11-3, are updated every few minutes.

7. Explore the other options or pick some of the links to find other weather-related information. The world is at your fingertips.

8. Use a search portal to locate five other weather-related sites and record your findings below. If you need more space, write your answers on a separate piece of paper.

Site Address and Description

1.

2.

3.

4.

5.

Leave your Web browser open for the next Step-by-Step.

FIGURE 11-2

Weather maps on *weather.com*

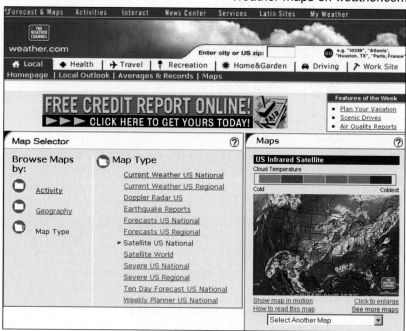

FIGURE 11-3
U.S. Satellite map in full motion

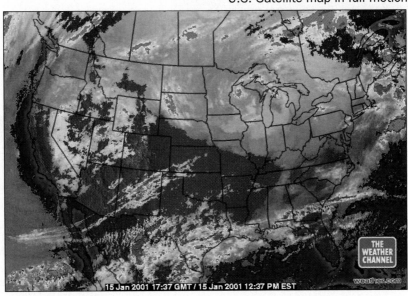

15 Jan 2001 17:37 GMT / 15 Jan 2001 12:37 PM EST

Astronomy and Space Exploration

As a society, we are fascinated with the exploration of space. While sci-fi has infiltrated many TV shows, hard science has also become a mainstay on major news programs.

In the past few years, we have witnessed the splendor of comets, explored nearby planets, and considered the possibility of extraterrestrial life. The Internet has fueled this interest by providing up-to-date pictures as well as virtual-reality tours of space.

INTERNET MILESTONE

ZEN AND THE ART OF THE INTERNET

Zen and the Art of the Internet was written by Brendan P. Kehoe in the earliest days of the popular Net. *Zen* remains one of the best ways to learn some of the tricky aspects of Net science. It is also a great guide to the culture of the Net. You can find early copies on the Net by keying *Zen Art Internet* in a search engine. Consider it required reading.

Kehoe introduces his book with the following very insightful quote: "One warning is perhaps in order—this territory we are entering can become a fantastic time-sink. Hours can slip by, people can come and go, and you'll be locked into cyberspace. Remember to do your work. With that, I welcome you, the new user, to the Net."

This advice applies particularly to those netizens who enjoy science. There is so much to see and learn—you may take a virtually endless Net field trip and never return to the report that is due at the end of the term.

1. Go to NASA's home page at **www.nasa.gov**.

2. Find a picture or link that will take you to the International Space Station home page, like the one shown in Figure 11-4. Choose it to go to *SpaceFlight,* the International Space Station's home page.

3. On the toolbar at the top, select **Station**. Enter the data below using the information you find at this site.
   Station time in orbit _____
   Crew time in orbit _____

4. Locate and record below five other space or astronomy-related sites.
   Site Address and Description
   1.
   2.
   3.
   4.
   5.

5. Leave your Web browser open for the next Step-by-Step.

Net Concept

The Net and the Web are the same thing, right? Wrong. The Internet started in the 1960s, linking computers together with the TCP/IP protocol. The World Wide Web wasn't born until the late 1980s. The Web and the Internet are now symbiotic organisms, which live and grow together. But any technical geek, like the authors of this text, will tell you they are different. There are many technical distinctions. Does it matter to the end-user? Not really. But we thought we would mention the distinction in the science section of this book so that we could use a really intelligent-sounding word like symbiotic.

FIGURE 11-4
NASA's Web site and the International Space Station link

Biology

In the next Step-by-Step, we'll introduce you to Fluffy the Frog, one of the interesting characters on the Internet. Fluffy was designed to give everyone the unforgettable experience of dissecting a frog without the mess.

One thing is for certain—biology may never be the same. Forget the formaldehyde and the scalpel. Kermit can rest a little easier.

STEP-BY-STEP ▷ 11.3

1. In a search engine, type in the phrase **virtual frog dissection kit** and press **Enter**.

2. Find and choose the link to the virtual frog dissection kit.

3. This site allows you to see many different views of Fluffy the Frog. It also allows you to download movies of the frog. Read the directions and then click the frog picture, as shown in Figure 11-5.

4. Follow the instructions for dissection and then describe below the purpose of each of the following organs and systems.
Nervous system:
Liver:
Brain:

Kidneys:
Small intestine:
Large intestine:

5. Search for and locate five other biology-related sites and record your findings below. If you need more space, write your answers on a separate piece of paper.
Site Address and Description

1.

2.

3.

4.

5.

Leave your Web browser open for the next Step-by-Step.

FIGURE 11-5
Meet Fluffy the Frog ... and then dissect him

Virtual Frog Dissection Kit

This <u>award-winning</u> interactive program is part of the <u>"Whole Frog" project</u>. You can interactively dissect a (digitized) frog named Fluffy, make <u>movies</u>, and play the <u>Virtual Frog Builder Game</u>. The interactive Web pages are available in a number of <u>languages</u>.

Jump into the kit.

NET ETHICS

HOW MUCH CAN YOU GET AWAY WITH AT WORK?

One of the big problems faced by corporations is that many employees use the Internet for personal reasons or to escape the dull routine of their jobs. When the author of *Zen and the Art of the Internet* suggested, "Remember to do your work." he was addressing this concern. Nowadays, you can listen to thousands of radio stations around the world or watch TV over your Net PC.

To prevent abuse, some companies have set up special *proxy servers* with *filters* to block out any Internet site that isn't work-related. A proxy server can be set up to track everywhere employees travel on the Internet and to block out unwanted sites.

How do you resolve the conflict of giving Internet access to employees who spend more time on the Web than working for the company?

Math

Many of the math sites on the Internet are set up to let users ask questions in a Usenet-style discussion. Other users can then post answers or questions.

Other sites provide formulas, games, and story problems to help you brush up on math concepts. Some even provide virtual-reality objects to help you visualize volume and other concepts that are hard to grasp from a drawing in a book.

Net Concept

Just as HTML uses simple text to instruct a browser how to format a Web page, VRML (virtual reality modeling language) is a language that simulates 3-D objects, lights, and textures. You use a VRML viewer within a Web browser. This language can create 3-D worlds, where users can interact with objects and other netizens in a virtual setting. After a VRML page has been downloaded, its contents can be viewed, rotated, and manipulated, and simulated rooms can be walked into.

STEP-BY-STEP ▷ 11.4

1. Go to a search portal and search for **math games AND math puzzles**.

2. Find a link that interests you and go to the site.

3. In the space below, write down a math game or puzzle from your site and see if you can get the solution to the problems. Team up with a friend if you need help solving them. Pay attention to what each site offers. Some give prizes to people who can solve the puzzles. If you need more space, write your answers on a separate piece of paper.

Site Address	Puzzle	Solution
1.		

4. Go back to your search portal and search for **geometry AND 3-D**.

5. Follow the link to **VRML Geometry Teacher** or another site that shows Geometry instruction. If you don't like one site, try another in the list of hits. Then check out the three-dimensional geometric shapes, such as the one shown in Figure 11-6.

6. If your browser has a VRML viewer, download one of the 3-D objects and try rotating it. (Note: Even if you don't have the necessary 3-D software, 3-D geometry sites still offer good information, such as formulas to calculate the areas of everything from a sphere to a trapezoid.)

7. Search for and locate five other sites related to math. Try to find a least one for algebra, calculus, and trigonometry. List them in the space that follows.

1.

2.

3.

4.

5.

8. Close your Web browser if you are done for the day.

FIGURE 11-6
A pyramid in 3-D

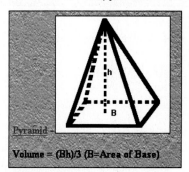

Volume = (Bh)/3 (B=Area of Base)

INTERNET MILESTONE

INTERNET MILESTONE — BLACK THURSDAY

The stock market has had a pair of Black Mondays. One occurred on October 19, 1987, when the market lost a gigantic 22 percent in a single day. The other was October 27, 1997, when it lost over 550 points. The computer world also has had a black day—November 3, 1988. This day is referred to as *Black Thursday,* the day of the *Internet worm.*

The worm was a malicious computer program unleashed on the Internet by a hacker. The program exploited security holes to gain entrance to Internet servers. It then bogged down the host server by replicating itself and using the server's own connections to infect other computers.

The worm managed to infect more than 6,000 computers, which was one-tenth of the computers on the Internet at that time. Eventually, all the systems infected by the worm had to be shut down. Some had to be shut down several times to purge themselves of all the copies of the worm. Some Net users were left without access to important research projects for over a week.

This devastating event did more to make netizens nervous about Internet usage than anything ever had before. It marked a sort of loss of innocence in Internet history.

Summary

In this lesson, you learned:

■ You can locate weather data for various locations.

■ NASA's home page can be visited and information about the International Space Station can be gathered.

■ It is possible to dissect a virtual frog and locate other biology-related sites.

■ You can find math puzzles and games, geometric shapes, and other math-related sites.

NET TERMS REVIEW

Define the following terms:

Black Thursday Internet worm Proxy server
Filters

LESSON 11 REVIEW QUESTIONS

TRUE/FALSE

Circle T if the statement is true or F if the statement is false.

T F 1. Black Thursday was caused by meteorological activity.

T F 2. You can conduct science experiments on the Internet.

T F 3. Weather information can't be found on search portals.

T F 4. If you go to NASA's Web site, you can find information on the International Space Station.

T F 5. Solutions to math problems can be found on the Internet.

FILL IN THE BLANK

Complete the following sentences by writing the correct word or words in the blanks provided.

1. _____ is the Internet language that creates 3-D worlds on the Net.

2. The frog dissected in Step-by-Step 11.3 is named _____ .

3. _____ _____ is the author of *Zen and the Art of the Internet*.

4. The World Wide Web wasn't born until the late _____ s.

5. _____ organisms live and grow together.

WRITTEN QUESTIONS

Write a brief answer to the following questions.

1. What are some benefits of getting a weather report from the Web versus getting the report from your local TV news program?

2. How does VRML enhance an educational Web site, such as one on geometry? How does VRML enhance a computer game?

3. What is *Zen and the Art of the Internet* and why is it considered an Internet milestone?

4. What are some pros and cons of using the Internet at work?

5. What are some advantages of using the Internet for science and math versus using a regular textbook?

LESSON 11 PROJECTS

SCANS

WEB PROJECT 11-1

Plan an Educational CD-ROM

GreatApplications, Inc., is very interested in creating an educational science CD-ROM. However, some team members have suggested that the Internet is so rich in scientific information that very few people today want to buy a CD-ROM on science topics.

You've explored some of the related sites available on the Internet. On the basis of your experiences online, write a memo to your boss describing the science information you've found. Then, answer this question: "Will a CD-ROM containing science lessons be marketable or will students rather use the Internet?"

In your memo, include a list of sites that were interesting to visit, as well as a list of sites that didn't impress you. Use the sites as examples to prove your opinion on the CD-ROM issue.

189

The Space Race

To expand your list of science-related sites, have a race to find scientific URLs about the following topics. See who can find the most resources about each of these topics in half an hour. Write down the URLs for each topic you find. Ready, set, here's the list.

Craters of the moon:

Mars exploration:

Galaxies:

Black holes:

Star Trek:

The space-time continuum:

PROJECT 11-3

Writing About Technology

Write a 100- to 250-word response on a separate piece of paper for each of the following questions.

1. How will virtual science, like the Fluffy the Frog dissection, change traditional science classes?

2. How will the Internet change the way high school students do science reports?

3. How will the Internet affect the way students use, depend upon, and learn from their science books, CD-ROM encyclopedias, and the school library?

CRITICAL THINKING

ACTIVITY 11-1

Weather Warning

Thousands of people around the world are killed every year by weather. In many cases, they just weren't prepared. Can the Internet help save lives in weather-related incidents? How? Prepare a 100- to 250-word answer to these questions.

ACTIVITY 11-2

Future Science

The Internet and science seemed to be a perfect match. Does the Internet make it easier for young people to become more interested in science? How will it help scientists in the future? Prepare a 100- to 250-word answer to these questions.

ACTIVITY 11-3

The Web Laboratory

You can probably see many benefits of virtual dissection. What are the benefits of having science experiments online as opposed to conducting the experiments in a laboratory? Are there any drawbacks? Prepare a 100- to 250-word answer to these questions.

ACTIVITY 11-4

Math Q & A

Find a resource that allows you to post questions for whatever math topic you are struggling with or that has bedeviled you in the past. Try posting a question and then answer the following questions.

How long did it take to get an answer? Was the answer helpful to you? Would you use the source again? Prepare a 50- to 100-word answer to these questions.

EXPLORING WRITING, JOURNALISM, AND HISTORY

OBJECTIVES

Upon completion of this lesson, you should be able to:

- Locate sources to help improve your writing skills.
- Research historical documents.
- Search for history-related sites.
- Find news and journalism sources.

⏱ **Estimated time: 2 hours**

NET TERMS

BITNET

Bulletin board system (BBS)

FidoNet

Gopher

Online writing labs (OWLs)

Writing

Net Tip

As we mentioned earlier, the Internet started as a research tool for scientists. It still is. However, now it is much more. It has quickly become the world's best tool to help you become a better writer.

Besides offering books and research data, the Internet can show you how to improve your writing. Many college Web sites are now offering **online writing labs** (*OWLs*), which help answer your writing questions and evaluate your writing skills. Note, however, that these online writing labs move around a lot, so it is best to use a search tool. In the search tool, key *Online Writing Labs*, *National Writing Center OWL*, or *University OWL*.

Can the Web help you become a better writer? Let's find out.

Forget your copy of *King Lear*? No problem. Just visit one of the many Shakespeare sites on the Internet and download another copy. While you are surfing, you may even find an online glossary so useful that you'll never bring home reference books again.

1. Launch your browser and go to the Internet Public Library at **www.ipl.org**. Click on the **Teen** link and browse through **A Plus** (or **+**) **Research and Writing Guide**. Check out this site's step-by-step approach to writing, illustrated in Figure 12-1.

2. Search IPL and record below the six steps to a good research paper. If you can't locate the IPL, try another OWL and record the site's suggestions. If you need more space, write your answers on a separate piece of paper.

Six Steps to Writing a Good Research Paper
1.
2.
3.
4.
5.
6.

3. Browse through each of the six steps. Look for a sub-step that you didn't know about or could do better. Write what you learned about that step.

4. OWLs are appearing everywhere. Many OWLs post reference documents for you to read and download for later reference. Using a search portal, locate five additional OWLs. Visit the five sites and browse through the documents they have posted. Read at least one article at each site and write what you learned. If you need more space, write your answers on a separate piece of paper.

College or University URL   What You Learned
1.
2.
3.
4.
5.

5. Search for, locate, and describe five other sites that can help you improve your writing skills. If you need more space, write your answers on a separate piece of paper.

Site Address   Content Description
1.
2.
3.
4.
5.

Leave your browser open until you complete the next Step-by-Step.

FIGURE 12-1
OWL at the Internet Public Library

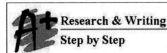 **Research & Writing** the Internet Public Library

Step by Step

 Why the Step by Step Approach?
Read below, then jump to:

Step 1 - Getting Started   Step 4 - Gathering Information

Step 2 - Discovering and   Step 5 - Preparing to Write
Choosing a Topic

Step 3 - Looking for and   Step 6 - Writing the Paper
Forming a Focus

Read me first!! **There's a ton of information available online about writing papers** for college classes, mostly provided by college and university writing departments. But when your political science or biology or economics instructor assigns you a research paper, writing the paper is only half the battle. **Before you can start writing, you have to explore the subject to find a topic, locate relevant information, analyze the issues and organize your arguments.** These activities take more time and require different skills than the final step--writing the paper. And many students haven't had a lot of formal training in how to do research and prepare information for writing a "research paper."

Librarians provide a lot of help to students in the exploring, finding and organizing phases of their writing projects. They've done **research on how students approach these tasks,** how they feel while they're doing them, and what kinds of activities lead to a successful research paper (Kuhlthau, 1993 and 1994).

 Net Concept

YOU ALREADY KNOW THAT CAPITAL LETTERS ON THE NET IMPLY SHOUTING AND ANGER. So don't use them unless you mean business. Many people mistakenly believe that any good news or important point should be capitalized. Unnecessary capitalization may send the wrong impression and is difficult to read.

INTERNET MILESTONE

CITING INTERNET SOURCES

As the Internet evolved into a regular source of information like an encyclopedia or magazine, it became necessary to set standards for citing Internet-based documents as sources. Citing Internet resources follows the same general pattern as other sources, although punctuation and location of elements vary depending on the reference guide you use.

Here is a general form: Author, Title of Article, Medium Available, e-mail address or URL of source, Access Date. Study the following examples.

E-mail example: Smith, Jared. *Bugs in Business*. Online. Available: e-mail: *MyName@host.edu* from *Author123@hotmail.com*, September 23, 2002.

WWW example: Bugs, Rabbit. *How to Succeed in Business*. Online. Available: *www.acme.com/bugsadvicefor/business.html,* December 25, 2003.

Online images example: Bugsinbusiness.jpg. Online Image. Available: *http://www.acme.com/bugsadvice/bugsbusiness.jpg,* December 26, 2003.

History

The Internet is a playground for surfers, a resource for academics, and a workhorse for the news media. It is also a virtual library of the past and an important tool for historians.

The Internet has become a repository for the world's greatest speeches and historical documents. Let's use what you have learned about researching the Web to locate a few of these speeches and documents.

Net Concept

The Net offers an unparalleled opportunity to share your thoughts in writing. But don't try presenting an argument with misspelled words in the text. You'll be flamed into extinction. Here is a common reaction to such errors: "If you can't spell DEMMOCRITIC, then get out of the thread!" Spell checkers and speech recognition software can help. As you know, it's impossible for speech software to make a spelling error.

STEP-BY-STEP 12.2

1. Start your search by entering **historical documents** in your favorite search portal.

2. Now narrow your search to the **Declaration of Independence**.

3. Read the Declaration of Independence online (illustrated in Figure 12-2) and answer the following questions. If you need more space, write your answers on a separate piece of paper.

   1. What were five reasons for separation from England cited in the document?
     1.
     2.
     3.
     4.
     5.

2. How many future presidents of the United States signed the Declaration of Independence? Who were they?

4. Locate five other sites related to history and write a description of their content. If you need more space, write your answers on a separate piece of paper.

   Site Address   Content Description
   1.
   2.
   3.
   4.
   5.

Leave your Web browser open for the next Step-by-Step.

FIGURE 12-2
The Declaration of Independence

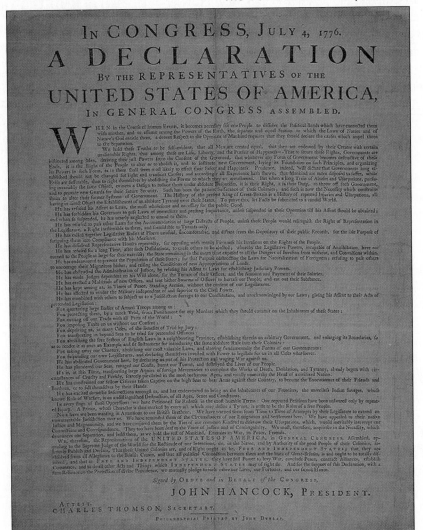

FIGURE 12-2
The Declaration of Independence

Journalism and News

News is everywhere on the Internet. You can find many forms of news on the Web, including content from newspapers, magazines, and television-based news. Like TV, the Net has the ability to broadcast pictures worldwide instantly. Additionally, the Internet has the unique capability of linking related newsworthy information from numerous sources quickly and reliably. The Web can present more in-depth coverage than a traditional 30-minute newscast.

In the next Step-by-Step, you'll explore various kinds of new media to disseminate the news. You can view browser-based news, like the *New York Times* as shown in Figure 12-3, or even view live video if you have a fast connection. We will talk about that more in Lesson 15. Also, most search portals have some form of news on them. Sometimes it is on the front page itself; other times, it is on a personalized Web page.

INTERNET MILESTONE

HISTORIC INTERNET SYSTEMS

Two of the earliest network communication systems serving educational users were *BITNET* and *FidoNet*. *BITNET,* short for Because It's Time Network, is a worldwide communications network created in 1981 by academic researchers who were tired of waiting around for electronic mail and file transfer capabilities. Not technically part of the Internet, BITNET pioneered and popularized e-mail among college professors and students. BITNET existed mainly on IBM mainframe computers and never achieved the popularity of the Internet.

FidoNet was a 1980s e-mail protocol that was mostly used for its bulletin board capabilities. A *bulletin board system* (**BBS**) is a computer system used as an information source and message system for a particular interest group. Users dial into the BBS, read and leave messages for other users, and communicate with other users who are on the system at the same time. BBSs are often used to distribute shareware.

Gopher was the most popular document cataloging system in use on the Net during the late 1980s. At one time, there were four Gopher servers in every Web server. Still around today, Gopher uses long descriptive filenames and hierarchical menus to catalog millions and millions of documents. Gopher was mortally wounded by Mosaic and the popularization of the World Wide Web. Netscape built Gopher capabilities into its early browser, but the system had already lost momentum to the Web and began an abrupt decline.

FIGURE 12-3

The New York Times on the Web

The Net is a great resource for students in journalism. Use a search engine to locate online newspapers, online magazines, and online publications in different categories.

Can you find school newspapers from your state? College newspapers? Local newspapers?

STEP-BY-STEP ▷ 12.3

1. Use a search portal to help you locate five college newspapers and complete the following table:

College	Name of Paper	Web Address
1.		
2.		
3.		
4.		
5.		

2. Locate five well-known nationally syndicated newspapers and complete the following table:

City	Name of Paper	Web Address
1.		
2.		
3.		
4.		
5.		

3. Locate five network TV stations and complete the following table:

Station	Web Address
1.	
2.	
3.	
4.	
5.	

4. Close your Web browser if you are done for today.

INTERNET MILESTONE

CYBERWORDS WERE CYBERRIFIC FOR A CYBERMOMENT

In the early days of the Net, everything was cyber-this and virtual-that. It all started with author William Gibson's term *CyberSpace*. A conversational thread on the Net or a chat group became known as a CyberChat. The Net's strange new vocabulary was called CyberSpeak or CyberEse. People even began to go on CyberDates. Virtual Universities and CyberSchools were started. The Net was called the Virtual- or CyberFrontier. Everything was Cyberized.

The overuse of cyber and virtual soon became apparent. It was no longer clever or cute to put the cyber prefix before every possible noun. Thankfully, this CyberTrend is beginning to die out.

Summary

In this lesson, you learned:

- There are online sources to improve your writing.
- You can locate historical documents.
- Historical sites can be found and researched.
- You can find online news sources.

NET TERMS REVIEW

Define the following terms:

BITNET   FidoNet   OWLs
BBS   Gopher

LESSON 12 REVIEW QUESTIONS

TRUE/FALSE

Circle T if the statement is true or F if the statement is false.

T F 1. The Internet can help you become a better writer.

T F 2. Gopher was an e-mail protocol.

T F 3. The Declaration of Independence can be found easily on the Internet.

T F 4. If you are preparing a report for an assignment, you don't need to cite online Web sources.

T F 5. You can have a newspaper delivered to you over the Internet.

FILL IN THE BLANK

Complete the following sentences by writing the correct word or words in the blanks provided.

1. In the early days of the Net, nearly every cool Net-related word began with _____ or virtual.

2. OWL stands for _____ _____ _____.

3. In the 1980s, _____ was the most popular document cataloging system on the Net.

4. It is a bad idea to write in _____ ALL OF THE TIME.

5. BBS is an acronym meaning _____ _____ _____.

WRITTEN QUESTIONS

Write a brief answer to the following questions.

1. How is a BBS different from e-mail?

2. How would you go about finding writing advice on the Internet?

3. What is the value of the Web from a historian's viewpoint?

4. What are some advantages of receiving news over the Internet? Are there any disadvantages?

5. How would you find a specific school newspaper on the Web?

LESSON 12 PROJECTS

PROJECT 12-1

News on the Run

You have been asked to look into online news technology for GreatApplications, Inc. The president of the company is interested in knowing how easily employees can find up-to-date news on economic and social trends that may have an impact on business. Visit major news sources on the Web. Test each site.

Start by finding and visiting the major sources of news and information. We won't give you the URLs because you need to figure those out yourself, but good starting points include ABC, CBS, NBC, FOX, CNN, CNNFN, NPR, MSNBC, and NYTimes.

PROJECT 12-2

Team up for the Big Push

Get together with your team and research the following Net technologies for use in your company: VRML, HTML, FTP, Telnet, BBS, Gopher, BITNET, and FidoNet. Divide up the list. Look up information about each on the Web using your favorite search portal. As a team, rank the technologies from top to bottom as to their value to the company. Give reasons why the company should or shouldn't use each of these technologies. Save the results in your Research folder.

PROJECT 12-3

Take a Newsstand

Do you think the Internet will be the end of printed newspapers and magazines as media for information delivery? Take a stand on this issue: will it or won't it? In a 100- to 250-word essay, describe why you have taken this stand. Feel free to use other sources to support your position.

CRITICAL THINKING

ACTIVITY 12-1

Clearly Reported

With the mass of information now available on the Internet, why is it more important than ever that online information be clearly written? Prepare a 100- to 250-word answer to this question.

ACTIVITY 12-2

The End of History As We Know It

Will there come a day when the traditional history textbook will be outmoded? Could an entire history class be taught using sources currently available on the Internet? Prepare a 100- to 250-word answer to these questions.

ACTIVITY 12-3

Fast-Breaking News

How can the information on the Internet speed up a journalist's job? What are some of the plusses and minuses, as well as some possible cautions about using the Internet for fast-breaking news? Prepare a 100- to 250-word answer to these questions.

EXPLORING BUSINESS, E-COMMERCE, AND THE ECONOMY ONLINE

LESSON

13

OBJECTIVES

Upon completion of this lesson, you should be able to:

- Locate economic forecasts from the Congressional Budget Office.

- Find tax information.

- Investigate the public debt.

- Go online window-shopping for various products.

- Locate historical and current stock market information.

- Discover various corporate ticker symbols.

⏱ **Estimated Time: 2 hours**

NET TERMS

Benchmark

Congressional Budget Office (CBO)

Dow Jones Industrial Average (DJIA)

E-commerce

Freeware

Internal Revenue Service (IRS)

Public debt

Ticker symbol

Government and Business: E-commerce Partners

The Internet is a growing partnership between government and business interests. In the beginning, it was financed almost exclusively by government grants. More recently, the Net has experienced many fundamental changes, paid for largely by investments from the business community.

The synergy between government and business investment has created a new economic force called *e-commerce*. E-commerce is the online sale and distribution of products, goods, and services.

Governments the world over support e-commerce as a tool to foster growth in their economies. They also use the Internet to conduct the business of government—to inform its citizens and to encourage high-tech investment in their countries. For example, the U.S. government tracks the public debt and e-commerce growth and reports its economic forecasts online. Governments also provide tax-paying businesses and individuals with the information they need.

 Net Concept

It is important for government to communicate clearly with its tax-paying businesses and citizens. In this regard, the Internet has helped. For example, the *Internal Revenue Service (IRS)* provides its tax forms and answers to the most common tax questions at *www.irs.gov*. The IRS is a part of the Department of the Treasury.

1. Let's find information about the public debt. Launch your browser and search for **U. S. public debt** or **United States Debt**. Check out some sites that sound interesting.

2. Now let's find out exactly how big the debt is. Look for a link among your hits called *public debt to the penny* or key this phrase into a search engine. A Web page similar to that shown in Figure 13-1 should be displayed.

FIGURE 13-1
Public debt to the penny

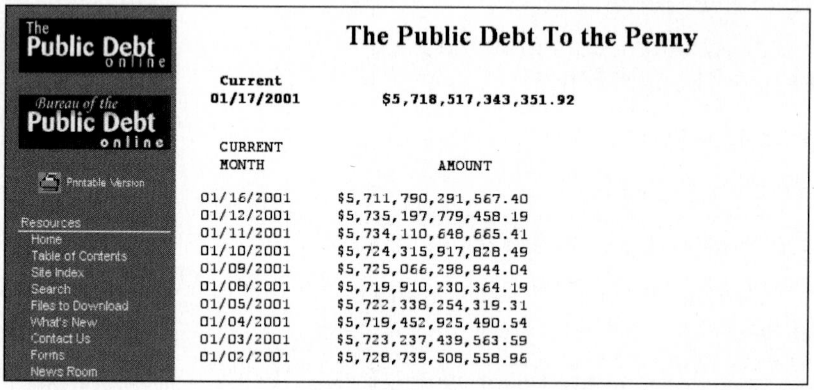

The Public Debt To the Penny

	Current 01/17/2001	$5,718,517,343,351.92
	CURRENT MONTH	AMOUNT
	01/16/2001	$5,711,790,291,567.40
	01/12/2001	$5,735,197,779,458.19
	01/11/2001	$5,734,110,648,665.41
	01/10/2001	$5,724,315,917,828.49
	01/09/2001	$5,725,066,298,944.04
	01/08/2001	$5,719,910,230,364.19
	01/05/2001	$5,722,338,254,319.31
	01/04/2001	$5,719,452,925,490.54
	01/03/2001	$5,723,237,439,563.59
	01/02/2001	$5,728,739,508,558.96

3. Find and record the following information about the U. S. public debt:

1. What is today's public debt?

2. How much did the debt increase/decrease from last month?

3. How much did the debt increase/decrease over the past year?

4. How much has the debt increased/decreased in the past ten years?

4. Search for the *Congressional Budget Office* and follow the link to the **CBO** home page.

5. The CBO is responsible for supplying Congress with reports, figures, and economic forecasts for the budget and the economy. Look through the list of CBO reports by checking under **Studies & Reports** in the **Documents** section, as shown in Figure 13-2.

6. List three reports that sound interesting and record their titles in the table below. Browse through each of the three reports and write a brief summary. If you need more space, write your answers on a separate piece of paper.

Name of Report   Brief Summary of Contents

1.

2.

3.

FIGURE 13-2
Economic forecasts by the CBO

7. Find tax help on the Web. Visit the Internal Revenue Service (IRS) at **www.irs.gov** (see Figure 13-3).

8. Visit three of the informative links found on the IRS site. Record your three choices and then describe the kind of people that can benefit from the information that appears under your links.

1.

2.

3.

Leave your Web browser open for the next Step-by-Step.

 Net Concept

The *public debt* is the sum total of all the money borrowed by the government to meet its obligations. If the government spends more than it collects in taxes, then it runs a deficit and adds to the public debt.

FIGURE 13-3
The IRS online

FRAUD ON THE WEB

Web fraud is a big business. There are as many scam artists on the Web as anywhere else. How can you protect yourself from Web fraud? One precaution you can take is to do your research. Ask questions about any company with which you are thinking about doing business.

Another precaution you can take is to pay attention to news stories about Web fraud. There are some really scary stories. One scam had users downloading a new, "free" Web page viewer. Once installed, the program routed the Web user's local phone Internet address to a long-distance line in an Eastern European country. The unwitting users had to pay the long-distance charges, which in some cases reached thousands of dollars. AT&T uncovered the fraud and reported it to the various governments in the countries where the fraud took place, saving some individuals a great amount of real (not virtual) cash.

What should be done to stop Web fraud? The U.S. Postal Service looks for mail fraud, and the Secret Service patrols bank fraud. What agency should patrol Web fraud?

Online Window-Shop Until You Drop

The Internet offers a unique shopping environment. In fact, the Internet has become a huge online shopping mall where you can find virtually anything at prices that are generally lower than those found in retail stores. You can buy anything from CD-ROMs and books to computers and new cars—all from the convenience of your own home.

In the old days, people would go window-shopping. The term means to look through the store windows with no real intent to buy. The purpose of window-shopping is to see what merchandise is available and to compare prices. The best place to window-shop these days is online. Let's do some online window-shopping.

Net Concept

The future of the Internet depends as much on business as the future of business depends on the Internet. With **e-commerce**, customers from around the world can access information and products quickly and easily. Orders can be placed and automatically processed for shipping without human intervention. Inventories can be instantly adjusted, and orders can be placed to replenish stock on hand.

STEP-BY-STEP ▷ 13.2

1. Use your search portal to locate online stores that sell the products listed in the table on the next page. List the names of the online store or vendor and a price for each product. In each section, you will be able to choose a product you're interested in along with three other standard products. Keep your Web browser open for the next Step-by-Step.

INTERNET MILESTONE

AMAZON.COM

While many large book companies shied away from the Web, *Amazon.com* jumped right online and began to sell books exclusively over it. This company was truly a pioneer. It started business without a physical store. Within a few years, book sales skyrocketed. *Amazon.com* proved that the Web could be a very lucrative place to sell books... and many other products as well.

Today, *Amazon.com* sells everything from books to DVDs, electronic devices to music, and kitchen appliances to cellular phones. You name it, they have it online just for you. Their success pushed Wal-Mart, Kmart, Sears, and other retailers online.

PRODUCT	NAME OF VENDOR OR ONLINE STORE	PRICE PER UNIT
CD-ROMs:		
The Beatles 1		
Frank Sinatra's Greatest Hits		
Saturday Night Fever		
Your Choice		
Books:		
Harry Potter: The Sorcerer's Stone		
The Hunt for Red October		
Star Wars: A New Hope		
Your Choice		
Computer systems:		
Gateway Computers		
Apple Computers		
Dell Computers		
Your Choice		
Automobile:		
Ford Mustang		
Volkswagen Jetta		
Dodge truck		
Your Choice		

Look Up Stock Prices

The recent status of the economy has generated more interest in the stock market than ever before. Billions of dollars are invested every month. Thanks to the Internet, investors have quick, easy access to all sorts of economic information. This allows them to make smart, educated decisions about their investments.

 Net Concept

Online investors can access corporate financial reports, historical stock information, and press releases from business sources. They can see up-to-the-minute stock reports to help them make decisions to buy or sell stock.

The ***Dow Jones Industrial Average (DJIA)*** measures the stock performance of 30 large U.S. companies. The Dow serves as a ***benchmark***, or standard, against which to judge the performance of individual stocks. By watching the DJIA, you can get a general sense of how stocks performed on a particular day. If your stocks did better than the DJIA, then you had a very good day.

STEP-BY-STEP ▷ 13.3

1. Go to **Yahoo!** and look for a link to **Finance/Quotes**, as illustrated in Figure 13-4. (Most major search portals offer stock quotes. As an alternative, try *Excite.com*, *msn.com*, or *cnnfn.com*.)

2. Locate the link to the Dow (DJIA) performance information. This leads to a table, similar to the one shown in Figure 13-6. This information is updated every few minutes. You will also see a graphic of historical Dow (DJIA) performance information, which is what we are interested in.

3. The Dow keeps track of its highs and lows. For example, it may reach a high of 10595 on one day and then drop to 10450 the next. What did the Dow (DJIA) reach today?

4. Select the five year (5y) link indicated in Figure 13-5.

FIGURE 13-4
Finance/Quotes in Yahoo!

FIGURE 13-5
Dow Jones information is updated every few minutes

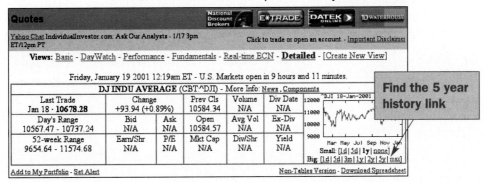

5. From the chart, try to determine the high that the Dow has reached in each of the past five years and record your answers below.

1. What has been the high this year?

2. What was the high a year ago?

3. What high was reached the year before that?

4. What high was reached four years ago?

5. What high was reached five years ago?

6. At the top of the page, you will see a *Get Quotes* box. Every company with publicly traded stock is issued a *ticker symbol*, which is a two- to five-letter abbreviation for the company. For example, Microsoft's symbol is MSFT and Apple Computer's is AAPL. As illustrated in Figure 13-6, you can enter a company's ticker symbol in the box to find that company's stock quote.

7. Pick five companies whose products you use on a regular basis. They can be computer, soft drink, fast food, clothing, automobile, or any other type of company you can think of. Find and record the following information for each company. Use the pull-down menu next to the **Get Quotes** box to find more detailed information as you search. Place your answers in the table below.

8. Close your Web browser if you are finished for today.

 Net Concept

Commercial games are given credit for attracting large numbers of customers to the Net. You must pay for some games before you download and play them. Shareware games can be downloaded and paid for later. Software games that you can download and never pay for are called *freeware*. Type "free software" in a search portal to find some good games. Be careful, however. Some freeware may contain viruses that can damage your computer system. Use at your own risk. Get permission before you download anything to your local network.

COMPANY NAME	TICKER SYMBOL	MOST RECENT PRICE	52-WEEK HIGH	52-WEEK LOW
1.				
2.				
3.				
4.				
5.				

FIGURE 13-6
Get quotes for individual stocks

FIGURE 13-6
Get quotes for individual stocks

Enter a ticker symbol to find a stock quote

Use the Symbol Lookup to find a ticker symbol

Net Tip

It isn't difficult to find ticker symbols for major companies. Most search portals provide a way to do a Symbol Lookup, as marked in Figure 13-6.

INTERNET MILESTONE

SECURITY FIRST NETWORK BANK

Worries about insecure transactions kept banks away from the Web for many years. The conditions before 1995 were dry for Internet banking. Many experts thought that customers would not use an online bank.

Then Netscape paved the way for banking by adding security features to its browser. (You can tell that you have a secure transaction by noticing the solid key or closed lock in the corner of your browser's status bar.)

Finally, taking the risk, a lone bank opened its Internet doors. Security First Network Bank (*www.sfnb.com*) went online, and everything changed overnight. Soon, the major banks took on Web banking too. Wells Fargo, Toronto-Dominion Bank, and Bank of America were among the first to offer online accounts. Today it is hard to find a bank that doesn't have an online presence.

Once banks believed that the Web was secure enough for their clients, other companies and consumers gained confidence in the security of Web transactions. This led the way to other kinds of e-commerce.

Summary

In this lesson, you learned:

- The Congressional Budget Office has economic forecasts and research reports.
- You can window-shop online for various products.
- Historical and current stock market information is available online.
- IRS information can be located online.
- You can research the public debt.

NET TERMS REVIEW

Define the following terms:

Benchmark	E-commerce	Public debt
CBO	Freeware	Ticker symbol
DJIA	IRS	

LESSON 13 REVIEW QUESTIONS

TRUE/FALSE

Circle T if the statement is true or F the statement is false.

T F 1. The Internet is safer today for online banking than it was in previous years.

T F 2. You can use the Internet only to look at products, not to actually buy them.

T F 3. The IRS was the first online bank.

T F 4. You can download software games for free over the Internet.

T F 5. You can get an up-to-the-minute stock quote on the Internet for MSFT.

FILL IN THE BLANK

Complete the following sentences by writing the correct word or words in the blanks provided.

1. DJIA is short for _____ _____ _____ _____.

2. The _____ is used as a benchmark for 30 companies that trade publicly on the stock market.

3. The IRS is a section of the Department of the _____ of the United States.

4. When it first started, *Amazon.com* sold _____ online without a physical store.

5. You can find free tax information and forms on the Web site of the IRS or _____ _____ _____.

WRITTEN QUESTIONS

Write a brief answer to each of the following questions.

1. Describe how you could locate the ticker symbol for a particular company and find information about that company's stock performance online.

2. Explain to a friend how to locate information about top-quality, yet inexpensive, computer systems online.

3. Give your opinion about the benefits and drawbacks of banking online.

4. Do you think it is in the public interest to distribute tax forms and tax information without cost over the Web?

5. Explain how taxpayers can locate critical tax information over the Web.

SCANS

WEB PROJECT 13-1

Online Investing

Several promotions at GreatApplications, Inc., have resulted in a healthy bankroll for you. You managed to save $15,000 and you want to invest in the stock market. Most investment firms look at financial reports to determine if a company is in good financial condition. Many companies post their financial reports on the Internet for potential investors to review.

Your job is to find the financial reports of five companies you are interested in. If you can save the financial reports to your personal folder, do so and then read through them later. You will make an investment in these companies.

Invest $3,000 in each company. On the day you start, divide the amount invested in each company ($3,000). Use the price of the stock that day to determine the number of shares you now own. For example, if the price of one share is $15.00, the number of shares you purchased would be $3,000/$15.00 = 200.

Perform the same calculation for all five companies and enter the starting numbers in the table below. Update the prices once a week for five weeks.

Calculate the net worth of your investments each week by multiplying the week's stock price by the number of shares you originally purchased. For example, if the price of the stock dropped to $14.50, then your stock's net worth that week would be $14.50 x 200 = $2,900.

After five weeks, how did your portfolio fare?

Company #1

	STOCK TICKER SYMBOL	DATE	PRICE PER SHARE	# OF SHARES	NET WORTH
Week 1.					$3,000
Week 2.					
Week 3.					
Week 4.					
Week 5.					

Company #2

	STOCK TICKER SYMBOL	DATE	PRICE PER SHARE	# OF SHARES	NET WORTH
Week 1.					$3,000
Week 2.					
Week 3.					
Week 4.					
Week 5.					

Company #3

	STOCK TICKER SYMBOL	DATE	PRICE PER SHARE	# OF SHARES	NET WORTH
Week 1.					$3,000
Week 2.					
Week 3.					
Week 4.					
Week 5.					

Company #4

	STOCK TICKER SYMBOL	DATE	PRICE PER SHARE	# OF SHARES	NET WORTH
Week 1.					$3,000
Week 2.					
Week 3.					
Week 4.					
Week 5.					

Company #5

	STOCK TICKER SYMBOL	DATE	PRICE PER SHARE	# OF SHARES	NET WORTH
Week 1.					$3,000
Week 2.					
Week 3.					
Week 4.					
Week 5.					

Take this project one step further by buying and selling shares. If one of your stocks isn't doing as well as you would like, sell your shares and invest in another stock that is doing better. If this stock has made money and you decide to sell those shares and invest in something else, then you can use whatever money you have gained. If your stock is losing money and you sell, you'll have lost some of your original investment and consequently will have less to reinvest.

TEAMWORK PROJECT 13-2

Team Stock Competition

With your teammates, create a stock portfolio by selecting five stocks. With the agreement of the team, invest $1 million of GreatApplications' money and buy the stocks. Watch the prices go up and down for seven days and then sell on day seven. Compare the performance of your team's five stocks with that of the other teams. The group that records the biggest gain and earns the most money from the mythical sale wins. These team members will then be promoted to become the next vice presidents of the Financial Department at GreatApplications, Inc.

PROJECT 13-3

Prevent Hacking

With more business transactions occurring online, major issues have surfaced surrounding the security of these transmissions. Unencrypted data transfers can be hacked into or intercepted by other people. How do you know that your credit card number is safe as it is flying through cyberspace? Do some research and write a 100- to 250-word report about what is being done to ensure online security.

CRITICAL THINKING

ACTIVITY 13-1

Voting on the National Debt

The national debt is a major issue in every national political race. Will the accessibility of this information over the Internet make any difference? Will it influence for whom we vote? Will this information help solve the problem? Prepare a 100- to 250-word answer to these questions.

ACTIVITY 13-2

Online Shop Until You Drop

How would you rate your online window-shopping experience from Project 13-2? Was it easy to find the information you needed? Would you rather talk to a salesperson than look at a computer screen? Why or why not? Prepare a 100- to 250-word answer to these questions.

ACTIVITY 13-3

Up-to-the-Minute Investments

In the past, investors were dependent upon investment houses and after-the-fact newspaper reports for stock information. How will having access to up-to-date information affect the average stock buyer? Prepare a 100- to 250-word answer to this question.

EXPLORING GOVERNMENT ONLINE

NET TERMS

Internet appliance

Microsoft.NET

Network computing

Oracle

Good Netizens Make Good Citizens

The Internet offers a unique and exciting opportunity for people to get involved in government. To become involved, you'll first need to be informed.

Nothing will get you up to speed faster than the Internet. Not only can the Net update you on current events, but you can also explore the ramifications of bills before legislative bodies or see what pressing issues are facing the Supreme Court.

Net Tip

The Senate and the House of Representatives make up the Congress or the federal legislative branch. The Congress makes the laws of the land. The executive branch, led by the President of the United States and members of the cabinet, enforces the laws. The judicial branch judges the law. You can watch these branches of government work online.

Government

Unless you spend the day watching C-SPAN, you probably don't know what the legislative and executive branches do every day. Few of us have time to follow congressional happenings very closely. Still, it's good to know what bills are currently before Congress.

The actions of our elected officials affect our lives. Let's see what's going on in Congress right now.

Net Tip

Use the top-level domain *.gov* to access government sites.

STEP-BY-STEP ▷ 14.1

1. Let's visit the Library of Congress to see what is happening in the legislative branch today. Launch your Web browser and go to **Thomas.loc.gov** (illustrated in Figure 14-1).

2. Look for **House Floor Now** to see what the legislative branch is working on today. Locate and record the information requested below. If the link is unavailable, you should be able to search bills from previous Congressional sessions.
House of Representatives
1. Name (number) of bill:

   2. What is the bill about?

FIGURE 14-1

The Thomas site tracks the activities in Congress

THOMAS
Legislative Information on the Internet

In the Spirit of Thomas Jefferson, a service of The Library of Congress

House Floor This Week | House Floor Now | Senate Schedule

Search Bill Text for 107th Congress (2001-2002)

By Bill Number [ ]   By Word/Phrase [ ]   [Search] [Clear]

For previous Congress, select Bill Text (below) and then select 106.

What's New in THOMAS?	LEGISLATION	CONGRESSIONAL RECORD	COMMITTEE INFORMATION
Frequently Asked Questions (FAQ)	**Bill Summary & Status** 93rd - 107th	**Most Recent Issue**	**Committee Reports** 104th - 107th
107th Congress: House Directories Senate Directories	**Bill Text** 101st - 107th	**Text Search** 101st - 107th	**House Committees:** Home Pages, Schedules, and Hearings
Congressional Internet Services: House · Senate Library of Congress GPO · GAO · CBO AOC · OTA · More	**Public Laws By Law Number** 93rd - 107th	**Index** 104th - 107th **Roll Call Votes:** House Senate	**Senate Committees:** Home Pages, Schedules, and Hearings
Library of Congress Web Links:			

3. Use a search tool and enter the name of the current president of the United States. Look for a site similar to the one shown in Figure 14-2. Search the site and find answers to the following questions:

1. What is the current president's full name?

2. Which state is the current president from?

3. Who is the current Vice President?

4. The President does not run the executive branch alone. Cabinet members head the various departments of government under the direction of the President. Use your search skills and find the names of these Cabinet members by their titles. Also find the Web site for each department that these cabinet members lead. Record the information in the table on the next page. Leave your Web browser open for the next Step-by-Step.

FIGURE 14-2
Searching for the President of the United States

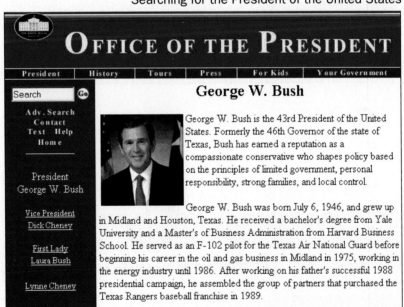

 Net Tip

Cabinet members usually go by the title of secretary, as in Secretary of Labor or Secretary of State.

Title of Cabinet Member	Name of Cabinet Member	URL to Department or Agency this Cabinet Member Heads
Secretary of Agriculture		
Secretary of State		
Secretary of Transportation		
Secretary of the Treasury		
Secretary of Defense		
Secretary of Education		
Secretary of Energy		
Secretary of Health and Human Services		
Secretary of Housing and Urban Development		
Secretary of the Interior		
Secretary of Labor		
Attorney General		
Secretary of Commerce		

NET ETHICS

NET ETHICS — WRITING TO ELECTED OFFICIALS

It is your right to e-mail elected officials. Freedom of speech is a great thing. However, the right to share your beliefs doesn't include the right to be rude, crude, and disrespectful to elected officials in e-mail messages. The Constitution gives us our freedoms, but our moms and grandmas taught us manners. Give every e-mail the mom test. When you write your elected officials, send a copy to a couple of higher authorities: your mother or your grandmother. If they approve, then your messages are ready for prime time.

Sure, elected officials make mistakes and, from our perspective, may even be totally wrong on the issues. However, reason and good manners must prevail. A congressperson or a president will be more likely to reconsider his or her views from a short statement that is well constructed and in good taste than from an e-mail full of trash talk.

Supreme Online Law

The Supreme Court is the highest court in the United States. It is responsible for interpreting the Constitution and applying this interpretation to laws that affect us.

How much do you know about the justices who make up the Supreme Court? Can you name any of them? What important decisions have been made in recent years?

STEP-BY-STEP ▷ 14.2

1. Search for information about the nine U.S. Supreme Court justices (see Figure 14-3).

Have changes been made to the U.S. Supreme Court since this picture?

FIGURE 14-3
Searching for U.S. Supreme Court justices

U.S. Supreme Court, 1998-99

Seated: Scalia, Stevens, Rehnquist, O'Connor, Kennedy
Standing: Ginsburg, Souter, Thomas, Breyer

Back Row (left to right): Ginsburg, Souter, Thomas, Breyer
Front Row (left to right): Scalia, Stevens, Rehnquist, O'Connor, Kennedy

2. Identify the current justices who make up the court. Fill in the following information:

	Name of justice	Date appointed	Which president appointed this justice?
1.			
2.			
3.			
4.			
5.			
6.			
7.			
8.			
9.			

3. Who is the current Supreme Court Chief Justice?

4. Using your search skills, find and list two recent court decisions. Briefly describe both decisions.
   1.

   2.

5. Select one of the decisions you wrote about in Step 4 and answer the following questions:
   1. Who wrote the decision?

2. What is the name of the case?

3. What is the case about?

4. What was the ruling of the court?

5. Which justice (if any) dissented?

Leave your Web browser open for the next Step-by-Step.

Political Issues

Every four years, we elect a President to govern the country. Before the election, we debate controversial issues. Then the election passes, and we go back to life as usual. The issues never seem to get resolved. Why is that?

The Internet provides a good forum for the debate over important issues. It allows people to inform themselves about what is fact and what is fiction. Information empowers people. In this Step-by-Step, you'll research a couple of important issues.

NET ETHICS

NET ETHICS — STAND BY YOUR E-MAIL

You can search for the e-mail addresses of your senators or congresspersons and send them messages. It is considered good netiquette to put your name on any e-mail you send to your elected officials. This sends the message that you stand by your position. It also says that you are a responsible person and that this e-mail message isn't a hoax written to stir up controversy. This rule applies to newsgroup discussions as well.

INTERNET MILESTONE

INTERNET MILESTONE — NETWORK COMPUTING AND .NET

Network computing, a system first developed by the technology company *Oracle*, stores every online tool you need—applications, data, and services—on a network of servers. These tools are downloaded to users' computers as needed. You can access these materials through a low-cost computer often called an *Internet appliance*.

Oracle sees this new system as "the dawn of the next generation of computing." According to a quote found on Oracle's Web site (*www.oracle.com*), "Inexpensive, easy-to-use computers linked to powerful, professionally managed networks of information are the keys of network computing." Complex tasks, such as updating software and maintaining virus protection, are moved from the end-user to professionals who maintain the network.

Microsoft has also developed its version of network computing with its *Microsoft.NET* project. The *.NET* concept allows information to be accessed from any device, including a small handheld personal organizer, a digital phone, or a small tablet computer. With *.NET*, the Web is always at your fingertips.

1. Search for four sites that discuss the greenhouse effect or global warming (see Figure 14-4). Make a list of the sources and their URLs in the following table.

FIGURE 14-4
Locate resources on global warming

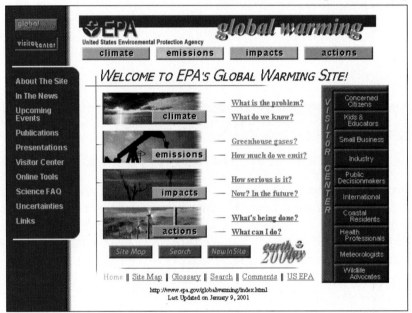

Global Warming Resource	Web Site URL
1.	
2.	
3.	
4.	

STEP-BY-STEP 14.3 CONTINUED

2. After reading some of the arguments, what is your position? Answer the following questions. If you need more space, write your answers on a separate piece of paper.

1. Is global warming an important and credible issue? Defend your answer.

2. Should the United States take steps to limit carbon dioxide emissions? Why or why not?

3. What might be the cost to the economy?

4. What new information did you learn from your online research?

3. For many years, Congress has debated the issue of campaign finance reform. Search for campaign finance reform and find two sites that present differing views on the issue. In the following table, identify two Web sites with different perspectives on this issue.

Campaign Finance Reform Resource	Web Site URL
1.	
2.	

4. On the basis of your findings in Step 3, answer the following questions. If you need more space, write your answers on a separate piece of paper.

1. Why do you think Congress has not been more successful in implementing campaign reform?

2. What are the best of the reform proposals?

3. What new information did you learn in your online research?

5. Close your Web browser if you are finished for today.

 Net Concept

Messages can be tracked from every Internet computer. Within seconds, government policing agencies, like the Secret Service and the FBI, can trace an illegal message back to the very computer that sent a message. They can then begin their investigation into the illegal activity.

Summary

In this lesson, you learned:

- There are executive, legislative, and judicial sites online.

- You can locate information on bills going through Congress.

- Information about Supreme Court justices and decisions is available online.

- You can find information about the various cabinet members and their departments.

- Political issues can be researched online.

NET TERMS REVIEW

Define the following terms:

Internet appliance   Network computing   Oracle
Microsoft.NET

LESSON 14 REVIEW QUESTIONS

TRUE/FALSE

Circle T if the statement is true or F the statement is false.

T F 1. It is possible to e-mail your senators over the Internet.

T F 2. Network computing allows data to be stored on a server rather than on an individual computer.

T F 3. You can decide who wins a court case by clicking "Yes" or "No" on the Justice Department's Web site.

T F 4. You should be disrespectful in your e-mails to your legislators because it will make them pay more attention.

T F 5. You can find out what is going on in the House of Representatives right now by going to the *Thomas* Web site.

FILL IN THE BLANK

Complete the following sentences by writing the correct word or words in the blanks provided.

1. The current Vice President of the United States is _____ _____.

2. The _____ branch of the government interprets the Constitution.

3. The _____ branch of the government makes the laws.

4. The _____ branch of the government enforces the laws.

5. *Thomas* is hosted by the _____ _____ _____.

WRITTEN QUESTIONS

Write a brief answer to the following questions.

1. Why is it important to be informed about legislative branch activities?

2. Do you think that network computing is "the dawn of a new generation of computing," as Oracle asserts? Why or why not?

3. Why is it important to be informed about the latest Supreme Court decisions? What can you learn from the Web sites about Supreme Court decisions that you probably won't find in your local newspaper?

4. An issue will be on the ballot next week asking voters to approve environmental reform. You want to be an informed voter before you go to the polls. Explain how you would research on the Internet the pros and cons of environmental issues.

5. Why do you think it is important to make your e-mail communications to your legislators brief and to the point?

SCANS

WEB PROJECT 14-1

Keeping up with the Government

   GreatApplications, Inc., needs to stay up to date on legislation that can affect the software business. Search the Web's legislative, executive, and judicial sites to find the important issues related to software and Internet regulation. Make a list of sources that can help you stay on top of the latest laws and court rulings that affect your company's business. Save this information in your Research folder.

SCANS

TEAMWORK PROJECT 14-2

E-mail Your Senator

   Get together with your team and agree on the most important issue facing the software industry and the Internet community today from among those you uncovered in Project 14-1. Research the e-mail addresses of your two senators and congresspersons. Draft a team e-mail to your state's senators and your local congresspersons that presents the team's position on the issue. Work together to craft a well-written, well-researched e-mail. Keep it to less than 150 words. Put all of the team members' names on the message, and e-mail it to your elected legislative representatives.

SCANS

PROJECT 14-3

Write a 100-word response to one of the following questions.

1.   How will access to online information about the three branches of government change how students view the workings of government?

2.   The Net allows us to take a more active role in government. If our founding fathers were here, how would they react to this new development?

3. Is it possible to view your elected officials in action and then e-mail your pleasure or displeasure instantly to them? How do you think our representatives will like this "instant feedback" from the voters?

CRITICAL THINKING

ACTIVITY 14-1

Keeping an Eye on Government

Will lawmakers act more responsibly if they know they are constantly being monitored by voters via the Internet? What information would you like to find out on the Internet about the government? Prepare a 100- to 250-word answer to these questions.

ACTIVITY 14-2

Public Influence on the Court

Supreme Court justices are not elected by popular vote. They are appointed by presidential recommendation. Once confirmed by Congress, justices serve for life. Supposedly, this keeps them free of outside influences and public opinion. However, as the public becomes more informed by the Internet, newsgroups, etc., they (the public) can raise a louder voice. Will this affect how the Supreme Court does its job? Is it good for the public to be so informed on judicial issues? Prepare a 100- to 250-word answer to these questions.

ACTIVITY 14-3

Warming up to Politics

Will the Internet help people become more involved in issues like global warming and campaign finance reform? Are you more or less likely to act on these issues now that you have information about these important topics? Prepare a 100- to 250-word answer to these questions.

EXPLORING JOBS ONLINE

OBJECTIVES

Upon completion of this lesson, you should be able to:

- Locate and research jobs online.
- Create an online resume.
- Find job salaries.

🕐 Estimated Time: 2.5 hours

NET TERMS

Monster.com
Telecommuting
Virtual office
Wizard

It's a Job Seeker's Virtual World

The Internet is an incredible tool not only for finding online museums or e-books but also for finding a great job in a very competitive marketplace. Many Internet companies offer services where employers can post job openings for prospective employees to search through, sites that provide job salaries, and even sites where you can post your resume and employers can search for your skills.

If you know where to look, finding a job online is a simple task. Go to a job site, search for a job you want, and contact that company. Many sites allow you to search for jobs in your local area. Let's give it a shot!

Net Tip

Most job search tools tell you how many jobs were found in the specific category and function that you selected. Sometimes there are too many jobs to review, so you need to narrow your search a little more.

STEP-BY-STEP 15.1

1. Start your Web browser and go to **www. flipdog.com**. Flipdog is an online job search service (see Figure 15-1). You can also enter **Online Job Search** into a search portal if you want to try another site.

2. Let's find your dream job. Choose **Find Jobs** at the top of the screen or choose a similar option in any other job-search Web site you may be using for this exercise.

FIGURE 15-1
Find a job at *FlipDog.com*

3. Narrow your search to the state and city in which you want to find a job. Select a state on the map and, when the list comes up, pick a nearby city and then click **next**.

4. On the next page, choose a **Job Category** from the list and, when the list comes up, select a **Job Function** or subcategory. Choose **next** again.

5. Choose an employer and click **finish** to view the listings for that company or job service agency.

6. Finally, select a job title to view details and contact information. Congratulations, you have found your dream job!

7. Locate three other sites that offer job listings and information about specific jobs.
    1.

    2.

    3.

Leave your Web browser open and available for the next Step-by-Step.

Net Tip

Most states and the federal government have job services that can help you find a government job. These agencies are often called Department of Workforce Services, Department of Workforce Development, or the like. Most of these agencies have information about finding jobs locally, and most have online job listings. Try searching for Department of Workforce Services or Department of Workforce Development and see if you can find an agency for your state.

Put Your Name Out There and Build an Online Resume

Now that you've found your dream job, make your name known by posting an online resume. Most job search sites that let you search for jobs also let you post your resume. This allows you to e-mail it to an employer at a prospective job or to post it so an employer can find your specific skills. For this Step-by-Step, we'll use *Monster.com,* one of the most well-known job search sites.

Net Tip

You will need to create an account with an online resume service before you can continue.

STEP-BY-STEP ▷ 15.2

1. Open your browser and go to **www.monster.com** or choose another job search site (see Figure 15-2).

2. Choose **Post Your Resume** to begin setting up your online resume.

3. Once you have logged in, choose the **Create My Resume** link to start the resume wizard. A *wizard* is a guide that takes you through several steps to create a finished product.

4. Fill in the requested information to create a resume that is as complete as possible.

FIGURE 15-2
Post your resume

5. When you are done, return to *my.monster.com*, where you can view your completed resume by selecting the title under **My Resumes**. You can create up to four additional resumes.

6. Choose **Resumes** near the top to view options for your resumes, as shown in Figure 15-3. On this page, you can view, edit, or make changes, delete, or e-mail your resume to an employer or friend to review using the **Send Resume** option. You can also see how many times your resume has been viewed by employers.

7. Locate three other sites that allow you to post your resume online and record them here.

1.

2.

3.

Leave your Web browser open for the next Step-by-Step.

Net Tip

An employer who is looking for someone like you wants as much information about your skills and experience as possible.

FIGURE 15-3
See how many times your resume has been viewed

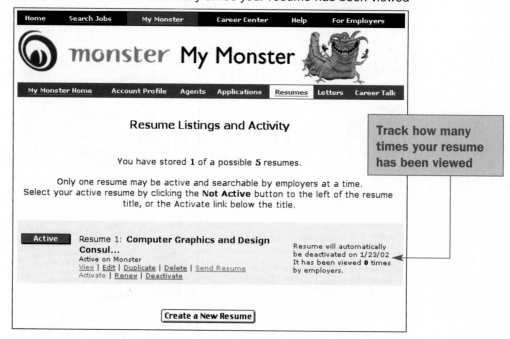

What Are You Worth?

Have you ever wondered how much money you could make in a certain profession? Is the salary different for a Web designer in Lubbock, Texas, than for one in Boston, Massachusetts? With the Internet, you can find answers to these questions online! Using the Salary Wizard at *Salary.com* or other job searching sites, you can find out what a person with your skills makes on average at various locations across the U.S.

STEP-BY-STEP ▷ 15.3

1. Start your Web browser and go to **www.salary.com**.

2. Using the Salary Wizard (shown in Figure 15-4), choose a job category and enter your ZIP code or a city near you.

FIGURE 15-4
Use the Salary Wizard to find how much you could make

INTERNET MILESTONE

VIRTUAL OFFICES AND TELECOMMUTING

More and more people don't drive to work. Instead, they work in the comfort of their homes. They have *virtual offices*, connecting to their employer over the Internet. The practice of working over the Internet is called *telecommuting*. Telecommuting reduces traffic on our nation's highways and provides an excellent opportunity for people to use that commuting time more effectively with their families. The advantage for a business is that they don't need to build office space for these employees.

3. Choose **Search** to narrow your query.

4. On the next page, choose a specific job title that interests you. If you're not sure, select **View Job Descriptions** to get more information.

5. Choose **Create Salary Report**. You will get a page that shows the low, median, and high salary range for your specified area as well as a detailed job description.

6. Scroll down to the **Compare** section. Now you can compare this job with a similar one or compare it with the same job at a different location. Choose a related job or the same job in a new location from the list and choose **Go**.

7. Now you will see a chart similar to the one shown in Figure 15-5. Try some different jobs and locations and see what you can find!

8. Close your Web browser if you are finished with your work for today.

FIGURE 15-5
A Web designer may make a
higher salary in Boston than in Lubbock

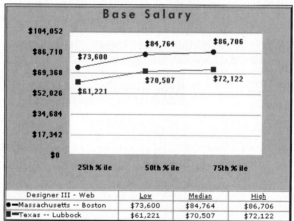

Designer III - Web	Low	Median	High
●— Massachusetts -- Boston	$73,600	$84,764	$86,706
■— Texas -- Lubbock	$61,221	$70,507	$72,122

INTERNET MILESTONE

NET MILESTONE — *MONSTER.COM* SUPER BOWL AD

In the 1999 Super Bowl, a relatively unknown dot.com company with a funny name (*Monster.com*) made Super Bowl history with an extremely clever advertisement. This little-known company with very little money paid a million dollars for a commercial that would make it a household name in its field.

The commercial featured children aspiring to unimpressive jobs, like "filing all day." The number of visitors to the Monster Web site skyrocketed. Within 24 hours following its critically acclaimed Super Bowl blitz, more than 2.2 million job searches were conducted on its site, which represented a 450% increase in searches.

The very next year, advertising dollars for high-tech company advertising flooded into the Super Bowl. Each of these companies tried to replicate this monstrous success.

Summary

In this lesson, you learned:

■ You can find and research a job online.

■ Resumes can be posted online.

■ Salaries for jobs all over the U.S. are given online.

NET TERMS REVIEW

Define the following terms

Monster.com   Virtual office   Wizard
Telecommuting

LESSON 15 REVIEW QUESTIONS

TRUE/FALSE

Circle T if the statement is true or F if the statement is false.

T F   **1.** *Monster.com* is a place where monsters chat on the Internet with humans.

T F   **2.** You can find almost any kind of job online.

T F   **3.** It is possible to find and compare competitive salaries on the Internet.

T F   **4.** Wizards manage job search sites.

T F   **5.** The Internet makes it easy to find a job online.

FILL IN THE BLANK

Complete the following sentences by writing the correct word or words in the blanks provided.

1. To find salaries online, you visited _____.

2. To locate jobs online, you visited _____.

3. To post a resume online, you visited _____.

4. A(n) _____ helps you complete a form step-by-step.

5. The Department of Workforce Services is a(n) _____ agency.

WRITTEN QUESTIONS

Give a short answer to the following questions.

1. Describe how you would help a friend find a job using the Internet.

2. List the steps required to post a resume online.

3. How would an employer benefit from having access to a search engine for resumes?

4. What are the advantages and disadvantages of online job searching as opposed to manually searching for a job?

5. In your opinion, if employees know that other people in other parts of the country are making more money than they are, will they become dissatisfied with their jobs?

LESSON 15 PROJECTS

WEB PROJECT 15-1

Help Wanted

A Web designer from GreatApplications, Inc., has recently left the company to go back to school and earn his doctorate. This creates a challenge, because GreatApplications, Inc., can't afford downtime on its Web site. The HR (human resources) director has assigned you to research information on hiring a new employee.

Prepare a 100- to 200-word report explaining how the HR director could find potential employees on the Internet and give the low, median, and high base salaries for a Web designer position in your area (*Hint*: search for *Designer III-Web*). Have the report ready for the HR director to present to the board of directors early next week.

TEAMWORK PROJECT 15-2

Help Needed

It seems that the Web designer is not the only person leaving GreatApplications, Inc. Five other job openings are now available in the areas listed below. Divide up the jobs within your group and find base salaries for each of the positions.

JOB OPENING	BASE SALARY
1. Administrative secretary (Secretary III)	
2. Errand boy (Photocopy operator)	
3. Customer service representative (E-commerce)	
4. Chief financial officer (Accounting)	
5. Audio-visual technician (Advertising)	

PROJECT 15-3

Thinking and Writing about Online Jobs
Write a 100-word response to two of the following questions:

1. How will the Internet make job seeking even more competitive than it is already?

2. How will the Internet change the way people look for jobs?

3. What can be done to improve the way people search for jobs online?

CRITICAL THINKING

ACTIVITY 15-1

Net Interviews

Do you think it makes much sense to hire someone over the Internet? Can you interview people over the Net? How would you do that? Would this be a good way to interview someone living far away? Prepare a 100- to 250-word answer to these questions.

ACTIVITY 15-2

Keeping the Best Employees

If you knew that employees could find a better salary elsewhere, what would you do to keep them with your company? Prepare a 100- to 250-word answer to this question.

Super-Sized Advertising

Why do you think that the Super Bowl has become such an important advertising medium? What kind of customers watch the Super Bowl? What are they interested in buying? Prepare a 100- to 250-word answer to these questions.

Exploring the Net for Fact and Fiction

REVIEW QUESTIONS

TRUE/FALSE

Circle T if the statement is true or F if the statement is false.

T   F   1.   The Internet was originally invented by Brendan P. Kehoe.

T   F   2.   Zen and the Art of the Internet is a famous Eastern religion.

T   F   3.   OWLs are Webmasters that work late into the evening to repair damaged Web servers.

T   F   4.   Using all CAPITAL letters in online messages implies shouting or anger.

T   F   5.   Few people worry about misspelled words online. Rather, it is the power of your arguments that will persuade people.

T   F   6.   FidoNet is a well-known Web site for dog and pet supplies.

T   F   7.   Gopher was a document cataloging system popular during the 1950s.

T   F   8.   E-commerce includes online marketing and sales.

T   F   9.   Web fraud is rare, but these cases attract a great deal of attention and scare customers away from e-commerce.

T   F   10.   The Internet appliance is an expensive, high-speed, and high-powered computer for accessing the Internet.

MATCHING

Match the correct term in column 2 to its description in column 1.

Column 1	Column 2

_____ 1. A high-tech laboratory in Switzerland.

_____ 2. A modeling language that simulates 3-D objects.

_____ 3. A government agency associated with space exploration and the International Space Station.

_____ 4. Communications network created in 1981 to facilitate e-mail and file transfers between academic researchers.

_____ 5. The tax collection agency of the U.S. government.

_____ 6. A virtual frog for dissection purposes.

_____ 7. A measurement of stock performance utilizing 30 large U.S. corporations.

_____ 8. An online resource for writers.

_____ 9. A software manufacturer advocating low-cost computers for Internet access.

_____ 10. Used as an information source and messaging system for a particular interest group.

A. Fluffy

B. BBS

C. CERN

D. OWL

E. DJIA

F. NASA

G. IRS

H. Oracle

I. VRML

J. BITNET

CROSS-CURRICULAR PROJECTS

The Web is a banquet of online information resources for every subject imaginable. It's like a smorgasbord of knowledge; you just need to learn where to find the information you're interested in. This unit allowed you to search for information on a variety of academic subjects. Complete the next few projects to see how much you learned.

SCIENCE 4-1

NASA has been deeply involved in space exploration from the manned exploration of the moon in the 1960s to the International Space Station of today. NASA has also explored the planets. Search the Internet and find four sources of information about the exploration of the planet Mars. Search for authentic sites that provide information about the planet itself and what we have learned from the many space probes that have landed on its surface. Name some of the projects and devices that have explored the surface of Mars in your list of resources. Save your list as **Science 4-1**.

SCIENCE 4-2

Use your list of sources found in the previous science activity (Science 4-1) to help you prepare a 250- to 500-word report on NASA's exploration of Mars. Save your report as **Science 4-2.**

LANGUAGE ARTS/SCIENCE 4-3

Search for three resources that can help students write quality science reports. Visit an online OWL and look for ways to improve the formatting and the writing of your Mars report. Seek advice on how to prepare a scientific report. What resources are there that help science writers produce quality reports? Create a list of resources. Explain each resource briefly and save it as **Language Arts 4-3**.

LANGUAGE ARTS/JOURNALISM 4-4

Visit the five online college newspapers that you located in Step-by-Step 12.3. Read each paper. After your review, state your opinion as to which of these five papers exemplifies the highest level of journalism and journalistic standards. Which of these papers do you feel presents the issues in the most unbiased and clear way? Prepare a 100-word report summarizing your findings and beliefs. Save this report as **Language Arts 4-4**.

HISTORY 4-1

The Internet is a wonderful resource to help people learn about obscure yet entertaining sport histories, such as skydiving, fly fishing, or badminton. Choose an obscure sport—something you have never done in your life—and search the Internet for the history of that activity. Create a 150-word report detailing some small part of the history of that sport. Save your work as **History 4-1**.

CIVICS AND GOVERNMENT 4-1

The United States has a unique form of government based on the principles of federalism in the separation of powers. However, most of the governments in the world do not follow this organizational plan. In fact, the United States is somewhat alone in its form of government. Most other governments in the world are modeled after the British or the French forms of government. Pick a country and find information on the Internet about its government. Prepare a 250- to 500-word report on this country and its form of government. Save your report as **Government 4-1**.

INTERNET ACTIVITIES

ACTIVITY 4-1

Of all the subject areas you have researched online (language arts, science, math, history, art, music, technology), which do you believe has the best coverage online? Which of the subject areas has the greatest amount of quality information? Pick one of the subject areas and explain why you think it is number 1 in terms of online Internet coverage. Defend your opinion in a 150-word essay. Save this essay as **Activity 4-1**.

ACTIVITY 4-2

How important do you think it is that governments explain how their systems work online for people from other countries? When you completed the **Government 4-1** paper, what did you find out about that country and its form of government that you didn't know? Are these positive things for outsiders to learn about? Explain your thoughts in a 100- to 250-word essay and save it as **Activity 4-2**.

SIMULATION

JOB 4-1

Where would you go online to find a good job working for the IRS in Washington D.C.? Explain the process you would follow to locate such a job. Save your plan of action in a short report of 100 to 250 words. Name the file **Job 4-1**.

JOB 4-2

How important do you think e-commerce is to the future of local businesses in your area? How much impact do you think e-commerce will have on the future of these businesses? State and defend your opinions in a short 100- to 250-word essay named **Job 4-2**.

SPRECHEN SIE INTERNET: HOW THE INTERNET SPEAKS AND SPARKLES

HOW THE WEB WORKS: YOUR FIRST WEB PAGE

OBJECTIVES

Upon completion of this lesson, you should be able to:

- View HTML source code.
- Identify parts of an HTML page.
- Define simple HTML tags.
- Create HTML pages with ordered and unordered lists.
- Format text using HTML.

⏱ **Estimated Time: 2.5 hours**

NET TERMS

Berners-Lee (Tim)

Generalized Markup Language (GML)

Gutenberg (Johannes)

Ordered (or Numbered) list

Standard Generalized Markup Language (SGML)

Tags

Unordered (or Bulleted) list

World Wide Web Consortium (W3C)

WYSIWYG

The Language of the Web

As you learned in Lesson 3, HTML (HyperText Markup Language) is the standard document format for creating Web pages. HTML commands define how Web pages will look, including such elements as text styles, graphic artwork, and hyperlinks. A great advantage of HTML is that all browsers can read it. And guess what? It's not complicated to learn, either!

Tags are written inside brackets <LIKE THIS>. HTML tags usually act like light switches that must be turned on and off. The tags tell the browser how to display the text between the on tag and the off tag.

The on tag indicates where the browser should begin applying the formatting instructions. The off tag includes a backslash </LIKE THIS>. The slash tells the browser to stop applying the formatting instuctions.

Now let's look at some real HTML.

 Net Tip

A Web page is created as an all-text file with an *.htm* or *.html* extension. The extension helps Web browsers identify HTML files. The files contain **tags:** instructions that tell the browser how to format the information between them. The browser displays the information according to the tags' commands.

STEP-BY-STEP ▷ 16.1

1. In your browser, go to your home page.

2. In Internet Explorer, select **View** and then **Source**. In Netscape, choose **View** and then **Page Source,** as shown in Figure 16-1. You can right-click in either browser and select **View Source** also. The source code will look something like Figure 16-2. Don't worry, it's not as confusing as it looks.

3. Viewing the source code of a complex page may be overwhelming, but look for these tags, which make up the basic framework of an HTML document, first:

   <HTML></HTML> This tag is loaded first and indicates the beginning and end of an HTML file.

   <HEAD></HEAD> Includes information about the Web page.

<TITLE></TITLE> Identifies the title that will be shown in the title bar of your browser.

<BODY></BODY> Identifies everything that will actually appear to other people in their Web browser.

These starting tags have the following basic order:

<HTML>

<HEAD><TITLE></TITLE></HEAD>

<BODY>

</BODY>

</HTML>

FIGURE 16-1
View Page Source in Netscape

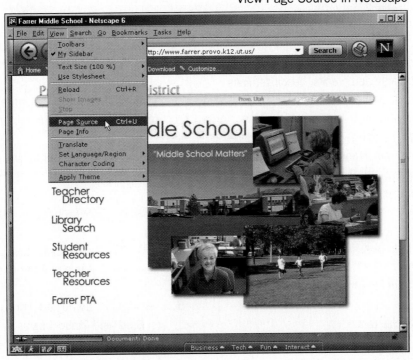

FIGURE 16-2
HTML source code

```
HTML: Farrer Middle School

<html>

<head>
<meta http-equiv="content-type" content="text/html;charset=iso-8859-1">
<meta name="generator" content="Adobe GoLive 4">
<title>Farrer Middle School</title>
</head>

<body bgcolor="white" link="#1d6174" vlink="#0099ff">
<center>
 <a href="http://www.provo.k12.ut.us/"><img height="50" width="624" src="images/psd_bar.gif" border="0"
 <p>
 <table border="0" cellpadding="0" cellspacing="0" width="637">
  <tr height="47">
   <td height="47" valign="top">
    <ul>
     <img height="47" width="172" src="images/farrer_title.gif" alt="Farrer Middle School">
    </ul>
   </td>
   <td rowspan="2" valign="top"><img height="342" width="429" src="images/collage.jpg" alt='&quot;Middl
  </tr>
  <tr>
   <td valign="top">
    <ul>
     <a href="http://ps4.provo.k12.ut.us/FMS/public/logon.html"><img height="28" width="128" src="image
     <p><a href="calendar.html"><img height="16" width="83" src="images/calendar_link.gif" border="0" c
     <p><a href="teacher_directory.html"><img height="34" width="96" src="images/directory_link.gif" bo
     <p><a href="http://lib.provo.k12.ut.us/farrer.html"><img height="32" width="80" src="images/librar
     <p><a href="student_resources.html"><img height="31" width="106" src="images/s_resources_link.gif"
     <p><a href="teacher_resources.html"><img height="31" width="106" src="images/t_resources_link.gif"
     <p><a href="pta.html"><img height="17" width="83" src="images/pta_link.gif" border="0" alt="Farrer
    </ul>
   </td>
  </tr>
  <tr>
   <td colspan="2">
    <center>
     <br>
     <br>
     <img height="18" width="417" src="images/address.gif" alt="100 N 600 E Provo, UT 84606 374-4970">
     <p><img height="2" width="571" src="images/bar.gif" alt="bar"></p>
     <p>[<a href="http://ps4.provo.k12.ut.us/FMS/public/logon.html">PowerSchool</a>][<a href="calendar.
     [<a href="http://lib.provo.k12.ut.us/farrer.html">Library Search</a>][<a href="student_resources.h
     <p>[<a href="http://www.provo.k12.ut.us/">Provo School District</a>]</p>
     <p><img height="2" width="571" src="images/bar.gif" alt="bar"></p>
     <p>Last Updated <csobj w="126" h="12" t="DateTime" format="LongDate" region="0">Tuesday, January 1
     Page by <a href="mailto:ryant@provo.k12.ut.us">Ryan Teeter</a></center>
   </td>
  </tr>
 </table>
</center>
</body>

</html>
```

4. Many other tags indicate changes in font styles, underlining, paragraph breaks, headings, lines, and lists. Look for the following tags:

<H1></H1> Heading – the number indicates the level of importance, with 1 being the most important and 6 being least important. Other examples include <H2></H2> and <H6></H6>.

<B></B> Bold text.

<U></U> Underline text.

<I></I> Italicize text.

<P></P> Begins a new paragraph. (Note:

This tag doesn't need an off tag.)

**
</BR>** Breaks a line and starts a new one. (Note: This tag doesn't need an off tag.)

<HR> Draws a horizontal line (rule) across the page. (Note: This tag doesn't need an off tag.)

<FONT></FONT> Indicates change of font style.

<FONTSIZE=X> Indicates change in font size, where X is a number between 1 and 7.

5. Tags can be combined. For example, text that is **Bold** and **Italic** begins with **<B><I>** and ends with **</B></I>**. Search your souce for text that looks like these tags.

6. Switch back and forth between your browser and the source page. What do other tags do? See if you can identify five additional tags and guess what they do.

Tag   Function

1.

2.

3.

4.

5.

Leave your Web browser open for the next Step-by-Step.

Net Tip

Don't be discouraged if the page you are looking at is hopelessly complex. HTML is a language that is constantly evolving to do more powerful things. You should still be able to find very basic tags. Be patient and look through the source, identifying what you know. Pretty soon, HTML will seem pretty simple.

INTERNET MILESTONE

TIM JOHANNES BERNERS-GUTENBERG-LEE

Johannes Gutenberg created a printing press with movable metal type containing letters, numbers, and symbols, and in 1454, printed multiple copies of a letter. The invention of the printing press allowed millions of inexpensive paper copies to be made quickly and easily. Gutenberg's press was the photocopying machine of the 15th century.

Gutenberg's invention started revolutions. Not only was there a revolution in mass communication, but the availability of inexpensive books greatly increased literacy and improved education. Gutenberg's invention made the Protestant Reformation possible, by allowing the people of the time to share new philosophies and ideas. Inexpensive printing allowed American and later French revolutionaries to share their ideas of freedom with the masses. The Gutenberg press had a major impact on the course of history.

One can only speculate on the impact the World Wide Web will have on the history of the planet. When *Tim Berners-Lee* invented his simple HTML version 1, he sparked a massive communications revolution that can only be compared with Gutenberg's invention in the scope of its impact.

A hundred years from now, the names Gutenberg and Berners-Lee may stand side by side in the history books as the two most significant individuals in the history of written mass communication.

Create a Simple Web Page

Now that you have seen the basics of a Web page, it's time to create your own. If you get confused, check out the figures along the way. They will guide you to ultimate success.

STEP-BY-STEP ▷ 16.2

1. Open a text editor such as **Notepad** for Windows or **SimpleText** for Macintosh.

2. Enter the starting tags in the basic layout shown here (press **Enter** after you key each tag):

   <HTML>

   <HEAD><TITLE></TITLE></HEAD>

   <BODY>

   </BODY>

   </HTML>

3. To make your page say something, first move your cursor between the <TITLE></TITLE> tags and type your first name followed by **Web Page** as in **<TITLE>Mark's Web Page</TITLE>.**

4. Next, position the insertion point before the second <BODY> tag and enter the text below. Fill in the blanks with information about yourself, as shown in Figure 16-3.

   **Hi! My name is _____.
**

   I live in _____,_____. (Insert the name of the city and state/province or country where you live.) **
**

   I was born in _____,_____. (Insert the name of the city and state/province or country where you were born.) **
**

   I _____. (Write something about yourself.) **
**

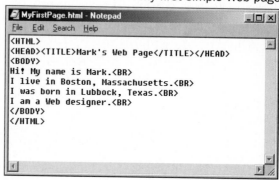

FIGURE 16-3
My first simple Web page

5. Save your document as **My First Page.html** and close your text editor.

6. In your browser, choose **File** and then **Open**.

7. Locate the file you just saved and open it. Does your Web page look similar to Figure 16-4? Leave your Web browser open so that you can complete the next Step-by-Step.

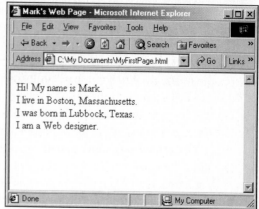

FIGURE 16-4
Opening an HTML file in your Web browser

Adding Content

You know how to create a very simple HTML Web page. Now, let's beef it up a bit and create lists of information. In a ***bulleted list,*** each item is preceded by a bullet or dot. A bulleted list is also an ***unordered list*** because it doesn't have a particular order of importance. For this, we use the <UL></UL> tag to start and end the list and the <LI> tag to insert a list item.

A ***numbered list*** or ***ordered list*** has items preceded by numbers and shows an order of importance. For this, we use the <OL></OL> tag to start and end the list and the <LI> tag to insert a new list item.

> **Net Tip**
>
> Be sure to put a line break <BR> tag after each line or it will look like one continuous line.

STEP-BY-STEP ▷ 16.3

1. Open your Web page in your text editor.

2. Position the insertion point just after the <BODY> tag and enter **<H1>Your Name WEB PAGE</H1><HR>.**

3. Now move to the end of the text on your page (just before the </BODY> tag and just after the <HR> tag). Enter the following information using your own list of things you like to do and your favorite TV shows (see Figure 16-5).

    <P>

    <H3>Things I Like To Do</H3>

    <UL>

    <LI>One thing I like to do

    <LI>Another thing I like to do

    <LI>Yet another thing I like to do

    </UL>

    <HR>

    <H3>My Favorite TV Shows</H3>

    <OL>

    <LI>Best Show

    <LI>2nd Best Show

<LI>3rd Best Show

</OL>

FIGURE 16-5
Lists in HTML

```
MyFirstPage.html - Notepad

File  Edit  Search  Help

<HTML>
<HEAD><TITLE>Mark's Web Page</TITLE></HEAD>
<BODY>
<H1>Mark's WEB PAGE</H1><HR>
Hi! My name is Mark.<BR>
I live in Boston, Massachusetts.<BR>
I was born in Lubbock, Texas.<BR>
I am a Web designer.<BR>
<P>
<H3>Things I Like To Do</H3>
<UL>
<LI>One thing I like to do
<LI>Another thing I like to do
<LI>Yet another thing I like to do
</UL>
<HR>
<H3>My Favorite TV Shows</H3>
<OL>
<LI>Best Show
<LI>2nd Best Show
<LI>3rd Best Show
</OL>
</BODY>
</HTML>
```

> **Net Tip**
>
> The <H1> tag creates a large title for your Web page that will show up in your browser. The <HR> tag places a horizontal bar beneath your title.

257

4. Save your file and open it in your Web browser (see Figure 16-6). Can you tell which items have header tags and which are part of ordered and unordered lists?

FIGURE 16-6
Lists on the Web

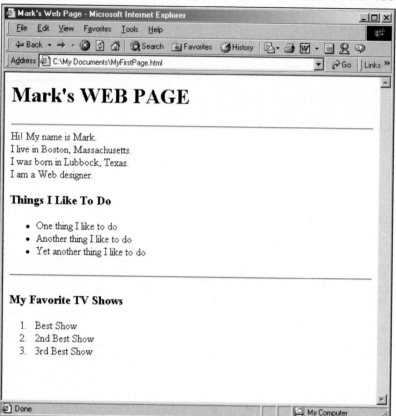

INTERNET MILESTONE

WYSIWYG

Companies like Adobe, Microsoft, Netscape, and others are trying to help Web authors and publishers get a better idea of how their work will look once it is posted on the WWW. To do this, they have created *WYSIWYG* HTML editors.

WYSIWYG (pronounced "wizzy-wig") stands for What You See Is What You Get, and that is essentially how this software works. Instead of having to spend a lot of time writing HTML code, Web designers can simply lay out their page and the software will do the coding for them.

Some companies, like Netscape, offer simple WYSIWYGs for free. For example, if you are using Netscape 4 or above, choose the *Composer* icon at the bottom of your window to get access to this powerful program.

5. Put the first thing you like to do in boldface. Use the **<B></B>** tags.

6. Italicize the second thing you like to do. Use the **<I></I>** tags.

7. Underline the third thing you like to do. Use the **<U></U>** tags. Your source should now look similar to Figure 16-7.

8. Save your file again and open it in your browser. Did you notice the formatting changes? (See Figure 16-8.)

9. Print your Web page to hang on the refrigerator at home. Your parents will be so proud!

10. Close your Web browser if you are finished for today.

FIGURE 16-7
Formatted lists in HTML

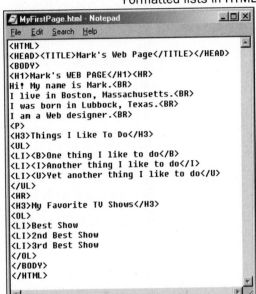

```
MyFirstPage.html - Notepad
File  Edit  Search  Help

<HTML>
<HEAD><TITLE>Mark's Web Page</TITLE></HEAD>
<BODY>
<H1>Mark's WEB PAGE</H1><HR>
Hi! My name is Mark.<BR>
I live in Boston, Massachusetts.<BR>
I was born in Lubbock, Texas.<BR>
I am a Web designer.<BR>
<P>
<H3>Things I Like To Do</H3>
<UL>
<LI><B>One thing I like to do</B>
<LI><I>Another thing I like to do</I>
<LI><U>Yet another thing I like to do</U>
</UL>
<HR>
<H3>My Favorite TV Shows</H3>
<OL>
<LI>Best Show
<LI>2nd Best Show
<LI>3rd Best Show
</OL>
</BODY>
</HTML>
```

FIGURE 16-8
Adding formats to your first Web page

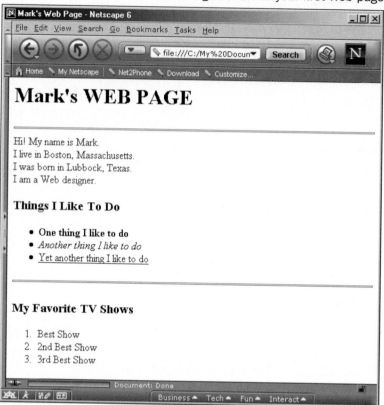

INTERNET MILESTONE

SGML + TB-L = HTML

In the beginning, there was *GML*, or *Generalized Markup Language*. GML was created by IBM in the 1960s as a way to share and edit documents. In 1986, an improved system called *SGML*, or *Standard Generalized Markup Language*, was adopted by the International Organization for Standardization (ISO). Tim Berners-Lee used SGML to help him create HTML.

HTML is maintained by the Editorial Review Board (ERB) of the *W3C*, or the *World Wide Web Consortium*. The W3C continues to organize, maintain, and publish improvements to HTML, which has various versions: HTML 1, HTML 2, HTML 3, HTML 4, and so on.

If you followed all this, you'll be able to follow this sentence:

"IBM created GML, which was improved as SGML and adopted by the ISO. TB-L used HTML to guide the development of HTML 1, 2, 3, 4, which is maintained by the ERB at the W3C."

And people actually speak like this! What is the W3 coming to?

Summary

In this lesson, you learned:

- HTML has commands in brackets called tags.

- HTML tags tell the browser how to display the text.

- You can create a simple HTML page.

- HTML has ordered and unordered lists.

- You can format text on an HTML page.

NET TERMS REVIEW

Define the following terms:

Berners-Lee	Ordered (or Numbered) list	Unordered (or Bulleted) list
GML	SGML	W3C
Gutenberg	Tags	WYSIWYG

LESSON 16 REVIEW QUESTIONS

TRUE/FALSE

Circle T if the statement is true or F if the statement is false.

T F   **1.**   Johannes Berners-Lee invented the printing press.

T F   **2.**   The <LI> tag defines a list item.

T F   **3.**   The <H1> tag creates exactly the same look as the <B> tag.

T F   **4.**   You can make text boldface on a Web page.

T F   **5.**   WYSIWYG HTML editors show only HTML code.

FILL IN THE BLANK

Complete the following sentences by writing the correct word or words in the blanks provided.

1.   Berners-Lee invented _____.

2.   A bulleted or _____ list shows items in no particular order.

3. An ordered or _____ list shows items in a numerical order.

4. You can make text _____ by using the <I></I> tag.

5. The _____ tag puts a horizontal line in your Web page.

WRITTEN QUESTIONS

Write a brief answer to the following question.

1. Describe what the <HTML> tag does.

2. Describe what the <TITLE> tag does.

3. Describe what the <UL> tag does.

4. Describe what the <BR> tag does.

5. Describe what the <B> tag does.

LESSON 16 PROJECTS

WEB PROJECT 16-1

Create a Web Presence

The Board of Directors at GreatApplications, Inc., has been watching you. The board members are impressed and have assigned to your group the daunting task of developing the company's Web site.

Create a simple Web page for GreatApplications, Inc., that describes what the company does and lists the members of your team.

TEAMWORK PROJECT 16-2

Web Site Hardware

The computer guru at GreatApplications, Inc., just took a job at Microsoft. The boss is in a bind and has asked your group to identify what hardware the company needs to present Web pages to its millions of customers. As a group, research the specifications and requirements for the new company Web server. What kind of equipment is necessary to set up and run a Web server for a large company like GreatApplications, Inc.?

Prepare a report for the board of directors showing what equipment will be needed and how much it will cost. Save your work in your common folder, with an additional copy in your personal research folder as a backup.

PROJECT 16-3

Thinking and Writing about Web Technologies

From your experiences so far on the Internet, select two of the following questions and write a 100- to 250-word response.

1. How important is it for a business to have a Web site?

2. How important is a Web site as a sales tool for business?

3. How important is it that the information on the Great Applications, Inc., Web site be honest and accurate?

CRITICAL THINKING

ACTIVITY 16-1

HTML's Simplicity

While computers and computer languages seem to get more complex all the time, HTML stands out as a fairly simple method of communication. Why do you think HTML is so simple? What advantages does it have? What disadvantages does this simplicity bring? Prepare a 100- to 200-word response to these questions.

ACTIVITY 16-2

Imagine a World without Gutenberg

What if the Gutenberg press had never been invented? How would the world be different? Prepare a 100- to 200-word response to this question.

ACTIVITY 16-3

Imagine a World without HTML

What if HTML had never been invented? How is the world different because of HTML? Would your really cool Web page have been possible? Prepare a 100- to 200-word response to these questions.

HOW THE WEB WORKS: ADVANCED WEB PAGE DESIGN

OBJECTIVES

Upon completion of this lesson, you should be able to:

- Learn and apply advanced HTML tags.
- Insert links and images into your Web page.
- Change the colors of your Web page.
- Change the font color of text on your Web page.

Estimated Time: 2.5 hours

NET TERMS

Anchor tag

Attribute

Hypertext reference (HREF)

Image source tag

Make Your Web Page Stand Out

Creating a Web page is the easy part. Making it stand out in a crowd of billions of other Web pages is more difficult. In this lesson, you will enhance the appearance of your Web page by adding hyperlinks and some graphics and changing the way your text looks.

But first we need to learn some new tags.

STEP-BY-STEP ▷ 17.1

1. Open your Web browser and go to your home page.

2. View the source of your home page as it loads (see Figure 17-1). (Note: Review Lesson 16 if you have forgotten how to view the source code of Web pages.)

3. An *anchor tag* is the HTML code that defines a hyperlink to another document or Web page. The anchor tag begins with <A> and ends with </A>. The text or graphic between the <A> and </A> is a hot spot that, when clicked, transports the user to the defined location. An anchor tag is a little bit longer than the tags you have learned so far, but its organization is simple when you understand the parts. Look for an anchor tag similar to the following:

   <A HREF="http://www.microsoft.com">Click here to go to Microsoft's home page</A>

FIGURE 17-1
The home page source

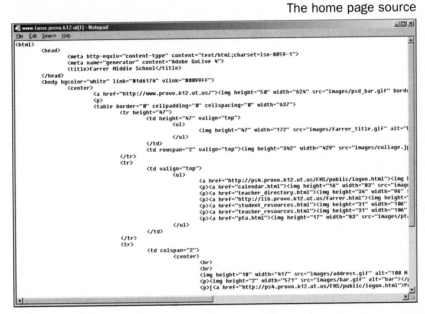

4. An ***image source tag*** tells a browser to load a specific image or graphic into your Web page. This tag is written *<IMG SRC="http://www.course.com/path/to/graphic.gif">*. Look for a similar tag in your source document.

5. If your page has a colored background or has an image, an attribute is added to the <BODY> tag. If you have a white background, look for a tag like *<BODY BGCOLOR=white>* in your source document. If you have an image in the background, look for something like *<BODY BACKGROUND="path/to/image.jpg">*.

 Net Concept

The HREF code stands for ***hypertext reference***. The HREF code is not the actual tag; it is called an ***attribute*** because it adds to another tag. This attribute followed by the = sign and an URL tells a browser where to go when the hot spot is clicked.

6. Now we will look for text with different font styles or font colors. Any tag that has to do with the font starts with the *<FONT></FONT>* tag. Text with the font Verdana uses the FACE attribute and looks like this: *<FONT FACE=verdana>*. Text that is blue has the tag *<FONT COLOR=blue>*. You can even combine many attributes in one tag. If you want a font that is purple and Courier, use the tag *<FONT COLOR=purple FACE=courier>*. If you have a page with a dark background, you can change the color of the text by adding the TEXT=color attribute to the BODY tag. Look for tags like these in your source code.

7. Locate three other advanced tags and guess what they do. Write the information in the table below.

8. Leave your Web browser open and proceed to the next Step-by-Step.

Tag	Purpose
1.	
2.	
3.	

Reach Out With Links and Images Too

Links allow you to reach out to the world and quickly transport information from one edge of the earth to the other. Let's add some links to your page.

S T E P - B Y - S T E P ⟹ 17.2

1. Open your browser and search for sites dedicated to three of your favorite TV shows. Record the URLs below.
   1.

   2.

3.

2. Open your Web page in a text editor.

3. For each of your favorite TV shows, add the anchor tags as shown below, substituting your shows and their respective URLs for those shown:

\<H3>My Favorite TV Shows\</H3>

\<OL>

\<LI>\<A HREF="http://www.crocodile-hunter.com">Crocodile Hunter\</A>

\<LI>\<A HREF="http://www.mondaynight-football.com">Monday Night Football\</A>

\<LI>\<A HREF="http://news.bbc.co.uk">BBC World News\</A>

\</OL>

4. When you have finished adding the tags, save your file. Open your Web page in your browser to view the changes. Did your hyperlinks appear underlined, as in Figure 17-2?

5. Go to **www.course.com/downloads/swep/ internetbasics**. Select the **Lesson 17** link. Find the image of Mark Web and download it to the same folder in which you have your HTML file. Note that you can use a different graphic if you like, but follow the same steps listed here. Make sure you remember the name of the file so you can enter it with exactly the same name as in Step 7.

FIGURE 17-2
Links in your Web page

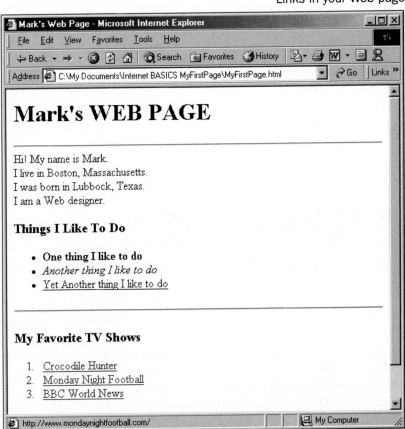

269

6. Go back to your text editor. Now let's add an image.

7. After the </OL> tag on your Web page, insert a **<P>** tag to add a new paragraph. Now add an image source tag with the name of your image, as shown below. (Note: The image search <IMG SRC> tag does not need a closing tag.)

<IMG SRC="markweb.gif">

8. Make your image a link. Add an anchor tag before and after the image source tag like this:

<A HREF="http://www.course.com/ downloads/swep/internetbasics"><IMG SRC="markweb.gif"></A>

9. Save your document. It should look similar to Figure 17-3. Refresh your Web page in your browser. It should look similar to Figure 17-4.

10. Add some additional links and images to your Web page. Continue to the next Step-by-Step, leaving your Web browser open.

FIGURE 17-3
Your HTML page now has images

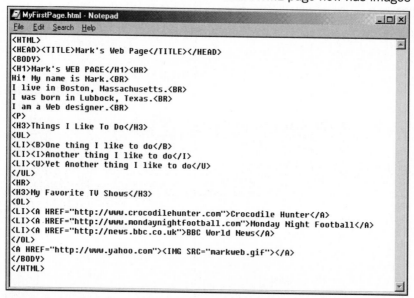

```
MyFirstPage.html - Notepad                          _|□|×|
File  Edit  Search  Help
<HTML>
<HEAD><TITLE>Mark's Web Page</TITLE></HEAD>
<BODY>
<H1>Mark's WEB PAGE</H1><HR>
Hi! My name is Mark.<BR>
I live in Boston, Massachusetts.<BR>
I was born in Lubbock, Texas.<BR>
I am a Web designer.<BR>
<P>
<H3>Things I Like To Do</H3>
<UL>
<LI><B>One thing I like to do</B>
<LI><I>Another thing I like to do</I>
<LI><U>Yet Another thing I like to do</U>
</UL>
<HR>
<H3>My Favorite TV Shows</H3>
<OL>
<LI><A HREF="http://www.crocodilehunter.com">Crocodile Hunter</A>
<LI><A HREF="http://www.mondaynightFootball.com">Monday Night Football</A>
<LI><A HREF="http://news.bbc.co.uk">BBC World News</A>
</OL>
<A HREF="http://www.yahoo.com"><IMG SRC="markweb.gif"></A>
</BODY>
</HTML>
```

NETIQUETTE

NET ETIQUETTE — HELPING OLDER BROWSERS ACROSS THE WEB

Today, browsers are more powerful than ever. They add capabilities to Web pages that go far beyond HTML. Tools like JavaScript, Java, and Shockwave add interest to Web pages.

Still, Web page creators often create two or three versions of Web pages to help out the folks in cyberspace who may not be able to upgrade to the latest and greatest browser. This is why you may be asked to select between a simple HTML version and a more enhanced version of a Web page. This is the highest form of Net Etiquette—going the extra mile to provide for the "browser-impaired."

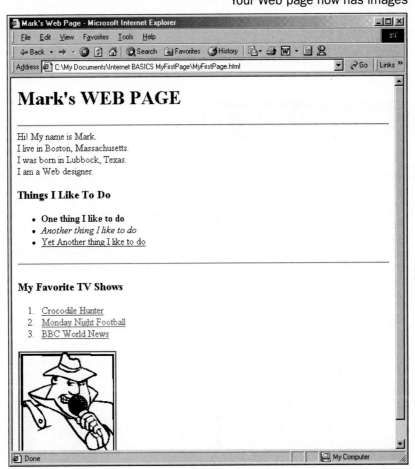

NET ETHICS

NET ETHICS — STEALING PICTURES

It is easy to "liberate" pictures off the Web. A couple of mouse clicks and it's yours. But should you take an image from the Web without permission? We were allowed to download the image for the last activity because it belongs to the publisher of this book. However, we found a really cool image of the Simpsons that we had to leave behind and not use because... well, you know.

Some people have taken copyrighted images, distorted them, and re-posted the mangled images back on the Web. This is considered unethical Web behavior. A Mickey Mouse vampire comes to mind. (Although a vampire Bart Simpson does seem in character.)

The Walt Disney Co., among others, has taken legal action against Web publishers who have used and misused their images without their express written consent. And a lawsuit is what such people deserve. What cyber-sicko would deface images meant for the child in all of us for the sake of a cheap joke? Come on…show some class!

Beautify Your Web World

In addition to images and links, you can use color in many creative ways to further enhance the appearance of a Web page. Let's change the background color of your page and make your list of favorite things all different colors!

STEP-BY-STEP ▷ 17.3

1. Open your HTML document in a text editor.

2. As you learned earlier, you can change the background color by adding the BGCOLOR= attribute to the BODY tag. Add this attribute to your Web page to change its background. It should look like this:

   <BODY BGCOLOR=beige>

3. If your text is too dark to read, add the TEXT and LINK attributes to brighten up all of your text and links as well, like this:

   <BODY   BGCOLOR=beige   TEXT=gray LINK=green>

4. Save your page and reload it in your browser. It should now look similar to Figure 17-5.

FIGURE 17-5
Now in living COLOR!

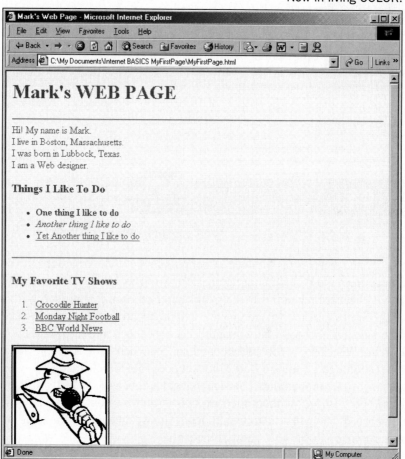

5. Now let's change the colors of your favorite things to your favorite colors. Switch back to your text editor.

6. Change the text color and font of your list of favorite things by adding the formatting tags as shown below:

<LI><FONT COLOR=red><B>One thing I like to do</B></FONT>

<LI><FONT FACE=courier><I>Another thing I like to do</I></FONT>

<LI><FONT FACE=verdana COLOR=purple><U>Yet Another thing I like to do</U></FONT>

7. Save your work and refresh your page in your browser. Did anything change? Your page should look similar to Figure 17-6.

8. Try playing around with what you now know about advanced HTML. Remember to close your browser if you are finished for the day. Before you end, however, print your page, take it home, and replace your first one on your refrigerator! Your parents will be even more impressed!

FIGURE 17-6
Fonts change too

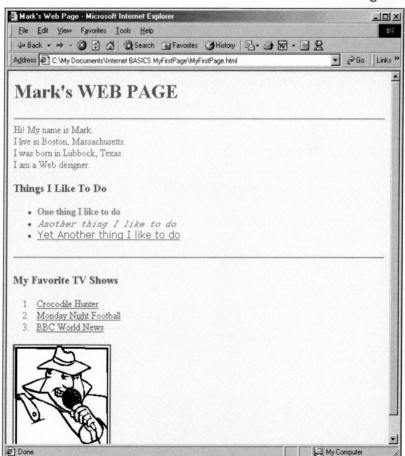

Summary

In this lesson you learned:

- You can use advanced HTML formatting tags.

- Links and images can be added to your Web page.

- You can change colors and fonts on your Web page.

- HTML can be used to bold, italicize, and underline text with HTML.

NET TERMS REVIEW

Define the following terms:

Anchor tag   Hypertext reference   Image source tag
Attribute

LESSON 17 REVIEW QUESTIONS

TRUE/FALSE

Circle T if the statement is true or F if the statement is false.

T F 1. You can add images to a page using the hypertext reference attribute.

T F 2. An attribute and a tag are the exact same thing.

T F 3. You can change text colors using the <FONT> tag with attributes.

T F 4. Your Web page will look exactly the same on every computer that pulls it up.

T F 5. You can link to another page using anchor tags.

FILL IN THE BLANK

Complete the following sentences by writing the correct word or words in the blanks provided.

1. The _____ tag doesn't need a closing tag because it simply places an image on a page.

2. A(n) _____ is not a tag, but it tells a tag to do something specific.

3. The _____ attribute to the <FONT> tag changes the font type to Verdana or to some other font.

4. You can create a link by using the _____ _____ attribute, which is entered as HREF.

5. The _____ attribute to the <BODY> tag will change the link's color.

WRITTEN QUESTIONS

Write a brief answer to the following questions.

1. What does BGCOLOR mean?

2. Explain what the <A HREF> tag and attribute do.

3. What does the <IMG SRC> tag and attribute tell the browser to do?

4. Describe what the <FONT> tag can do.

5. What does the FACE attribute do?

WEB PROJECT 17-1

CREATE A WORLD-CLASS SITE FOR GREATAPPLICATIONS, INC.

GreatApplications' board of directors liked the content you put in your Web site but feel that it could be spiced up a bit. They want a world-class site.

Using what you now know about Web design, sketch some ideas on a piece of paper. Will you use a lot of graphics? What about fonts? How will you organize the page?

If you need more ideas, visit more sites. Look for Top 5% sites, or sites that have won Internet awards. Follow some links from sites you've visited to find out where they lead.

Prepare a new Web site with new colors and graphics to present to the Board. Keep in mind that colors that are too bright or too dull won't look very good.

TEAMWORK PROJECT 17-2

HOSTING YOUR SITE

Now that you've put the site together and have the hardware to host it, get together with your team and figure out how much it will cost to host your site. Split up the following list among team members to see how much it will cost GreatApplications, Inc., to host its site for one year.

Domain Registration

Salary for the Webmaster

WYSIWYG HTML Editor

Online connection fee

Other

Create a report of prices on the costs for the Board to discuss and save it in your group's common folder.

CRITICAL THINKING

ACTIVITY 17-1

COLOR STATEMENTS

From your experiences with the Internet, why wouldn't you want a site with colors that are too bold or too dull? Write a 100- to 250-word response giving examples of Web sites where the colors just don't make it.

ACTIVITY 17-2

THE VALUE OF TAGS

Many software products on the market can make HTML coding very simple. Using these products, you might not even have to see the HTML tags. Is it still valuable to understand something about the way tags work? Why or why not? Write a 100- to 200-word response to these questions.

ACTIVITY 17-3

REASONS TO UPDATE

Some Board members at GreatApplications don't want to invest more money in an updated Web site. Write a 100- to 200-word report that explains to the Board how a poorly organized site can harm a business.

MULTIMEDIA ON THE NET: ENHANCING THE USER EXPERIENCE

OBJECTIVES

Upon completion of this lesson, you should be able to:

- Discuss and view Shockwave and Flash.
- Discuss Java and run Java applets.
- Identify and discuss several Internet programming languages and graphic file formats.
- Explore VRML worlds.
- Search for information about other Web technologies.

⏱ **Estimated Time: 2 hours**

NET TERMS

.gif

.jpg or .jpeg

ActiveX

Applets

Common Gateway Interface (CGI)

Dynamic Hypertext Markup Language (DHTML)

Extensible Markup Language (XML)

Flash

Java

JavaScript

Just in Time (JIT)

Platform

Plug-ins

Practical Extraction and Report Language (Perl)

Shockwave

Hot Languages For Cool Web Effects

HTML is a very simple language. Although it is evolving all the time, it can go only so far in presenting information. Now there are some new tools on the block, and they are turning the Internet upside down.

Two of the most important newcomers are **Shockwave** and its little brother **Flash**. Shockwave and Flash can add a high level of interactivity to any Web site. Rather than simply clicking links, you navigate through a whole site using fully animated buttons and text. You can even play Shockwave and Flash games. Many online sites use these tools. For example, NASA added some excitement to its International Space Station Team site, as seen in Figure 18-1.

FIGURE 18-1
NASA used Shockwave to promote its Space Station

Another important Web technology is *Java*. Java is a complex programming language that allows a program to be written once and used on any operating system *platform*. Windows, Macintosh, Linux, and Unix are all different operating system platforms. Java saves a lot of time since programs don't have to be rewritten for each platform. Java Web programs are called *applets:* tiny programs that can be attached to HTML pages. Examples include animated characters, scrolling text, and simple games.

JavaScript is a less powerful computer language than Java, but it is easier to learn and use. Instead of creating programs attached to Web pages, JavaScript places a list or scripted set of commands in the HTML page itself. JavaScript requires less software to create and works very well for certain specialized tasks.

ActiveX is Microsoft's answer to the problem of linking traditional software to the Internet. ActiveX transforms applications like Word or Excel into powerful Web tools.

Another newcomer is Virtual Reality Modeling Language (VRML). VRML is a language used to create 3D "worlds" where you can interact with objects in a virtual setting that seems almost real.

> **Net Tip**
>
> You may need to install *plug-ins* or special adapters to use some of these tools. Check with your instructor to see if your computer has plug-ins already installed. Upgrading your software is the best way to keep up with all of these new enhancements for the Web.

News Flash — Interactive Web Sites

Shockwave and Flash give incredibly high interactivity to any Web site. Not only can you click buttons that make sounds or load pages that play music in the background, but you can also play video games and watch short movies. Many sites use Shockwave and Flash to introduce their site with a bang. Let's find some examples.

STEP-BY-STEP 18.1

1. Start your browser and go to **www.shockwave.com**.

2. Select the **Games** link at the top of the page and choose **Puzzles,** as seen in Figure 18.2.

FIGURE 18-2
Puzzles on *Shockwave.com*

3. Try some of the puzzles and see if you like them.

4. Return to the Shockwave **Games** link and choose a game category. Select a game from the next page. Have fun for a minute or two and watch how Shockwave and Flash can make high-quality Internet games!

5. Find three other sites that use Shockwave to add interactivity to their sites and then list the Shockwave site URL or Web address on the lines below:
   1.

2.

3.

Keep your Web browser open for the next Step-by-Step.

NET ETHICS

COMPETITION OR STANDARDIZATION?

It always happens. A healthy competition between companies causes them to create differences in their products. Product differences run counter to the spirit of the Web and to HTML, which stresses a common set of standards that everyone can use and access. Because of the browser wars, Microsoft, Sun, Oracle, and Netscape have added all sorts of enhancements to the Web experience. These exciting new features go way beyond the carefully constructed open standards produced by the Executive Review Board (ERB) at the World Wide Web Consortium (W3C).

Java — What Can You Do For Me Today?

Java was created to enable household appliances to communicate with each other, believe it or not. Although the development of the smart appliance didn't go very far, Java programmers found another way to keep the language alive: the Internet.

Because all kinds of computer platforms have access to the Internet, it made sense to create a language that would allow programs to be written once and played via any Web browser on any kind of computer system. This feature is called "write once, deliver anywhere."

We'll visit a few sites that use Java, so you can see how it enhances your Internet experience.

Net Concept

Microsoft is taking a lead in extending HTML in new directions. One new innovation is called *Dynamic Hypertext Markup Language,* or *DHTML*. Dynamic HTML allows users to move and manipulate objects on the Web page as easily as they manipulate icons on their Window's computer desktop. Visit Microsoft's site at *www.microsoft.com* and use the *Search* feature to find demonstrations of DHTML in action.

STEP-BY-STEP 18.2

1. Visit **java.sun.com**.

2. Choose the **Products & APIs** link, then the **Applets** link.

3. Read about applets available online and describe below what two of them do:
   1.

   2.

4. Look for a link to **Hangman**. Play the Java game and see if you can make Duke dance with glee (see Figure 18-3). (Note: As an alternative assignment, visit the free applets available on the site and see if there are any you would like to add to your personal Web page!)

5. Now check out some other applets. Which applet do you like the best? Why? Keep your Web browser open for the next Step-by-Step.

FIGURE 18-3
Duke survived...this time

Hang Duke

Try to guess the secret word and save Duke.

Type in a letter you think is in the secret word; you only get five wrong guesses so be careful.

p o k

circumstance

The source.

A Walk in the Virtual Park

VRML allows the creation of three-dimensional worlds. You can walk through these worlds, look up or down, turn around, or change your camera angle.

Many believe that the Internet of the future will be a true virtual reality experience. You will be able to walk into buildings and open doors to view the information for which you are searching. Hollywood has certainly provided some interesting views of the possible future in movies like *Toy Story*. Will virtual reality ever be like that? Only time will tell. Meanwhile, find out what VRML is being used for here in the present. Note: You will need a VRML plug-in for the following Step-by-Step to work correctly. Make sure your instructor has installed a plug-in like *Cosmo* so you can explore the VRML world.

INTERNET MILESTONE

SUN'S JAVA LANGUAGE

Java was created by Sun Microsystems (*www.sun.com*) as a compact programming language for electronic appliances, such as VCRs, satellite receivers, and microwaves. First called Greentalk and later Oak, Java was apparently named after a type of coffee several of the Sun developers were drinking one day. Little did the creators at Sun know that Java would become the next big milestone in Internet history.

Java is to programming languages what HTML is to publishing. Java solves the problem of how to create software programs that can be delivered quickly and easily through the Web to any kind of computer. The theory is that you can write one program and have any computer—Macintosh, Windows, or Unix—run the program with the help of a ***Just in Time (JIT)*** compiler built into a Java-enabled Web browser. JIT turns commands into programs as soon as you wish to run them.

1. First, let's meet Floops, one of the most interesting VRML characters on the Internet. Go to **www.protozoa.com/backstage/floops.html**. Figure 18-4 shows the buttons that control movements through this virtual world.

2. Choose one of the Floops categories.

3. On the next page, pick one of the Floops scenes and choose embedded (small) or full screen (large) to load the *.wrl* file.

FIGURE 18-4
Meet Floops

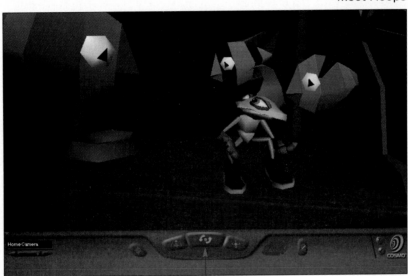

Use these buttons to manipulate the environment

INTERNET MILESTONE

GRAPHICS ON THE WEB

The two most commonly used graphics formats on the Web are *.jpg* (or *.jpeg*) and *.gif*. The .jpg or .jpeg graphics format was defined by an international committee called the Joint Photographic Experts Group. JPEG images can contain millions of colors for photographs or other high-quality graphics.

The .gif extension stands for Graphics Interchange Format and was originally created by CompuServe to share graphics easily over the Web. GIF files can contain only 256 colors, but they can be animated and have transparency effects that allow them to blend into a Web page background. Both formats compress the large graphics files so that Web browsers can display the pictures quickly.

4. When the Floops scene has finished loading, click inside the frame to start the animation. What do you think of the little guy?

5. While the animation is playing, experiment with the plug-in controls and see what happens.

6. Search for other cool VRML sites and record below what you found. Have fun exploring!

7. Close your Web browser if you are finished for today.

Net Tip

VRML uses *.wrl* files for its worlds. These files tend to be rather large and can take a while to download. Be patient.

	Address	What does the site contain?
1.		
2.		
3.		

INTERNET MILESTONE

SUN'S JAVA LANGUAGE

Other scripting languages and markup language tools are also popular, including CGI, XML, and Perl.

Common Gateway Interface (CGI) is a recognized standard for interfacing applications, like database programs, with Web servers and Web pages. CGI allows users to interact through Web pages. For example, with CGI you can create a form in which site visitors enter data and the data go to the server for processing.

Practical Extraction and Report Language (Perl) is designed to handle a variety of system administrator functions. Both CGI and Perl can link programs and databases together with Web pages to perform complex functions.

Extensible Markup Language (XML) allows Web page designers to create styles of Web pages and to define how things will look in a browser, which goes far beyond what HTML provides.

Summary

In this lesson, you learned:

■ Shockwave and Flash add interactivity to Web sites.

■ Java has animated applets.

■ You can identify and discuss several Internet programming languages.

■ There are different Web graphic file formats.

■ The 3D VRML worlds are yours to explore.

■ You can search for information about other Web technologies.

NET TERMS REVIEW

Define the following terms.

.gif	DHTML	JIT
.jpg or .jpeg	XML	Platform
ActiveX	Flash	Plug-ins
Applets	Java	Perl
CGI	JavaScript	Shockwave

LESSON 18 REVIEW QUESTIONS

TRUE/FALSE

Circle T if the statement is true or F if the statement is false.

T F **1.** Shockwave sites are normally dull and nondynamic.

T F **2.** VRML sites allow you to browse through and manipulate 3D environments.

T F **3.** You can run a Java program only on Windows computers.

T F **4.** Java Applets work with HTML exactly like JavaScript commands do.

T F **5.** Java was originally created to power electronic appliances.

FILL IN THE BLANK

Complete the following sentences by writing the correct word or words in the blanks provided.

1. _____ is Microsoft's product that allows products like Microsoft Word to integrate with the Web.

2. Java was once called _____ and then _____.

3. Files in the ._____ format can have only 256 colors but can be animated.

4. Files in the ._____ format can have millions of colors and are used for photos on the Web.

5. DHTML stands for _____ HTML.

WRITTEN QUESTIONS

Write a brief answer to the following questions.

1. What is the main advantage of the Java programming language?

2. What is VRML and how does it differ from HTML?

3. How would you go about searching for VRML sites?

4. How does an applet work?

5. In what way is Shockwave a valuable interactivity and advertising tool?

LESSON 18 PROJECTS

WEB PROJECT 18-1

A Virtual-World Site for GreatApplications, Inc.

You've already given a report to the board of directors at GreatApplications, Inc., on how to build an effective Web site for the business. You even helped to design the site. You have been introduced to Java and VRML and have gained a vision of the future of the Internet. Locate Java and VRML sites that are being used for commercial purposes and bookmark them for a new presentation to the board of directors.

Your presentation should be a 250-word report in the form of an e-mail message that you will send to the Board.

You may want to include links to a couple of the fun sites you've seen in your e-mail report, but only do so to illustrate ways of making the site practical in a business setting.

Remember that the board of directors is open-minded as long as the company makes money from the site. They want to be sure that whatever money they spend setting up Web sites or creating VRML worlds is going to come back in increased revenues.

TEAMWORK PROJECT 18-2

Web Technologies for the Future

The board of directors at GreatApplications, Inc., was not pleased with your earlier report about Java and VRML. The report came back with a huge "INCOMPLETE" stamped over the cover page. A note was attached stating the following:

"Oops. Time to get the team together and fix the mistake. We have heard of other technologies that may serve our company's needs better than Java and VRML. Please investigate the following: JavaScript, JScript, DHTML, Animated GIFs, ActiveX, XML, VBScript, Perl, and CGI. If you find any Net technologies worth knowing about, put them in your team report."

This task is too big to do alone. Divide up the list and learn as much as you can about the technologies listed by the Board. Add *streaming technology* to the list and see what you can find out about the Web browser Opera. That should impress them. Also, don't leave out Shockwave and Flash.

Here are some obvious places to start looking:

Microsoft *www.microsoft.com*
SunMicrosystems *www.sun.com*
Netscape *www.netscape.com*
Oracle *www.oracle.com*
Internet Week *www.internetweek.com*

Also, try searching technical magazines. Use your search portals to find these resources. You may not be able to find information on all the technologies, but if you do your homework, you can make an impressive report at the board meeting.

Sites like the Internet Week Web site *www.internetweek.com*, illustrated in Figure 18-5, offer top-quality reviews of Internet technologies. This site will help you research some of these difficult technical topics.

FIGURE 18-5
Technology reviews on Internet Week

Save your research in your personal research folder.

Prepare a 250-word report detailing the following information for each technology your team has researched:

1. Describe what the technology can do. What are its major effects on the Net and how can it help the customers of GreatApplications, Inc.?

2. Explain who invented or created the technology and who supports it.

3. Describe its potential five years from now. Will the technology still be in use?

4. Define what would be needed in terms of personnel, money, equipment, software, and resources to use this technology. Is this technology cost-effective?

CRITICAL THINKING

ACTIVITY 18-1

Breaking Standards

New Internet features force people to upgrade their software or miss out on the special effects the new features provide. Should companies be allowed to go beyond the recognized Web standards? Should they be able to push users into new products and software? Are companies free to compete, to innovate, and to create a better mousetrap? Can competition produce better browsers, better Net features, and a more exciting and powerful Internet? Would anyone really want to hold Microsoft, Netscape, Oracle, Sun, and other companies back as they seek to gain a competitive edge? Write a 250- to 500-word response to these questions.

ACTIVITY 18-2

Predicting the Future of the Web

You've seen a lot of exciting things through this course. You have also learned valuable skills that will help you through college and in the working world. For this assignment, evaluate the current state of the Internet. How was your experience? Will the Internet be helpful and useful to you in the future, or will it be merely entertaining? What technologies do you think will be more developed in the future? What is missing from the Internet that could make it a better experience? Can you live a productive life without it? Write a 250- to 500-word response to these questions.

MOVIES, TV, MUSIC: THE WEB'S GOT YOU COVERED

OBJECTIVES

Upon completion of this lesson, you should be able to:

- Discuss new technologies that enable audio, video, and animations on the Web.

- Find movie reviews and show times.

- Watch movie trailers online.

- Search for television-related sites and watch streaming TV.

- Find music-related sites and listen to the radio over the Internet.

- Locate sports-related sites.

⏱ **Estimated Time: 2.5 hours**

NET TERMS

MP3

Napster

Plug-in

Shawn Fanning

Streaming

Trailer

WebTV

All Work and No Play...

All work and no play makes for a pretty dull day. Even the scientists who invented the Internet thought so. Remember the first newsgroup you learned about in this book? It wasn't about the project the scientists were working on. It was a group for people to talk about science fiction books.

In this lesson, you'll discuss some of the resources available to help make the most of your recreation time. The Internet isn't going to replace all other forms of media or entertainment, but it will add to your fun.

 Net Tip

New technology and new data-handling processes are making Web browsing a full multimedia experience. With technologies such as QuickTime and Windows Media Player, you can now watch the foreign news, pull up your favorite movie trailers, or listen to Internet radio stations all over the world while you're online.

Let's Go to the Movies!

The Internet is becoming a marketing vehicle for the movie industry. Months before a movie is released, a Web site can be set up to increase the hype. You can even visit Web sites where you can download full movie *trailers*, which are short advertisements for an upcoming movie.

Reviews of current and past movies are posted all over the Net. You can even find lists of what some people believe are the best and worst movies ever made. More and more theaters are posting movie times on the Web, which is great. No more busy signals when you're trying to find out when a movie is playing.

Let's see what's playing right now!

STEP-BY-STEP ▷ 19.1

1. Go to your favorite search portal and find and select a **Movies** link.

2. Most search portals contain links to what is playing and when, along with reviews of new movies. Many portals also allow you to enter your ZIP code, city, or the title of the movie to find a theater closest to you (see Figure 19-1).

3. Record on the next page the movie theaters and times for five movies you want to see.

FIGURE 19-1
Movies at Yahoo!

MOVIE THEATER	SHOWTIME
1.	
2.	
3.	
4.	
5.	

4. Select a movie that is currently playing. If you follow the link, your search portal will take you to a review and synopsis of the movie.

5. Return to your search portal and search for the **QuickTime Movie Trailers** page (shown in Figure 19-2) hosted by Apple. This page contains QuickTime movies of current and recent movie trailers.

FIGURE 19-2
QuickTime Movie Trailers Theater

6. Find your favorite new movie from the list and follow the link to its trailer. Click the movie to play it. Try to search for other Web sites that contain movie trailers for upcoming movies. Leave your Web browser open for the next Step-by-Step.

 Net Tip

To fully experience the really cool animations and multimedia effects on most entertainment Web sites, you may need to have the Shockwave or Flash plug-in installed in your browser. A ***plug-in*** is an auxiliary program that works with major browsers to enhance its capability. For example, if your browser doesn't have the Shockwave player or you want to update your version of it, go to *www.macromedia.com* and download it!

Couch Potato's Guide To TV

You can now watch live streaming TV over the Internet because new processes for transferring data are improving the distribution of audio and video on the Internet. *Streaming* is a data-handling process that enables music and video to flow continuously. With QuickTime, RealPlayer, and Windows Media Player, it is now possible to watch your favorite show or news programs without turning on your television.

Web sites for TV shows are extremely popular. While only one site can be the official site, hundreds of unofficial sites are likely to spring up all over the Internet. You can find lists to past episodes, hear sound bites, and view pictures from the latest episodes of popular programs.

INTERNET MILESTONE

INTERNET MILESTONE — CONNECTING ANYWHERE, ANYTIME, WITH MULTIPLE DEVICES

Larry Ellison, founder of Oracle Corporation, wondered why people needed to buy expensive computers to connect with the Internet. If the resources are already on the Net, why can't the resources be accessed by inexpensive network computers so that nearly everyone can afford to take advantage of the Web?

Wireless telephone companies weren't far behind in this way of thinking. They realized that if you can access information on inexpensive Internet appliances, you can also access your e-mail and favorite Web pages from your wireless phone. As a result of this thinking, more people in the world access the Net from their phone than from a PC.

Not to be outdone, Microsoft announced they would be supporting tablet computers. Tablet computers look like notebooks with a computer screen. You can write on the screens with the pen-like device. Tablet computers don't have keyboards and can connect wirelessly to the Web.

Need to pick up some tickets quickly for the game tonight? Log onto the Net with your wireless telephone or a network computer in a kiosk at the mall and order your tickets. Leave your research paper home? No problem. Download it to your palm-held computer and beam the paper to the nearest printer. Today you can connect anytime, anywhere, with multiple kinds of devices.

1. Most search portals feature categories devoted to television, usually located in the *Recreation* or *Entertainment* sections. (For example, in Yahoo!, click the **Entertainment** section.) Find your favorite portal and start searching!

2. Browse until you see a menu of TV show categories, as illustrated in Figure 19-3.

FIGURE 19-3
Yahoo! TV categories

Categories

- Action and Adventure *(238)* NEW!
- Animation *(1384)* NEW!
- Arts and Humanities *(61)* NEW!
- Business and Economy *(21)* NEW!
- Children *(331)* NEW!
- College and University *(12)*
- Comedies *(1273)* NEW!
- Cop Shows *(272)* NEW!
- Dramas *(820)* NEW!
- Education *(3)*
- Game Shows *(123)* NEW!
- Health *(11)*
- Horror *(454)* NEW!
- Lawyer Shows *(71)*
- Medical Dramas *(127)* NEW!
- Military Shows *(69)*
- Movie and Film Reviews *(7)*
- Movies on Television *(34)*

- Music *(39)* NEW!
- Mystery *(55)* NEW!
- News *(84)*
- Prime-Time Soaps *(109)* NEW!
- Public Access *(123)*
- Real-Life Mystery *(11)*
- Reality Television *(358)* NEW!
- Recreation and Sports *(216)* NEW!
- Science *(99)*
- Science Fiction and Fantasy *(1713)* NEW!
- Sketch Comedy *(103)*
- Soap Operas *(410)* NEW!
- Society and Culture *(89)*
- Spy Shows *(24)*
- Talk Shows *(162)* NEW!
- Variety *(29)*
- Web Directories@
- Westerns *(65)* NEW!

3. Find an episode guide to *Friends*, one of the longest-running, most watched television shows in history, and answer the questions below.
   1. When did the first episode air?

   2. How many episodes total have been aired so far?

4. Now find the show called *Who Wants to Be a Millionaire?* and answer the questions below.
   1. How many categories at Yahoo! are dedicated to *Who Wants to Be a Millionaire*?

   2. What is the address of the official Web site of *Who Wants to Be a Millionaire*?

5. Now, let's actually watch some TV. Go to **headlinenews.cnn.com**.

6. Choose **Video**, then look for the link that says **CNN QuickCast** and choose it.

7. In the window that pops up, select your media player (QuickTime, RealPlayer, or Windows Media Player) and Internet connection speed (see Figures 19-4A, 19-4B, and 19-4C). In a few moments, that page will refresh and you will be watching CNN Headline News live over the Internet! What are today's top three news headlines?

1.

2.

3.

8. Find some other TV stations that you can watch live on your computer over the Net. Leave your Web browser open for the next Step-by-Step.

FIGURE 19-4A
CNN Headline News live in QuickTime

FIGURE 19-4B
RealPlayer's version of the News

FIGURE 19-4C
Full streaming video in Windows Media Player

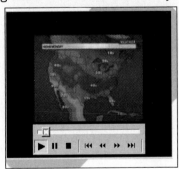

Lesson 19 Movies, TV, Music: The Web's Got You Covered

The Digital Music Revolution

In case you haven't noticed, there's a music revolution going on. New audio formats allow you to listen to the radio right over the Internet. A format known as *MP3* allows songs to be compressed to one-tenth their normal size without losing the CD quality of the sound. The format has become very popular as a means of sharing audio on the Web. QuickTime, Windows Media Player, and RealPlayer all allow you to play this special format on your computer.

Let's find some online music!

NET ETHICS

NET ETHICS — NAPSTER

Napster was founded in May 1999 by **Shawn Fanning** as a way for Net users to share music over the Web. The service has grown to have over 40 million users. Over 9 terabytes (9,000 gigabytes) of music files are shared with Napster at any given time.

Because users can share any MP3 files, many music artists filed lawsuits against Napster claiming that their copyrights have been infringed. In fact, the Recording Industry Association of America (RIAA) filed a lawsuit claiming that Napster promotes music piracy.

On the other hand, many artists feel that Napster is a cheap and easy way for new musicians to make their music available online and many feel it is a good way to promote their music.

What's your opinion on this issue?

INTERNET MILESTONE

NET MILESTONE — STREAMING

Audio and video streaming is a process for compressing audio and video signals so they can be sent easily over the Net. The compressed signals are then captured in a buffer, decompressed, and played as continuous sound and video.

The player that made streaming popular was RealPlayer from RealNetworks. Other companies like Apple and Microsoft have added QuickTime and Windows Media Player. Visit their sites (see below) and download the players. Some are free, and others charge a fee. Try a free player and experience streaming. You'll like it.

RealPlayer www.real.com
QuickTime www.apple.com/quicktime
Windows Media Player www.microsoft.com/windowsmedia

STEP-BY-STEP ▷ 19.3

1. Conduct a search for online digital music. For example, you can go to the AltaVista search portal at **www.altavista.com** or choose another search portal.

2. At AltaVista you can choose **Multimedia Search** and choose **MP3/Audio,** as illustrated in Figure 19-5. You can also search using the keyword **MP3** with another search tool.

FIGURE 19-5
MP3/Audio search at AltaVista

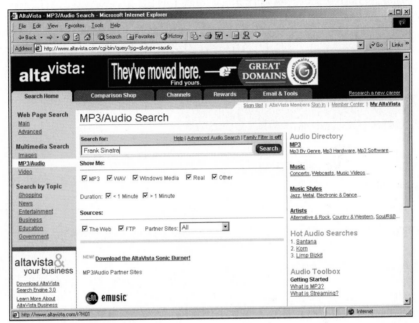

3. Search for your favorite artist or song. AltaVista and other search portals will look for MP3 files as well as WAV and program specific files.

4. Choose a song to listen to. It will open in your default player and play as it downloads. See if you can locate a radio station that plays your type of music. If you can find one, AltaVista or another portal will open a new window and stream the radio station right to your computer!

5. Search for music and radio stations using other search portals.

6. Don't close the Web browser just yet. See if you have enough time left to complete the next exercise!

Sports for the Armchair Quarterback

The Internet is a great place for major sports. You can find schedules, stats, records, reports from last night's big game, player profiles, and video of the game-winning last-second shot.

But what if you like obscure sports, like camel racing or curling? Or what if you want to find out the best places in the country to fly fish? The Internet probably has a page for you to visit, too. Let's find some of the many resources available for sports fans.

Net Tip

You can now track all the major sporting events on the Web. For instance, take pro football at *www.nfl.com*. At a site like this, you can keep track of every NFL game as the games progress. You can also watch game highlights and review game stats.

S TEP-BY-STEP ▷ 19.4

1. Find five sports sites with information about major league sports.

SITE SPONSOR OR OWNER	URL OR WEB ADDRESS
1.	
2.	
3.	
4.	
5.	

2. Find five sites related to less familiar or less popular sports.

NAME OF SPORT	URL OR WEB ADDRESS
1.	
2.	
3.	
4.	
5.	

3. Locate schedules for the following organizations. (Note: See an example in Figure 19-6.)

PROFESSIONAL ORGANIZATION	URL OR WEB ADDRESS
1. Women's Professional Volleyball Association	
2. Ladies Professional Golf Association	
3. National Basketball Association	
4. National Football League	
5. Women's Tennis Association	

FIGURE 19-6
Track sports all through the season online

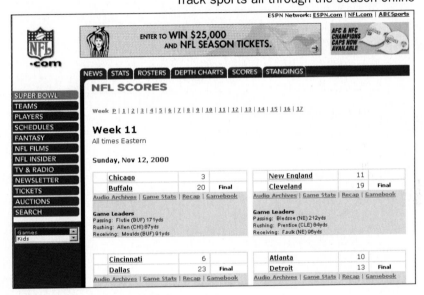

4. Here's a challenge. Search and find a current roster for the U. S. National Volleyball Teams. Record in the table on the next page.

WOMEN'S NATIONAL VOLLEYBALL TEAM ROSTER	MEN'S NATIONAL VOLLEYBALL TEAM ROSTER
1.	1.
2.	2.
3.	3.
4.	4.
5.	5.
6.	6.
7.	7.
8.	8.
9.	9.
10.	10.
11.	11.
12.	12.

5. Find three Internet TV stations that broadcast sporting events. Close your Web browser if you are finished with this book!

NET TV STATION	URL OR WEB ADDRESS
1.	
2.	
3.	

INTERNET MILESTONE

INTERNET MILESTONE — WEBTV

WebTV was the first attempt to merge the Internet and your TV set. Using any Internet TV receiver and your phone line, you can get online without a computer! Not a big seller in its first years, WebTV has started to take hold. WebTV provides another great entertainment option for less cost than a traditional computer system. For more information about WebTV, visit *www.webtv.com.*

Summary

In this lesson, you learned:

■ You can enjoy audio, video, and animations on the Web.

■ Movie reviews and show times are on the Net.

■ Movie trailers can be found online.

■ You can find television-related sites.

■ Streaming TV can be viewed over the Internet.

■ The radio can be listened to over the Internet.

■ You can locate sports-related sites.

NET TERMS REVIEW

Define the following terms.

MP3	Shawn Fanning	WebTV
Napster	Streaming	
Plug-in	Trailer	

LESSON 19 REVIEW QUESTIONS

TRUE/FALSE

Circle T if the statement is true or F if the statement is false.

T F 1. MP3 stands for Multi-Player games that support three players at once.

T F 2. Streaming video allows you to watch TV without having to download the whole file first.

T F 3. You can watch news anytime from any computer using the Internet.

T F 4. QuickTime is a program that acts like a digital clock on your computer.

T F 5. A network computer requires only an Internet connection; everything else is provided by a server.

FILL IN THE BLANK

Complete the following sentences by writing the correct word or words in the blanks provided.

1. _____ allows you to surf the Web on your television.

2. You can watch movies online using _____ technology, meaning you can watch it as it downloads.

3. Network computers were first developed by a company called _____.

4. _____ is a program that allows you to share MP3s for free, but its legality has been challenged in court.

5. Three major programs — _____, _____, and _____ _____ _____ — allow you to play MP3s, video, and TV over the Internet.

WRITTEN QUESTIONS

Write a brief answer to the following questions.

1. You are on a business trip to Boulder, Colorado. You have finished your business for the day, but it's still early, so you thought you would take in a movie. After a long day, a good comedy will help you relax. But you don't know where any theaters are in this city or what movies are playing. Explain the steps you would follow to select a comedy to watch online.

2. Explain how WebTV differs from a traditional personal computer accessing the Net.

3. You have always liked the TV show *Frasier* and you'd like to find out what other shows Kelsey Grammer has acted in. How would you find this information?

4. More and more, the Net is being used by the entertainment industry to promote its products. Is this increase in commercialization a good thing or a bad thing? Who benefits from commercialization: the entertainment companies, Net users, or both?

5. Discuss how you would listen to music on the Net.

LESSON 19 PROJECTS

WEB PROJECT 19-1

MOVIE CRITIC

The office isn't all work. Most of the folks at GreatApplications, Inc., are moviegoers. Several of your friends at work have asked you to circulate a weekly newsletter containing movie reviews that can be read on their lunch break. Find reviews for new movies being released this week. Summarize the reviews or paste them into a document named **Movie Reviews**.

TEAMWORK PROJECT 19-2

GAMES DEBATE

Debate the ethical issues of playing games on the job. Should employees be allowed to use the company computers to play games? If so, when and under what conditions? Summarize your team's discussion in a short report. Be sure to save your work.

CRITICAL THINKING

ACTIVITY 19-1

THE WEB AND THE MOVIES

Why do you think moviemakers are so eager to have a presence on the Net? Do you think there is a correlation between box office sales and Net promotions? What other entertainment businesses do you think could increase their sales by offering a Web site? Prepare a 100- to 250-word answer to these questions.

ACTIVITY 19-2

TELEVISION ADVICE FROM THE WEB

How much attention do you think TV producers should pay to comments and e-mail from Internet users? Do you see a time when Internet feedback will affect programming? Plots? The quality of programming? Commercials? Prepare a 100- to 250-word answer to these questions.

ACTIVITY 19-3

BLOCKING THE STREAM

Streaming is one of the more exciting data transfer processes developed for online media. Sound and movie files tend to be large and require a lot of time to download before they can be played on your computer. Streaming allows them to play as they download. However, streaming can fall apart when Internet traffic is too high. How was your experience? Can you think of ways online radio and television can be improved? Prepare a 100- to 250-word answer to these questions.

ACTIVITY 19-4

CLIPPING THE CLIPS

Many Web sites post screen shots and sound bites from their favorite TV shows. The problem is that this material is copyright-protected property of the network that owns the show. These unofficial sites can be shut down and the site owners can be prosecuted for breaking the law. Some people argue that posting small pieces of TV shows on the Web site shouldn't be illegal. After all, these sites are feeding the popularity of the show. What do you think about this issue? How can it be resolved fairly for both sides? Write a 100- to 250-word response.

Sprechen Sie Internet: How the Internet Speaks and Sparkles

REVIEW QUESTIONS

TRUE/FALSE

Circle T if the statement is true or F if the statement is false.

T F   1. HTML files contain tags.

T F   2. The </HTML> tag is usually the first tag on a Web page.

T F   3. Modern Web browsers don't allow the user to view the source HTML code.

T F   4. The <PICTURE => tag places graphics and photos in Web pages.

T F   5. All pictures found on the World Wide Web are in the public domain and are free from copyright restrictions.

T F   6. Netiquette is a software program used to download MP3 files over the Internet.

T F   7. Java is a more complex language than JavaScript.

T F   8. Shockwave and Flash can add high levels of interactivity to Web pages.

T F   9. HTML Web pages are also called applets.

T F   10. Streaming is a data handling process enabling music and video to flow continuously to listeners on the Internet.

MATCHING

Match the correct term in column 2 to its description in column 1.

Column 1   **Column 2**

___ 1. Extension used to identify an HTML file.   **A.** <IMG SRC=>

___ 2. Displays information about the Web page in the title bar.   **B.** <I>

___ 3. Allows images to become the background to a Web page.   **C.** <BODY BACKGROUND =>

___ 4. Identifies everything that will actually appear in a Web browser. **D.** <A HREF=>

___ 5. Tag used to create hypertext links.   **E.** <OL>

___ 6. Creates a line in a Web page.   **F.** <HR>

___ 7. Will make text boldface in a Web page.   **G.** <B>

___ 8. Will italicize text in a Web page.   **H.** <TITLE>

___ 9. Will create numbered lists in a Web page.   **I.** <BODY>

___ 10. Allows images to be inserted into a Web page.   **J.** htm

CROSS-CURRICULAR ACTIVITIES

In this final unit review, organize some of the best information resources you have found in previous units and create Web pages to catalog these sources. Build your own Web library of academic and technical information.

ART 5-1

Create a Web page with hypertext links to ten museums or cultural organizations that you can use for future reference as you study the arts and humanities. Save this file as **Art 5-1.html**.

MUSIC 5-1

Create a Web page with ten hypertext links leading to your top ten music sites. Make sure you include sites from a broad range of music. Save this file as **Music 5-1.html**.

LANGUAGE ARTS 5-1

Create a Web page containing ten hypertext links leading to information about your ten favorite authors. Save this Web page as **Language Arts 5-1.html**.

MATH 5-1

Organize a Web page with ten hypertext links leading to sources of information that may help you in your mastery of mathematical subjects. Save this Web page as **Math 5-1.html.**

HISTORY 5-1

Organize a Web page with a dozen sources of information regarding history. Have at least four of the sources lead to resources concerned with local history. Have another four links lead to national history sources. Finally, make the final four sources link to information about world history. Save your creation as **History 5-1.html**.

SCIENCE 5-1

Create a Web page containing three sections covering three areas of science, such as biology, zoology, and chemistry. Add at least five hypertext links to sources of research for each branch of science that you have selected. Save your creation as **Science 5-1.html**.

FOREIGN LANGUAGE 5-1

Create a Web page that contains at least three resources with information that will help you in your study of a foreign language. If you are not currently studying a foreign language, create a Web page with links to at least three different countries where a language you would like to study is spoken. Save your file as **Foreign Language 5-1.html**.

CRITICAL THINKING

ACTIVITY 5-1

How would education be different without HTML? Has HTML helped shaped learning in schools? Defend your opinion in a 150- to 250-word essay. Save your essay as **Activity 5-1**.

ACTIVITY 5-2

In your opinion, what is the most important and exciting part of the Internet? Explain your views in a 150- to 250-word report. Save your thoughts as **Activity 5-2**.

JOB 5-1

Of all of the possible careers you can think of that involve using the Internet, which career do you find the most exciting? Explain why you find this area so interesting in a short 150- to 250-word report. Name this file **Job 5-1**.

JOB 5-2

Research the career you described in Job 5-1. Create a Web page with ten links providing information about this career. Save this file as **Job 5-2.html**.

GLOSSARY

A

Accessibility options Changes made to software to make it user-friendly for individuals with handicaps. For example, for visually impaired users, font sizes can be adjusted and icons can be enlarged.

Active server pages Web pages that allow you to change their appearance by resizing their windows and moving them around.

ActiveX Microsoft programming that allows traditional applications to work on the Web.

Address/Location box The box on a Web browser where you enter and access URLs.

Algorithms Mathematical formulas and programmed mathematical subroutines that perform computer calculations.

Anchor tag HTML codes that define a hyperlink to another document or Web page. The anchor tag begins with <A> and ends with </A>. The text or graphic between <A> and </A> is the link's hot spot that, when clicked, transports the user to the linked button.

Anonymous To be unknown. Users often log on to Internet servers as anonymous users.

Applets Tiny programs written in Java that can be embedded in HTML pages.

Archive A folder or hard drive where data and files that someone wishes to preserve are stored. Archives often hold historical records or reference information such as e-mail messages between business partners or research results that individuals may wish to access in the future.

ARPANET Advanced Research Projects Agency Network, the earliest ancestor of today's Internet. This network was created to maintain a communications system in the event that a nuclear war or natural disaster knocked out large sections of the Net.

Attachments Files linked to an e-mail message so that they travel to their destination together. Any type of file can be attached, but usually database, spreadsheet, graphics, or program files are sent as attachments.

Attribute A description or definition of a characteristic that an element or object should have. For example, a size attribute may limit the size of a graphic on a Web page. A font attribute may change the appearance, style, or size of a font.

B

Benchmark A standard or level of performance used for comparison. For example, computer benchmark tests are conducted to determine the relative performance of various computer systems.

Berners-Lee (Tim) Credited with the creation of the World Wide Web and Hypertext Markup Language.

Binary A numerical system consisting only of zeros and ones. All computers perform their calculations using this system of mathematical computation.

BITNET One of the earliest mail systems serving educational users. Short for "Because It's Time Network," BITNET was created by academic researchers tired of waiting for electronic mail and file transfer capabilities.

Black Monday On Monday, October 19, 1987, the market lost 22 percent in a single day. On Monday, October 27, 1997, it lost over 550 points.

Black Thursday On November 3, 1988, the Internet worm virus took down one-tenth of all Internet servers, which were forced to shut down as a result of this malicious attack.

Blind copy (BC) A copy of an e-mail message that can be sent to an individual or individuals without other recipients of the message knowing that they have received a copy. Blind copy recipients are listed in the BC field.

Bookmark Also known as a "favorite," a bookmark records Web site URLs for easy and quick retrieval.

Boolean logic System of logic invented by George Boole, a nineteenth century mathematician. This system uses operators to manipulate data, based on a simple yes or no ranking system. The primary operators in Boolean logic are AND, OR, and NOT.

Boolean operators The operators such as AND, OR, and NOT used in search strings to refine the scope of the search.

Broadband A high-speed Internet connection capable of transporting files, music, voice messages, and multimedia video at high rates of speed.

BTW Internet lingo for "by the way."

Bulleted list Unordered list in which dots or "bullets" precede each item.

Bulletin Board System (BBS) Computer system used as an information source and message system for a particular interest group. Users dial into the BBS, read and leave messages for other users, and communicate with other users who are on the system at the same time. BBSs are often used to distribute shareware.

C

Call for Votes (CFV) A request for supporters approving and supporting the creation of a new newsgroup.

Chat An online, two-way, interactive communication between users utilizing instant messaging technology.

Chatter's jargon Abbreviated typed phrases used by chatters sending instant messages. For example, BTW means "by the way" and ROL means "rolling over laughing."

Click and drag Use of a pointing device, such as a mouse, to latch onto an object on screen and move it. You place the pointer over the object you want to move and click the mouse button to grab it. Then, you hold the button down while you slide the object to its destination. Finally, you release the mouse button.

Client A personal computer that is part of a server-client network.

Common Gateway Interface (CGI) Recognized standard for interfacing applications, like database programs, with Web servers and Web pages. CGI allows users to interact through Web pages. For example, with CGI you can create a form in which site visitors enter data and the data go to the server for processing.

Compressed files Files that are compacted from their normal size to save space. These files are smaller and therefore can be transferred over the Net at faster speeds.

Congressional Budget Office (CBO) Congressional agency given the task of preparing budget figures and analysis for the U.S. Congress.

Cookie Information created by a Web site and stored on the user's hard disk. It provides a way for the Web server to keep track of the user's patterns and preferences and, with the cooperation of the Web browser, to store this information on the user's own hard disk in a cookies.txt file.

Courtesy copy (CC) A copy of an e-mail message sent to a secondary recipient as a courtesy.

Cyberspace A popular 1990s term used to describe the Internet and the World Wide Web.

Cybersquatters Individuals or companies who purchase and control top-level domain names hoping one day to sell these domain names to corporations or individuals at a profit.

D

Data Individual pieces of information that a computer processes. Data are stored in computer files and can take any form: numbers, text, image, and even voice and video.

Dialog box A box or window in which you are required to enter information before the software can execute a command.

Directory or folder Logical places to store related files and other data. Folders can contain applications, data, video, music, and text related files.

Dock A screen location where graphical icons can be organized and grouped using a graphical user interface.

Domain name A description of a computer's "location" on the Internet.

Domain Name Server/System (DNS) A computer with software that enables it to compare domain names that people can remember, like *www.disney.com,* with the actual IP (Internet Protocol) number that defines a server on the Internet. The DNS computer makes the association so that the requested server can be found by its number (such as 158.91.6.45).

Dow Jones Industrial Average (DJIA) A measure of stock performance of 30 large U.S. companies, often used by investors as a benchmark, or standard, against which to judge the performance of individual stocks.

Download To transmit a file from one computer to another. Generally, "download" means receive and "upload" means transmit.

Drivers Programs that allow hardware, like printers and sound cards, to communicate with a computer's operating system. The operating system calls the driver, and the driver "drives" the device.

Drives Hardware devices in a computer that stores data.

Dynamic Hypertext Markup Language (DHTML) Microsoft's extension to HTML that allows users to move and manipulate objects around the Web page as easily as they manipulate icons on their Windows computer screen.

E

E-book Book that has been digitized and put into online libraries for public distribution online.

E-commerce The online sale and distribution of products, goods, and services.

Ellipses Three little dots following some command options that indicate that a dialog box will appear if this command is selected. You see them in pull-down menus.

E-mail Electronic mail; memos, messages, and attachments transmitted over a network.

Emoticons Keyboard symbols arranged to express emotion, as in : -) for smile.

Emulate The process of converting input and output from one computer system to another computer system or input and output device.

Executable files An application program that begins the execution of its programmed operation after the command is given to start the program. In Windows, executable files are known by their .exe extensions.

Extensible Markup Language (XML) Format for structured documents and data in a text file. Data can include spreadsheets, address books, database information, or even drawings. XML defines the style and the parameters of the data.

Extensions File types, or file categories, added to the end of file names preceded by a dot, as in the following form: filename.doc.

F

Fanning, Shawn The controversial 19-year-old who programmed Napster and spurred an online phenomenon of music-sharing involving over 40 million users and raised new Internet-related copyright issues and litigation.

Favorites A term used for bookmarks or records of URLs or Web addresses in Microsoft Internet Explorer that the user wishes to return to again and again. Favorites provide one-click access to these URLs.

FidoNet A 1980s e-mail protocol that was most used for its bulletin board capabilities.

File Data storage areas created and named using an application program.

File extensions Three-character acronyms used to describe the type of file or file format in which the data are saved. For example, a .txt file stands for a text file. The .exe file indicates an executable file. A .doc file indicates a Word file.

File Transfer Protocol (FTP) A program that allows you to move files from computer to computer on the Internet.

Filters Software that blocks or filters out unwanted information. For example, a filter may block unwanted e-mail messages from a particular source. Filters can interrupt the transmission of inappropriate Web pages so that they are unable to pass through to the client computer.

Flaming Emotional electronic communication. In other words, online cursing.

Flash Tools created by Macromedia to create excellent low-bandwidth multimedia presentations online.

Folders or directories Simulated file folders that hold data, applications, and other folders. Folders are logical places to put related files.

Freeware Any software that customers never have to pay for.

G

Generalized Markup Language (GML) Originally created by IBM, this system of display standards allows documents to be interpreted and displayed in specific ways.

Gopher Document cataloging system on the Net, popular during the late 1980s. Still around today, Gopher uses long descriptive file names and a hierarchical menu system to catalog millions and millions of documents but has been in decline because of the rise of the World Wide Web.

Graphical User Interface (GUI) The use of pictures or icons to communicate commands from the user to the software. Click a GUI icon with your mouse and something happens. For instance, click the Print button and your document will print.

Graphics Interchange Format (.gif) Widely used Web graphics format developed by CompuServe.

Gutenberg (Johannes) The inventor of the printing press in the 1450s.

H

Hard drive The primary storage area on your computer. It offers large storage capacity and fast retrieval.

Header First part of an e-mail message, which contains controlling data, such as who sent the e-mail, who it was mailed to, who should receive copies, the priority level, and the subject of the message.

History folder Folder in which your browser keeps track of the recent URLs you've visited. Entries in the History folder show the name of the page that appears in your Title Bar and the Internet address of the sites you visited.

Hits The number of times a Web page has been accessed or the number of items found in response to a search query.

Home page A page of information that appears in a Web browser window. Often called a "Web page," the home page is usually the first page that users see when they come to a Web site. However, some people call all Web pages home pages.

Host computers Computers that store information to be shared with other computers, called clients. For example, client computers can request information from host computers on the Web running Web server software.

Hover To rest a mouse pointer over an icon.

Hyperlink (links) A link between one object and another. The link is displayed either as text or as an icon. On World Wide Web pages, a text hyperlink is displayed as underlined text, typically in a different color, whereas a graphical hyperlink is a small image or picture.

Hypertext Links that transport you to the selected information. Hypertext can link to information within a document, in another document on the same computer, or in a document residing on any Web server on the Internet.

Hypertext links See hypertext.

Hypertext Markup Language (HTML) The standard document format used on the World Wide Web. The HTML tags define how the Web page will look when displayed by a Web browser.

Hypertext reference (HREF) HTML code HREF= within an anchor tag that signifies to the browser the address or URL where the target document can be found.

Hypertext Transfer Protocol (HTTP) The communications protocol used to connect to servers on the World Wide Web. Its primary function is to establish a connection with a server and transmit HTML pages to the client browser. Addresses of Web sites begin with an http:// prefix.

I

Icons Pictures or graphics that represent applications, data files, or other information on a computer display.

Image source tag HTML code that inserts a graphic image on a Web page. The image tag begins with <IMG SRC= followed by the address of the image's file location and ends with a closing bracket.

IMHO Internet lingo for "in my humble opinion."

Inbox The first thing you see when you sign on.

Information Infrastructure Task Force (IITF) Committee put together by the Clinton/Gore administration to implement the administration's vision of how the National Information Infrastructure (NII) should work.

Information overload The condition in which people feel overwhelmed and overburdened by too much information and constant change.

Instant Messenger (IM) A communications system enabled by instant messaging software that allows individuals to communicate quickly and easily over the Internet.

Instant messaging client Software that allows instant messaging between Internet users.

Interface System of interaction between the user and the computer.

Internal Revenue Service (IRS) The government agency in the United States charged with collecting and monitoring the payment of national taxes. Currently provides much of its information online at www.irs.com.

Internet appliance A low-powered, low-cost computerized device connecting to the Internet and the World Wide Web.

Internet Corporation for Assigned Names and Numbers (ICANN) The international organization responsible for assigning and maintaining top-level domain names.

Internet Network Information Center (InterNIC) Provided Internet domain name registration for the Net through Network Solutions until the creation of ICANN.

Internet Protocol (IP) A number that uniquely identifies a specific computer on the Internet. IP numbers appear as four numbers separated by periods, such as 193.45.67.123.

Internet relay chat (IRC) An early form of instant messaging allowing instant messages to be relayed to other individuals over the Internet.

Internet Service Provider (ISP) A business that physically connects its customers to the Internet.

Internet Telephony Technologies enabling traditional telephone services over the Internet.

Internet worm Program unleashed on the Internet on November 3, 1988 that infected host computers by finding security holes and then overloaded system resources by replicating itself. The program infected over 6,000 computers, which was about one-tenth of the number of computers on the Internet at that time.

J

Java A platform-independent programming language. Java programs have to be written only once, and it can be executed on any computer platform.

JavaScript A programming language that is easier to use but less powerful than Java. JavaScript uses the HTML page as its interface, whereas Java can generate a completely customized interface.

.jpg (or .jpeg) Standard graphics format developed by the Joint Photographic Experts Group. Its compact nature makes it ideal for the Internet.

Just in time (JIT) The practice of receiving needed information or training "just-in-time" to complete a job or task.

K

Keyword Any word used to begin a search for related information. Used by search engines and search portals to narrow down the range of information being requested.

L

Leaseware Software that is leased to the user for a monthly or yearly fee.

Linux A popular Internet operating system.

Link(s) See hypertext.

List box A list of options that you can scroll through to make your section.

LOL Internet lingo for "laughing out loud."

M

Macintosh An operating system for personal computers.

Maximize button A button in a corner of your Windows screen that will make a window larger, usually to fill the entire screen. This button is called the "zoom box" on a Macintosh.

Maximized A window expanded to its greatest possible screen size.

Meteorology The study of weather and weather phenomena. Meteorological sites are very popular on the Internet.

Microsoft.NET A computer operating system for Internet devices.

Minimize button A button in a corner of your screen that will make a window smaller. Clicking the minimize button shrinks the window down to a button and puts it on the Taskbar or Dock, out of the way.

Minimized A window that has been reduced to a fraction of the computer screen.

Mirror site Copy of the original site that resides in a computer in another location. The purpose of a mirror site is to lessen Net traffic to the original site and speed up transmission by allowing users to go to the closest site.

Monster.com An online job search site.

Mosaic The first GUI Web browser, created by the National Center for Supercomputing Applications (NCSA). This browser made the World Wide Web popular. Mosaic was user-friendly and free to users.

MP3 A popular music format commonly used to share music over the Internet.

N

Napster A peer-to-peer system of sharing files over the Internet. Napster allows music MP3 and other files from one client computer (which doesn't have to be a server) to be shared and copied by another client.

National Center for Supercomputer Applications (NCSA) Located at the University of Illinois in Champaign-Urbana. The first graphical user interface browser, called Mosaic for the Internet, was born at NCSA.

National Information Infrastructure (NII) An integrated communications system planned by the Clinton/Gore administration that will be based on a nationwide network of networks and will supposedly allow all Americans to take advantage of the country's information, communication, and computing resources.

National Science Foundation (NSF) The organization that founded much of the development of the early Internet during the 1980s and 1990s.

National Telecommunications and Information Administration (NTIA) The executive-branch agency responsible for domestic and international telecommunications and information policy issues.

Natural language searching A search method, still in its developmental stage, in which a query is expressed in English, French, or any other spoken language in a normal manner.

Netizen A citizen of the Net, or a fellow traveler on the Information Superhighway.

NetNews All the news that runs over the Internet.

Network A group of computers that can communicate or "talk" to each other through connections or links. The Internet is the largest computer network ever created and is often called "the network of networks."

Network computer (NC) Low-cost computer that accesses resources from a professionally managed network server linked to the Internet to provide computing services to the customer instead of requiring the programs and capabilities to reside on the local computer.

Network computing System developed by Oracle that stores everything—applications, data, and services—on a network of servers and downloads them to users' computers, as needed. Complex issues such as updating software and maintaining virus protection are moved from the end-user to the professionals who maintain the network.

Network drives Drives that are shared by a network of computers.

Network interface card (NIC) A circuit board that connects your computer to the others on the network so that the computers can exchange information.

Newbies New users of the Internet.

Newsgroup Collection of messages on the Internet about a particular subject. People subscribe to newsgroups to meet and talk electronically with others interested in the same subjects.

NSFNET The National Science Foundation network of supercomputers was established for scientific research. This network became the foundation for today's Internet.

Numbered list A list in which the items are sequentially numbered, indicating the order of importance.

O

Online writing labs (OWLs) Online writing labs established on many university Web sites to help students improve their writing.

Operating system (OS) The master program that runs the computer. All applications must be able to "talk" to the operating system.

Operators Symbols used to perform computer operations, such as to filter data in a query.

Oracle The second-largest software manufacturer in the world, noted primarily for its SQL database software and its advanced technologies for the Internet.

Ordered (or numbered) list List in which the items are displayed in order of importance. The tag <OL> denotes an ordered list in HTML.

P

Patches Fixes to bugs in software that has already found its way to the customer.

Peer-to-peer networks Networks in which every computer has access to every other computer's resources—drives, folders, and files.

People finder Search feature provided by search services on the Internet that helps you find people's e-mail addresses, street addresses, and phone numbers.

Phrase searching Searching for exact sequences of words in a query by enclosing the words in quotation marks.

Platform A computer hardware and its accompanying software operating system.

Plain Old Telephone System (Pots) Name applied to the traditional telephone system.

Plug-in An auxiliary program that works with a major software package, such as a browser, to enhance its capability.

Post To upload or place information, data, files, or multimedia online for access by others.

Post Office Protocol (POP) A popular protocol used for Internet e-mail.

Practical Extraction and Reporting Language (Perl) A programming language designed to handle a variety of system administrator functions.

Proprietary software A program owned and controlled by a company or person.

Protocol A communications system used to transfer data over networks. A language that similarly configured computers can speak and understand.

Proxy server A computer that interrupts a client computer's request for Internet information in order to assist, process, or filter the information being requested.

Public debt The amount of money borrowed by a government.

Pull-down menu A bar displayed usually at the top of the program screen that lists options from which the user can select. Once an option is selected by a mouse-click, a vertical list opens, giving the user a choice of commands.

Pull media Internet content delivery system in which users access content one site at a time by clicking a link or entering a URL.

Push media Internet content delivery system in which the user specifies the information to be delivered and the system searches and downloads (or pushes) the information automatically to the user's computer.

Q

Query Method of filtering data to find information that meets the search criterion.

R

Real-time Happening at that moment, as in "happening live."

Remote access Contacting a computer from a remote location, often with a modem over phone lines.

Request for Discussion (RFD) A request for comments concerning the establishment of a new newsgroup.

Rich Text Format (RTF) Text format that enables the use of enhancements, such as bold, italic, and different fonts and colors. You can also insert pictures, sound, and video clips or documents created in a variety of programs.

ROTFL Internet lingo for "rolling on the floor laughing."

S

Scroll bars Horizontal and vertical bars usually containing a small box at the side or bottom of windows. Clicking and dragging the small box allows you to slide around the window to view previously hidden content.

Search engine Computer software that searches for data, based on some criterion such as a keyword.

Search portal Web sites, such as Yahoo! and AltaVista, that maintain a directory database of other Web sites. You can look for information on the Web by entering a search criterion, such as a keyword, where indicated on the search portal Web site. Portals may also offer free services including e-mail, news, and other content.

Search Tool Also called a search engine, a search tool may use keywords, phrases, or natural language sentences to help locate specific types of information on the Internet. Search tools often use Boolean logic.

Second-level domain name A part of the domain name that identifies the organization, corporation, agency, or individual that controls and maintains a Web site. Second-level domain names include such notables as disney.com, ibm.com, microsoft.com, and speakingsolutions.com.

Self-extracting files Executable files that decompress themselves automatically when launched.

Server A high-speed computer on a server-client network that stores information and distributes it to requesting clients.

Server-client network A network of clients sharing information distributed by servers. This is the type of network on which the Internet is based.

Shareware Software you can download for free, try for a certain length of time, and then purchase if you find it valuable.

Shockwave A multimedia viewing plug-in for a Web browser that allows users to experience the animations and full multimedia effects on some Web sites.

Spam Unwanted and unsolicited advertising or other messages, such as political or social commentary.

Speech recognition Software that enables users to use their voice to write and give commands to a computer. Speech has become a popular input device for many Internet applications, such as e-mail.

Standard Generalized Markup Language (SGML) A more sophisticated markup language than GML, it served as the basis for the popular HTML language used to create the first Web pages.

Streaming A data handling process that enables data to flow continuously, allowing Web site audio and video to play without requiring a full file download.

Subject line The place in an e-mail header where the sender inserts a brief description of the message contents.

Subscribe The process of joining a newsgroup or listserve.

Surfing The act of exploring the Internet and World Wide Web.

Symbiotic Two mutually beneficial systems that exist together. Hardware and software are considered symbiotic.

T

Tags HTML instructions that tell the browser how to display the Web page information. Tags are enclosed in brackets <LIKE THIS>.

Taskbar A toolbar that displays the applications (tasks) that are running. Clicking on a taskbar button restores the application to its previous size.

Telecommuting The process of working at home while making use of high-speed Internet access and other telecommunications systems that allow a traditional office-like environment in remote locations.

Telephony Term used to describe any kind of two-way voice communication system like the telephone system and Internet voice systems.

Text-to-speech (TTS) Speech recognition system where text is converted to synthesized speech. Available on many voice portals and other Internet sites.

Thread Several newsgroup postings related to information on the same topic.

Ticker symbol A two-to-five letter abbreviation that represents a company in stock listings.

Toggle A control that allows the user to alternate between two options.

Toolbar A bar of GUI icons that usually provide one-click access to frequently used commands.

Top-level domain name (TLD) The highest category of domain name extensions identifying Internet providers and Web sites, including .com, .net, .edu, .biz, and .museum.

Trailer A clip from a movie featuring promotional highlights, often posted on the Internet for marketing purposes.

U

Uniform Resource Locator (URL) The Internet addressing scheme that defines the route to a file or program. The URL is used as the initial access to a resource.

Unix An important and influential operating system developed by Bell Laboratories. Many versions remain free for users. Unix has served as one of the most important operating systems in the establishment of the Internet. Linux is derived, in part, from Unix. Macintosh OS X also has Unix roots.

Unordered list List that shows no particular order of importance among its items. The tag <UL> denotes an unordered list in HTML.

Unsubscribe A process whereby someone discontinues participating in a newsgroup or Internet listserve.

Unvisited color The color of a hypertext link before it has been selected.

Usenet Comes from USEr NETwork. A giant public-access network on the Internet, maintained by volunteers, that provides user news and e-mail. Newsgroups get their messages from the Usenet network.

User-friendly Easy to learn and use.

V

Viruses Programs written to alter the functioning of the infected computer. The virus code is buried within an existing program. When the program is executed, the virus code is activated and attaches copies of itself to other programs in the system. The virus may be a prank that causes a small annoyance or it may be malicious vandalism that destroys programs and data.

Virtual office An office without a physical office space. Virtual offices usually consist of portable computers and Internet connections. Sometimes they appear in home offices.

Virtual Reality Modeling Language (VRML) Language used to simulate 3D objects, lights, and textures, viewable using a VRML viewer within the Web browser. This language can create 3D "worlds," where users can interact with objects in a virtual setting. After a VRML page has been downloaded, its contents can be viewed, rotated, and manipulated, and simulated rooms can be "walked into."

Visited color The color a hypertext link becomes after it has been selected.

W

Webmasters People who create, organize, and manage Web sites.

Web servers Computers on the Internet that allow others to access their drives, folders, and files. They accept requests from Web browsers to transmit HTML pages and other stored files.

WebTV An Internet TV terminal that allows you to access the Internet through your TV and phone line, without a computer.

Windows The dominant operating system, produced by Microsoft. The term is also used to describe open applications or dialog boxes on the computer screen. These windows can be maximized, minimized, and moved around the screen.

Wizard A term used to describe executable programs that guide a user through a specific process. For example, a new user Wizard might guide a new Internet user through the installation and setup process or help the user create a new connection to the Internet.

Workgroup A smaller network within the larger network. The computers of those in the workgroup are linked together so they can share resources and accomplish group tasks.

World Wide Web Consortium (W3C) An international council that helps organize content and World Wide Web related events and information distribution.

WYSIWYG An acronym that means "what you see is what you get." WYSIWYG software works to ensure that what is created by an author or Web page developer on their computer screen will look the same when printed or shared over the World Wide Web via a Web browser.

Z

Zoom box A box in a corner of your Macintosh screen that will make your window larger, usually to fill the entire screen. This box is called the "maximize button" in Windows.

INDEX

writing to officials, 224

Graphical user interface (GUI), 3

Graphic background, 70

Graphics
downloading, 14
formats, 283

Graphics Interchange Format (.gif), 283

GroupWise, 97

Gutenberg, Johannes, 255

H

Hacker, 187

Hart, Michael, 165

Header, e-mail, 99

High-speed connection, 31

Historic Internet systems, 198

History folder, 32

History sites, 196–197

Hit, 144

Home button, 31

Horton, Mark, 129

Host computer, 46. *See also* Server

Host server, 51

Hotbot, 151

Hotmail, 98–100, 104

Hover option, 70

.hqx, 80, 82

.htm, 252

.html, 252

HTML (Hypertext Markup Language)
commands, 252–255. *See also* Source code
defined, 46
as evolving, 255
hidden tags, 47
inventor of, 255
lists in, 257, 259

HTTP (Hypertext Transfer Protocol), 46

Hyperlinks
creating, 47–48
defined, 44–45
locating, 45

speaking, 3
transport via, 25
URLs and, 46
visited and unvisited colors with, 70
See also Hypertext links; Links

Hypertext links, 3. *See also* Hyperlinks; Links

Hypertext Markup Language (HTML), 46. *See also* HTML

Hypertext reference tags, 47–48, 267

Hypertext Transfer Protocol (HTTP), 46

I

ICANN, 52–56

Icons, 3

Icon view, 11

Images, distorting, 271

Image search tag, 270

Image source tag, 267

"In the dark," 167

.info, 53

Information overload, 147

"Information superhighway," 166

Instant messaging, 113–125
attaching files with, 120–121
multiple-buddy chat, 118
number of users, 115, 117
sending messages, 117–118
signing in, 115

Instant messaging client (IM), 113

.int, 52

Interactive Web sites, 279–280

Interface, 61

Internal Revenue Service (IRS), 205, 207–208

International Organization for Standardization (ISO), 260

International Space Station site, 184, 278–279

Internet
addresses, 28–29
communicating with, 3
historic systems, 198
other names for, 2
as political forum, 227–229

servers, 12

Internet appliance, 227

Internet Explorer (IE), 3, 10, 26–27, 30

Internet Network Information Center, 52

Internet protocol (IP) numbers, 48–49

Internet Public Library, 162, 194–195

Internet Relay Chat (IRC), 117

Internet Service Provider (ISP)
defined, 97–98
e-mail with, 97–98, 102

Internet sources, citing, 195

Internet telephony, 119–120

Internet worm, 187

InterNIC, 52

Investors, online, 210

IRC. *See* Internet Relay Chat

ISP. *See* Internet Service Provider

J

Jargon, chatter's, 122

Java, 270, 279, 281–282, 284

JavaScript, 270, 279

Job search, 235–246
Flipdog.com, 235–236
government job, 236
Monster.com, 237–238, 240
online resume, 237–238
salaries, 239–240

Joint Photographic Experts Group (JPEG), 283

Journalism sites, 197–200

.jpg (.jpeg) graphics format, 283

Jughead, 33

Juno.com, 98

Just in Time (JIT) compiler, 282

K

Kehoe, Brandan P., 183
Keyword, 144
Keyword searches, 144–147

L

Languages
    Flash, 278–279, 292
    HTML. *See* HTML
    Java, 281–282, 284
    Shockwave, 270, 278–289, 292
    VRML, 282–284
Library, virtual, 160–173
Library of Congress, 160–162, 222
Links, 44
    adding to Web page, 268–271
    See also Hyperlinks; Hypertext
        links
Linux OS, 71
List
    in HTML, 257, 259
    on Web page, 257–258
List box, 64
List view, 11
Lotus Notes, 97
Louvre, 165–166
Lycos, 152
Lynx, 33

M

MacBinary files, 82
Macintosh dock, 4
Mac OS X, 71
Mail server, 102
Math sites, 186
Maximize button, 7, 63
Media Player
    movie trailers in, 290
    music with, 296
    streaming and, 296
    television with, 293, 295
Menu, pull-down, 5
Meteorology sites, 180–183
Microsoft Exchange, 97

Microsoft Internet Explorer, 3, 10.
    See also Internet Explorer
Microsoft.NET, 227
Microsoft Network (MSN), 26
    as large ISP, 98
    MSN Messenger, 113–114,
        116–118
.mil, 52
Minimize button, 7
Mirror site, 83, 167
Mom test, 224
Monster.com, 237–238, 240
Mosaic, 25, 28, 71, 198
Mouse button, click and drag with, 8
Mouse pointer, on hyperlink, 45
Movies, 290–292
Moving files, 14
MP3, 296
Multimedia, languages for, 278–289
.museum, 53
Museums, virtual, 164–166
Music, digital, 296–297
My Documents, 12

N

.name, 53
NASA Web site, 184
National Center for Supercomputing
    Applications (NCSA), 25, 28
National Gallery of Art, 165–166
National Science Foundation
    (NSF), 71
Natural language searching, 147–148
Navigator. *See* Netscape Navigator
NCSA. *See* National Center for
    supercomputing Applications
.net, 52
.NET, 227
Net, the, 2
Net ethics
    copying information, 19
    cybersquatters, 56
    e-mail to elected officials, 227
    encryption software, 168
    mom test, 224

Napster, 296
    newsgroup anonymity, 128
    newsgroup netiquette, 131
    proxy servers, 186
    shareware and leasing
        dilemma, 86
    spam, 101
    stealing images, 271
    subscription ethics, 101
    Webmasters, 153
    Web standardization, 280
Netiquette
    mirror sites and, 167
    newsgroup, 131
    old vs. new browsers, 270
Netscape Navigator, 3, 10, 26–27, 30
    e-mail system, 97
    founder of, 28
    Gopher and, 198
    security features on, 213
    WYSIWYGs with, 258
Network
    defined, 7
    meanings of term, 15
    peer-to-peer, 18
    personal, 21
Network computing, 227
Network Solutions, 50
Newbies, 2
Newsgroups, 126–141
    anonymity in, 128
    first, 126
    freedom to create, 131
    netiquette in, 131
    posting response to, 130–131
    reading posts, 129–130
    searching for, 127–128
    spam and, 130
    subject line in, 131
News sites, 197–200
New York Times, 199
NFL Web site, 298
Notepad, 16
Novell GroupWise, 97
NSF. *See* National Science
    Foundation
Numbered list, 257

O

Online investors, 210

Online resume, 237–238

Online shopping, 209–210

Online writing labs (OWLs), 193–195

Open dialog box, 28–29

Open Web Location dialog box, 28

Operating systems (OS)
differences between, 6
Unix, 71

Operators
AND/OR, 149
Boolean, 149–151
defined, 148
NEAR/ADJ, 151–152
NOT/–, 150–151
parentheses with, 153

Oracle Corporation, 227, 293

Ordered list, 257

.org, 52

Outlook Express, 97

OWLs. *See* Online writing labs

P

Page Source, 253

Palm-held computer, 293

Parentheses, in Internet searches, 153

Pasting, copying and, 16–19. *See also* Copying information

Patches, 79

Peer-to-peer network, 18

Pegasus, 33

People finders, 166–167

Perl, 284

Personal digital assistant, 117

Personal network, 21

Phrase searching, 147–148

Platform, operating system, 279

Plug-ins, 279, 292. *See also* Flash; Shockwave

Political issues, 227–229

Post, 126, 129–130

Post Office Protocol (POP), 97, 108

Practical Extraction and Report Language (Perl), 284

President of the United States, 223

Pretty Good Privacy (PGP) encryption software, 168

Privacy
e-mail systems and, 101
encryption software and, 168
Webmasters and, 153

.pro, 53, 56

Project Gutenberg, 165

Proportional list box, 65

Proprietary e-mail, 97

Protocol
defined, 46
FTP, 46
HTTP, 46
TCP/IP, 184

Proxy servers, 186

Pull-down menu, 5

Q

Query, 144

QuickTime
movie trailers in, 290, 292
music with, 296
streaming and, 296
television with, 293, 295

QWERTYIOP, 97

R

Real-names searches, 154–155

RealPlayer
music with, 296
streaming and, 296
television with, 293, 295

Recording Industry Association of America (RIAA), 296

Refresh/Reload button, 31

Reply button, 102

Request for Discussion (RFD), 131

Research evaluation forms, 73–75

Restore button, 8, 63

Resume, online, 237–238

RFD. *See* Request for Discussion

RTF (Rich Text Format), 105

Run option, to open .exe file, 81

S

Salary.com, 239

Save Picture As command, 14

Save This Image As command, 14

Save Web page dialog box, 12

Science
astronomy sites, 183–184
biology sites, 185–186
meteorology sites, 180–183
space exploration sites, 183–184

Scroll bars, 8–10

.sea, 82

Search button, 49

Search engines
advanced searches, 161
keyword searches, 144–147
natural language and phrase searches, 147–148
operators, 148–152
phrases, 147–148
real-names, 154–155
trial and error with, 151
WebCrawler, 33

Search portal, 29, 34, 38

Second-level domain name, 52, 54–55

Secure transaction, 213

Security First Network Bank, 213

Selecting text, 16–17

Self-extracting files, 82

Server
defined, 16
Internet, 12
mail, 102
proxy, 186
See also Web server

Server-client network, 16

SGML (Standard Generalized Markup Language), 260

Shareware
    defined, 77
    finding, 78
    games, 212
    leasing dilemma, 86
Shareware.com, 78–80
Shockwave, 270, 278–280, 292
Shopping, online, 209–210
.sit, 80, 82
Software
    downloading FTP, 83–86
    encryption, 168
    online repairs, 79
    proprietary, 97
Source code
    viewing, 253–254
    See also HTML
Source command, 47
Sources, citing Internet, 195
Space exploration sites, 183–184
Spam
    advertisement-based e-mail
        and, 101
    newsgroups and, 130
Speech recognition software
    real-name searches with, 155
    spelling skills and, 196
    surfing and, 3
Spell checkers, 196
Sports sites, 298–300
Spry, 28
Starting tags, 253, 256
Status bar
    toggling, 62
    URL on, 45
Stock prices, 210–213
Stop button, 31
Streaming, 293, 296
StuffIt Expander, 80–82
Subject line
    e-mail, 99–100
    newsgroup, 131
Subscribe, 126
Sun Microsystems, 284
Supreme Court, 225–226
Surfing
    defined, 2
    speech recognition software and, 3

T

Tablet computers, 293
Tags
    anchor, 266, 269
    combining, 254
    defined, 252
    horizontal bar, 257
    HTML, 47, 252–255
    hypertext reference, 47–48, 267
    image search, 270
    image source, 267
    line break, 257
    starting, 253, 256
    title, 257
Taskbar, Windows, 4
TCP/IP protocol, 184
Telecommuting, 239
Telephony, 119–120
TextEdit, 16
Text Size option, 65
Text-to-speech (TTS)
    technologies, 66
Text Zoom option, 65
Thomas Web site, 222–223
Thread, 129
Thumbnail view, 11
Ticker symbol, 212
Toggle
    defined, 62
    status bar, 62
    toolbar, 62–63
Tomlinson, Ray, 97
Toolbar
    defined, 4
    Internet Explorer, 5
    one-click commands on, 30
    personal, 64
    toggling, 62
Top-level domain (TLD) names,
    51–55
Trailers, movie, 290–292
Tucows Web site, 83–84
TV shows
    streaming, 293
    Web sites for, 294
Type style. *See* Font options

U

Uniform Resource Locator (URL)
Unix, 71, 108
Unordered list, 257
Unsubscribe, 126
Unvisited color, 70
URL (Uniform Resource Locator),
    28–29
    absence of *www* in, 53
    History folder for, 32
    hyperlinks and, 46–47
Usenet, 129
User-friendly, 25

V

Veronica, 33
Video streaming, 296. *See also*
    Streaming
View Page Source, 253
Virtual clipboard, 16
Virtual encyclopedias, 163–164
Virtual library, 160–173
    people finders, 166–167
    virtual encyclopedias, 163–164
    virtual museums, 164–166
    worldwide knowledge web, 160
Virtual museums, 164–166
Virtual offices, 239
Virtual Reality Modeling Language
    (VRML), 186–187, 279, 282–284
Virus
    defined, 79
    freeware and, 212
Visited color, 70
VRML (Virtual Reality Modeling
    Language), 186–187, 279,
    282–284

W

Walt Disney Co., 271
Weather sites, 180–183
Web, the, 2